American Cinema of the 1960s

SCREEN

AMERICAN CULTURE / AMERICAN CINEMA

DECADES

Each volume in the Screen Decades: American Culture/American Cinema series presents a group of original essays analyzing the impact of cultural issues on the cinema and the impact of the cinema in American society. Because every chapter explores a spectrum of particularly significant motion pictures and the broad range of historical events in one year, readers will gain a continuing sense of the decade as it came to be depicted on movie screens across the continent. The integration of historical and cultural events with the sprawling progression of American cinema illuminates the pervasive themes and the essential movies that define an era. Our series represents one among many possible ways of confronting the past; we hope that these books will offer a better understanding of the connections between American culture and film history.

LESTER D. FRIEDMAN AND MURRAY POMERANCE
SERIES EDITORS

American Cinema of the

1960s

Themes and Variations

EDITED BY

BARRY KEITH GRANT

RUTGERS UNIVERSITY PRESS

NEW BRUNSWICK, NEW JERSEY, AND LONDON

LIBRARY OF CONGRESS CATALOGING-IN-PUBLICATION DATA

American cinema of the 1960s : themes and variations / edited by Barry Keith Grant.
    p.   cm. — (Screen decades)
  Includes bibliographical references and index.
  ISBN 978-0-8135-4218-8 (hardcover : alk. paper) — ISBN 978-0-8135-4219-5
(pbk. : alk. paper)
  1. Motion pictures—United States—History. I. Grant, Barry Keith, 1947–
PN1993.5.U6A8576 2008
791.430973'09046—dc22

                           2007015496

A British Cataloging-in-Publication record for this book is available from the British
Library.

This collection copyright © 2008 by Rutgers, The State University

Individual chapters copyright © 2008 in the names of their authors

Visit our Web site: http://rutgerspress.rutgers.edu

Manufactured in the United States of America

This book could only be dedicated to my mother, whose love of movies gave us something to share during a turbulent decade.

CONTENTS

ACKNOWLEDGMENTS

I wish to thank series editors Lester Friedman and Murray Pomerance for all their support and advice as I worked on this book. Thanks, too, to the contributors, with whom it has been a pleasure to collaborate and whose work has been so insightful about the 1960s. I am indebted to Leslie Mitchner for having the vision to see the value of the Screen Decades series for scholars as well as the general reader. Thank you also to Eric Schramm for his careful copyediting of the manuscript. All the staff members at Rutgers University Press were thoroughly professional and delightful to work with. Curtis Maloley and Olga Klimova, graduate students in the M.A. Program in Popular Culture at Brock University, offered invaluable research assistance, the former with the bibliography and the latter with the timeline. A Chancellor's Chair Research Award at Brock provided the financial support for research and preparation of the manuscript.

T I M E L I N E

The 1960s

1960

24 JANUARY	Insurrection against French rule breaks out in Algiers. State of siege declared.
29 FEBRUARY	Hugh Hefner opens the first Playboy Club in Chicago.
6 MAY	President Dwight D. Eisenhower signs the Civil Rights Act of 1960, intended to remove barriers for Blacks who want to vote in the South.
16 MAY	Berry Gordy founds Motown records in Detroit.
8 NOVEMBER	John F. Kennedy (D) defeats Richard M. Nixon (R) in the U.S. presidential election.
16 NOVEMBER	Clark Gable dies of a heart attack days after completing *The Misfits*.

1961

3 JANUARY	The United States terminates diplomatic relations with Cuba.
17 JANUARY	In his farewell address President Eisenhower warns of "the military-industrial complex."
23 JANUARY	Bob Dylan makes his debut performing at an open-mike hootenanny at the Café Wha? in Greenwich Village, New York City.
12 APRIL	Yurl Gagarin of the USSR becomes the first man to orbit the Earth.
17 APRIL	The failed Bay of Pigs invasion takes place.
13 AUGUST	Construction begins on the Berlin Wall.
22 DECEMBER	James Davis of Livingston, Tennessee, becomes the first American soldier to die in Vietnam.

1962

20 FEBRUARY	John Glenn orbits the Earth three times in *Friendship 7*.
3 JULY	France cedes independence to Algeria.

9 JULY   Andy Warhol's first art exhibit, consisting of thirty-two paintings of Campbell's soup cans, opens at Ferus Gallery in West Hollywood, California.

23 JULY   Jackie Robinson becomes the first African American to be inducted into the Baseball Hall of Fame.

4 AUGUST   Marilyn Monroe dies at age thirty-six from an overdose of prescription drugs.

22 OCTOBER   The Cuban missile crisis begins.

1963

17 JUNE   The U.S. Supreme Court rules that no state or locality may require recitation of the Lord's Prayer or Bible verses in public schools.

28 AUGUST   At a civil rights demonstration in Washington, D.C., Martin Luther King Jr. gives his "I Have a Dream" speech.

30 AUGUST   An emergency hotline between Washington and Moscow is set up.

27 SEPTEMBER   Joseph Valachi identifies Mafia families in his testimony before the McClellan Committee on national television.

22 NOVEMBER   JFK is assassinated in Dallas; Lyndon B. Johnson is sworn in as the thirty-sixth president.

1964

7 FEBRUARY   The Beatles arrive in the United States for the first time at the newly renamed JFK Airport in New York. Two days later, the band makes its first appearance on "The Ed Sullivan Show," viewed by more than 72 million.

13 APRIL   At the 1963 Academy Award ceremonies, Sidney Poitier wins an Oscar for Best Actor for *Lilies of the Field*, the first African American actor to win the award.

7 AUGUST   Congress passes the Gulf of Tonkin Resolution, approving U.S. action in Vietnam and giving President Johnson discretionary power.

27 SEPTEMBER   The Warren Commission releases its report on the investigation into the assassination of JFK, claiming that Lee Harvey Oswald acted alone.

1 OCTOBER   The first student arrest in the Free Speech Movement at the University of California, Berkeley. Two months later over seven hundred demonstrators are arrested during a demonstration on campus.

1965

21 FEBRUARY   Influential and militant black nationalist Malcolm X is murdered by three gunmen while giving a speech in Harlem in New York City.

13 MARCH   LBJ authorizes the use of napalm in Vietnam.

MID-JULY   *Mariner 4* Mars probe flies to within 6,100 miles of Mars, sending back pictures of the planet's surface.

11 AUGUST   Six days of rioting begins in the Watts section of Los Angeles.

4 OCTOBER   Pope Paul VI, the first pope to visit North America, arrives in New York City.

18 OCTOBER   The first public burning of a draft card is carried out by David Miller in New York City.

1966

22 JUNE   Samuel Goldwyn wins an out-of-court settlement of a sixteen-year-long antitrust suit against Twentieth Century Fox and other companies.

30 JULY   The United States bombs the Demilitarized Zone (DMZ) in Vietnam for the first time.

13 AUGUST   The Cultural Revolution is officially announced as state policy in China.

8 SEPTEMBER   The first episode of "Star Trek" ("The Man Trap") is broadcast on NBC.

29 OCTOBER   The National Organization of Women is officially launched, with Betty Friedan as president.

15 DECEMBER   Walt Disney dies of lung cancer at the age of sixty-five.

1967

15 JANUARY   The Green Bay Packers beat the Kansas City Chiefs 35–10 in Superbowl I in Los Angeles.

13 MARCH   Senator Eugene McCarthy (D-Minn.) introduces the equal rights amendment to Congress.

5 JUNE   Beginning of the Six Day War between Israel and the Arab states of Egypt, Syria, Jordan, and Iraq.

10 JUNE   The American Film Institute is established.

17 JUNE   China announces its first successful test of a hydrogen bomb.

14 DECEMBER   Biochemists at Stanford University announce the successful synthesis of DNA.

1968

2–3 MAY Leftist students occupy a lecture hall at the University of Paris and clash with police, setting off the events of May '68. A general strike begins on 13 May.

10 MAY Peace talks begin between the United States and North Vietnamese delegations in Paris.

4 APRIL Martin Luther King Jr. is assassinated on a motel balcony in Memphis, Tennessee; several days of rioting follow in cities across the United States.

5 JUNE Senator Robert Kennedy is assassinated in Los Angeles moments after declaring victory in California's Democratic presidential primary. Three days later, James Earl Ray, the alleged assassin of Martin Luther King Jr., is arrested at Heathrow Airport in London.

27 JULY Alexander Dubcek, Czech party leader, announces that the country will manage its affairs independent of the USSR. On 20 August, Soviet tanks invade and Dubcek and others are arrested, ending the Prague Spring.

26 AUGUST The tempestuous Democratic National Convention opens in Chicago.

1 NOVEMBER The Motion Picture Association of America (MPAA) announces its new ratings system.

1969

20 JANUARY Richard Nixon is inaugurated as the thirty-seventh president.

6 JUNE John Lennon and Yoko Ono stage their bed-in for peace in a Montreal hotel.

27 JUNE Beginning of Stonewall raids and rebellion in New York City.

20 JULY Astronaut Neil Armstrong makes his "giant step" for mankind on the moon.

9 AUGUST Actress Sharon Tate and four others are murdered by Charles Manson and his "family" in Tate's Hollywood Hills home.

15–18 AUGUST The Woodstock Music Festival in upstate New York.

5 SEPTEMBER Military authorities charge Lt. William Calley with premeditated murder in the My Lai massacre of eighteen months earlier.

6 DECEMBER The Rolling Stones' free concert at Altamont Speedway in northern California results in violence and the death of one fan.

American Cinema of the 1960s

The shocking violence of *Psycho* (Alfred Hitchcock, Universal, 1960) anticipated many events to come in the 1960s. Personal collection of the editor.

INTRODUCTION

Movies and the 1960s

BARRY KEITH GRANT

The Eve of Destruction

"What happened in the sixties was no one's deliberate choice, but one of those deep-seated shifts of sensibility that alters the whole moral terrain," writes Morris Dickstein (x). Of course one might say the same of any decade—the 1930s, for example, brought the Great Depression and the international rise of fascism, the 1940s World War II and the Atomic Age, the first decade of the new century 9/11, and so on, each event requiring a radical rethinking of the world and our place in it. Still, the 1960s are frequently regarded as a special, unique period in American history, and not just because of the romantic patina cast over the era by the Baby Boomers (of which, for the record, I am one). For the profound changes of this particular decade brought the United States closer to social revolution than any time in the twentieth century.

"We all want to change the world," sang John Lennon in "Revolution," released on record in late 1968, the same year that saw real revolutionary fervor in places as diverse as China, Prague, Paris, and Quebec. The push for self-recognition by Third World colonies appeared as soon as the decade began, with the insurrection against French rule in Algiers. Several nations gained their independence from colonial oppressors in the 1960s, including Algeria in 1962 and Kenya and Zambia (formerly Northern Rhodesia) from Britain in 1963 and 1964, respectively, while Singapore and Biafra seceded from other countries. The decade also saw a growing resistance to South Africa's apartheid policy and the founding of the Palestine Liberation Organization in 1964. In the United States, an era of consensus built by the national effort of World War II and reinforced during the Red Scare of the 1950s was shattered in the 1960s, replaced by a plurality of voices demanding to be heard, all growing increasingly militant if not violent as the decade progressed. If the decade began with the unfurling of the new fifty-star American flag, it came to a close with flags and draft cards being publicly burned in protest of the Vietnam War. Jimi Hendrix's performance of "The Star-Spangled Banner" at the Woodstock music festival in August 1969, its melodic beauty alternating with screaming electronic distortion, perfectly captured the social and political tensions of the era.

The 1960s was a decade in which, as Bob Dylan knew, "The Times They Are a-Changin'" (1964). Drawing our attention in his song to the momentous social changes taking place at the time ("The order is rapidly fadin'"), Dylan warned listeners that, awash in this sea-change, "you better start swimmin' or you'll sink like a stone." This is exactly the fate of poor Marion Crane as the car containing her body is swallowed up by the swamp near the Bates Motel in Alfred Hitchcock's *Psycho* (1960), a film that in several ways signaled the nature of the decade to come. The brutal killings of eight student nurses by Richard Speck in Chicago in July 1966, and the shooting of forty-six people (fifteen of them fatally) by Charles Whitman from the clock tower at the University of Texas at Austin a month later (a tragedy that inspired Peter Bogdanovich's first feature, *Targets* [1968]) were only two of the decade's violent events that revealed the prescience of Hitchcock's film. Random violence seemed poised to strike at any moment, as it does to the apparent star of *Psycho*. The film's shocking violence, its gender tensions, its critique of the normal, and its permeating pall of death are qualities also characteristic of the cultural and social history of the 1960s, a decade marked by social rebellion, insurrection, assassination, and mass murder.

American society fragmented during the decade as the various challenges to state power were met with increasing and violent resistance. The dichotomy between hip and square of the '50s Beat Generation hardened into the New Left versus the establishment. The "generation gap" (the divide between increasingly alienated young people and their parents) was for awhile as newsworthy as the "missile gap" (Kennedy's term for a purported American military inferiority under Eisenhower). Posters and pins of the time like "Make love, not war," "America—Love It or Leave It," and "If you're not part of the solution, you're part of the problem" reinforced the polarization of the day. "Don't trust anyone over 30," advised Berkeley Free Speech Movement activist Jack Weinberg. Already in 1962 Michael Harrington revealed to Americans in his best-selling book that there was an affluent America and there was *The Other America*. Harrington's book inspired President Lyndon Johnson's "War on Poverty," the term unintentionally revealing the extent to which Americans were in conflict with each other. "We have evidently a great imbalance in American society," explains a teacher in Frederick Wiseman's shocking documentary on the educational system, *High School* (1968), talking about Harrington's book. But his description applies not only to the economic disparities of class in the United States that Harrington discusses, but also to the several other social imbalances that came to the fore in the 1960s. As Dylan sang, "There's a battle outside and it's ragin,'" and it was being fought on a number of fronts simultaneously.

Most ominously, the Cold War continued to heat up. American and Soviet tanks faced each other in August 1961 as construction began on the Berlin Wall, an edifice that seemed to literalize Winston Churchill's postwar observation that an "iron curtain" had descended across the European continent. People were still buying and building fallout shelters in 1960, and "duck and cover" drills continued to be practiced in the nation's public schools. Nuclear tests proliferated in the decade by both Russia in its Semipalatinsk test range and the United States in the Pacific and, beginning with a hydrogen bomb at the Nevada proving grounds in July 1962, within its own borders. America seemed to be losing the space race, as the USSR was first to put a man into space with Yuri Gagarin's orbital flight in April 1961 (the United States followed a month later with flights by Alan Shepard and then by John Glenn, who orbited Earth three times in February 1962). Communist China detonated its first atomic bomb in 1964, joining the ranks of the superpowers. And during the Cuban missile crisis in October 1962, the world waited for almost a week at the brink of nuclear war until Soviet premier Nikita Khrushchev offered to remove Soviet missiles from Cuba if the United States did the same in Turkey.

Americans became increasingly polarized by the Vietnam War, with opposition growing from a small faction early in the decade to become the most significant antiwar movement in American history. By 1966 "teach-ins" about Vietnam sprung up on college campuses across the country. As the decade unfolded, the split between firepower and flower power, those who supported the war and those who opposed it, was cast as one between hawks and doves, a simple binary iconography that, like black hats and white hats in the western genre, pervaded the popular culture of the time. The intensity of the debate, which tore apart families, was graphically revealed when thousands of protestors gathered at the Democratic National Convention in Chicago in August 1968 and Mayor Richard J. Daley responded by sending in the police with nightsticks and tear gas, precipitating three days of violent clashes caught on national television. For many in the New Left this was the inevitable repressive display of state power about which President Dwight D. Eisenhower had warned in his reference to the "military-industrial complex" in his farewell address in January 1961.

It was just such a critique of the nation's dominant ideology—militant, covert, interventionist, even racist—that helped make the television show "Star Trek" so popular with younger viewers. From its debut in September 1966, "Star Trek" delivered its message using the alternate world of science fiction to present an enlightened contrast with U.S. foreign policy, although it ultimately endorsed American culture overall. (Thus there was little irony that the TV spaceship was named for the USS *Enterprise*, which was commissioned as the world's first nuclear-powered aircraft carrier in 1961.) Although ideologically conservative, even old-fashioned, in many ways, the program's concept of a "United Federation of Planets" with a "Prime Directive" that forbids interference with indigenous cultures expressed some viewers' fantasy for a new approach to U.S. foreign policy.

The anger over the nation's history of racial oppression reached its inevitable breaking point in the 1960s. President Eisenhower signed into law the Civil Rights Act, intended to remove barriers for Blacks in the South who wanted to vote, in May 1960, and President Johnson signed another such law in 1964. Certainly the decade saw some major racial barriers broken, perhaps most melodramatically when Black students began registering for the first time at universities in the South against hostile state resistance from the likes of Alabama governor George Wallace, who personally blocked the entrance to the University of Alabama in Tuscaloosa in June 1963 when Vivian Malone and James Hood, escorted by federal troops, arrived. In July 1962, Jackie Robinson became the first Black player to be inducted into the Baseball Hall of Fame, and one month later Mal Goode became the first Black network news commentator, on ABC. Bill Cosby became the first Black actor to co-star in a network TV dramatic series, "I Spy," in 1965. The following year, Edward Brooke (R-Mass.) became the first African American elected to the U.S. Senate since Reconstruction. The crossover success of the Motown sound with groups like The Temptations and Smokey Robinson and the Miracles made black culture seem safe for whites—Diana Ross and the Supremes even introducing a new sense of black glamour by appropriating white styles—but more aggressively, there was James Brown singing "Say It Loud, I'm Black and I'm Proud." Against the racial stereotypes of the past, the idea that "Black is Beautiful" found expression in the afro hairstyle worn by political activist Angela Davis, jazz musician Herbie Hancock, and funk-rock band Sly and the Family Stone, among others. The last vestiges of minstrelsy faded out of popular entertainment in North America in the 1960s, and coon caricatures like Stepin Fetchit of previous decades were replaced by the likes of the articulate and self-confident boxer Muhammad Ali, who, instead of shuffling, noted his ability to "float like a butterfly and sting like a bee."

Martin Luther King Jr. spoke of his famous American dream of peaceful coexistence between the races in 1963. But such a harmonious vision of race relations was challenged by events to follow, not the least of which was the assassination of King himself on 4 April 1968, which sparked violent protests around the country. Just one month after President Johnson first highlighted the phrase "The Great Society" in a commencement address in May 1964, civil rights workers James Chaney, Michael Schwerner, and Andrew Goodman were arrested in Philadelphia, Mississippi, then murdered, their bodies found buried in an earthen dam outside of town weeks later. For several summers the nation experienced violent riots in ghettos across the country as African American frustration at economic and social disparity overheated. Inspired by activists like Stokely Carmichael, the civil rights movement grew less rural, more urban, and more militant as it increasingly turned to expressions of "Black Power." In May 1967, the Black Panthers, led by Huey Newton and Bobby Seale, marched into the State Capitol in Sacramento, California, and in July H. Rap Brown threatened, "If America don't come around, we're going to burn America down." A month later, Carmichael, broadcasting from Havana, urged African Americans to arm for "total revolution," but by the end of the decade most of the Panthers' leadership would be killed in suspicious circumstances or in prison.

The sexual revolution, with its openness to alternate sexual experiences and relationships other than those prescribed by the traditional family and heterosexual monogamy ("free love"), evolved over the course of the decade. The emerging feminist movement began in 1960 with the introduction of the first birth control pills for women, Enovid, which was immediately successful, giving women empowerment over their own bodies even as Hugh Hefner opened his first Playboy Club in Chicago the same year, with the lifestyle of the "Playboy philosophy" suggesting otherwise. Journalist Gloria Steinem worked undercover as a Playboy bunny in 1963, publishing her diary of the experience with a harsh attack on the company's exploitation of women. Betty Friedan's *The Feminine Mystique*, also published in 1963, and Kate Millett's *Sexual Politics* (1968) were influential in raising awareness of patriarchal assumptions and privilege. Friedan's book, which critiqued the traditional homemaker role assigned to women, launched "second wave" feminism and by the end of the decade had sold more than five million copies. Designer Mary Quandt's mini-skirts seemed to further liberate women, and her high boots influenced Nancy Sinatra's proto-feminist hit "These Boots Are Made for Walkin'" in 1966. Friedan and other activists formed the National Organization of Women that same year, and drew attention by trashing their bras in protest at the 1968 Miss America pageant and then by lobbying for passage of the equal rights amendment at the White House in 1969; the proposed amendment, which would have prohibited the infringement of equal rights on the basis of sex, was never ratified.

Gay liberation came out of the closet early in the 1960s and turned violent by decade's end. The decade began with the lesbian organization Daughters of Bilitis holding its first national conference in San Francisco in 1960, although it was not until 1967 that the *Los Angeles Advocate,* the first national gay and lesbian news periodical, began publication. With the acceptance of camp in the cultural mainstream by 1966, most visibly in the retooled "Batman" television series, gay culture seemed to be everywhere, as witnessed by the ubiquity of the fey Paul Lynde on television variety and talk shows and dramatic series at the time. Such representations were more implied than explicit, but that changed dramatically on the night of 27 June 1969, coincidentally the day that gay icon Judy Garland was buried. When police, for reasons not entirely clear, raided the Stonewall Inn, a gay bar in New York City, the patrons, including Beat poet Allen Ginsberg, resisted. Violent confrontations ensued, lasting for the next three nights during which people were arrested and injured, including several policemen. The Stonewall Riots marked a turning point for homosexuals—the Gay Liberation Front was formed in New York a month later—and initiated the Gay Pride movement in the decades to follow.

Although environmentalism had yet to become a significant issue in American society, those with ecological foresight were beginning to sound the alarm. The decade began with the founding of the World Wildlife Federation in 1961 and the publication of Rachel Carson's *Silent Spring,* a best seller of 1962 that exposed the problems of pollution resulting from the use of pesticides. Not coincidentally, at the same time the eco-protest song "Where Have All the Flowers Gone?" by the Kingston Trio scored high on the pop charts. For the first time in American history since Emerson, Thoreau, and the Transcendentalists more than a century before, the idea that nature was a delicate ecosystem that could be destroyed by the meddling of technological progress entered popular consciousness. Further proof that better living through chemicals was debatable was provided in the same year when it was discovered that the anti-nausea pill thalidomide caused severe birth defects in the babies of pregnant women who took it. The decade was marked by a growing anxiety about pollution, culminating in the winter of 1969 when an oil rig ruptured off the coast of Santa Barbara, dumping millions of gallons of crude oil into the coastal waters, killing thousands of sea birds and fish, and then in summer when the Cuyahoga River in Cleveland caught fire as a result of being so polluted.

The Whole Earth Catalogue, published twice a year for four years beginning in 1968, was a *de rigueur* tome for every hippie's bookshelf. With sections like "Shelter and Land Use" and "Community," the *Catalogue*'s purpose was to empower the reader ("access to tools") to "conduct his own education" and "shape his own environment." The hippie movement included a back-to-the-land idealism that was expressed by the appropriation of Native American iconography (beads, feathers, fringes, headbands) as part of subcultural fashion. "We've got to get ourselves back to the garden," sang Joni Mitchell in the song "Woodstock," about the legendary music festival in August 1969 (which Mitchell missed on the advice of her manager), when close to half a million people gathered peacefully in upstate New York despite inadequate facilities, insufficient supplies, and thunderstorms that turned the fields of Max Yasgur's farm into mud. Rejecting the military-industrial complex, many in the counterculture chose to "turn on, tune in, drop out," as former Harvard psychology professor Timothy Leary proclaimed, preferring to drop acid rather than bombs. In opposition to straight culture, the counterculture developed alternative (FM) radio, underground newspapers like the *Los Angeles Free Press, Berkeley Barb, San Francisco Oracle,* and *East Village Other* in New York, and underground comics, most famously by Robert Crumb.

The counterculture had its most profound impact in popular music. Deliberately working against the romantic love songs of Tin Pan Alley, performers such as Arlo Guthrie, Phil Ochs, Bob Dylan, Joan Baez, and others sought to make music more relevant with the development of folk rock and protest music. "Hate your next door neighbor, but don't forget to say grace," growled Barry McGuire in his number-one hit, "The Eve of Destruction," a scathing attack on bourgeois American hypocrisy that could never have been imagined by Irving Berlin. The blues, a musical form developed by Black musicians in the South, experienced a revival with white audiences who identified with the social oppression it expressed. Dylan plugged in his guitar and went electric at the Newport Folk Festival in July 1965, and then at a concert in Forest Hills, New York, outraging folk purists who ran on stage attempting to disrupt the concert in protest. At the beginning of the decade Mitch Miller, an influential A&R man at Columbia who also had a hit TV show, "Sing Along with Mitch," which featured a constipated Miller leading a choir and the audience in middle-of-the-road vocal arrangements of standard pop tunes, was an outspoken opponent of rock 'n' roll. Consequently, the label avoided rock acts, and the company's fortunes lagged. But the words of the rock prophets were written on vinyl, with the help of record company executives, rather than on the subway walls and tenement halls, and by 1967 Miller was history ("For he who gets hurt will be he who has stalled," sang Dylan). His influence at Columbia ended with the coming of the hipper Clive Davis, who immediately signed such progressive psychedelic rock bands to the label as Janis Joplin with Big Brother and the Holding Company, the Byrds, and the Electric Flag, in the process converting Columbia into one of the country's most successful record companies by the end of the decade. Miller's tepid TV show likewise left the air, replaced by more dynamic pop shows like "Shindig" (1964–66) and "Hullabaloo" (1965–66) that featured contemporary music. One has only to listen to the sound track of *Easy Rider* (1969), a film that altered the ethos of Hollywood, to understand how the rock music of the time expressed "the sacred squeal of now" (Goldstein 11).

Jazz, at one time virtually synonymous with popular music, had grown more remotely intellectual by the beginning of the 1960s. As the decade began, Gunther Schuller introduced the notion of Third Stream Music, a highbrow combination of classical music and jazz improvisation. Saxophonist John Coltrane also formed his pioneering quartet in 1960, and as the decade progressed he explored spiritual directions in extended free jazz solo improvisations with *A Love Supreme* (1965) and *Ascension* (1965) through *Stellar Regions* and *Interstellar Space*, both recorded shortly before his death in 1967. Eric Dolphy, after leaving Coltrane's group, was *Out There* and *Outward Bound* (both 1960) and, for some, *Out to Lunch* (1964). Spiritually searching, this music had soul, but lacked a beat you could dance to. Some jazz musicians, eager to return to earth and recapture the mainstream audience siphoned off by rock, absorbed pop and rock songs of the day into their repertoire, playing Bacharach along with Berlin, and Lennon-McCartney along with Arlen and Harburg. Jazz-rock ensembles Blood, Sweat and Tears, the Electric Flag, and Chicago Transit Authority (later Chicago) used horn arrangements that recalled the big band era. And Miles Davis, one of the pioneers of cool jazz in the late 1940s, changed his sound radically, embracing rock's insistent rhythms, heavy bass lines, and electrification in a new style of jazz-rock or fusion. Davis's 1969 release *Bitches Brew*, influenced by rock groups like Sly and the Family Stone, sold well enough to place on the pop charts and paved the way for important bands to follow in the next decade, such as John McLaughlin's Mahavishnu Orchestra, Herbie Hancock's Headhunters, Chick Corea's Return to Forever, and Weather Report.

While pop artists like Claes Oldenburg, Roy Lichtenstein, and, above all, Andy Warhol blurred the boundaries between junk culture and fine art, and happenings erased the distinction between stage and audience in theater, rock music offered similar challenges to cultural taste as it aspired to art. The formula pop tunes churned out by Brill Building tunesmiths in the early 1960s were replaced by the extended works by singer-songwriters who considered themselves poets in the bardic tradition. Jim Morrison's unbearably pretentious lyrics to "The End," an extended twelve-minute Oedipal meditation on masculine identity ("He took a face from the ancient gallery and walked on down the hall") that concludes The Doors' self-titled first LP in 1965 clearly indicates the creative ambitions of the era's rock musicians. As the Beatles began to be taken seriously in the middle of the decade, the pages of cultural magazines were filled with academic debates about whether the music of the Beatles, who had evolved in just a few short years from covering simple rhythm and blues hits to composing more complex and ambiguous tunes, was art or not. *Sgt. Pepper's Lonely Hearts Club Band*, which ushered in the "summer of love" when it was released on 1 June 1967, introduced a number of technical recording innovations and was immediately regarded as a profound cultural event. But if some considered "I am the walrus" as more posturing than profundity, Frank Zappa, with his band the Mothers of Invention, dispelled any doubt about the viability of "art rock." Bursting on the scene with the startlingly innovative double-LP *Freak Out!*—arguably the first true "concept album"—in 1966, it included in the liner notes a list of his musical influences that ranged from Gene and Eunice to Ravel and Varèse, Elvis as well as Ives. Zappa and his group introduced postmodernism to pop, playing everything from straight-ahead R&B to free jazz to Brechtian performance pieces about popular music.

As rock music became increasingly intertwined with the drug culture, those whom Dylan called old-fashioned "sinking stones" gave way to the stoned soul picnic of the late 1960s. Ray Charles moaned "Let's Go Get Stoned" (1966) and Sly and the Family Stone got down singing "I Want to Take You Higher" (1969). In "Rainy Day Women # 12 & 35" (1966) Dylan himself democratically declared that "Everybody Must Get Stoned." The celebratory, drug-infused bus tour by author Ken Kesey and the Merry Pranksters in 1964 was immortalized in Tom Wolfe's best-selling 1968 work of new journalism, *The Electric Kool-Aid Acid Test*. Songs like the Beatles' "Lucy in the Sky with Diamonds," included on *Sgt. Pepper*, were understood by everyone at the time to be about LSD. Psychedelia entered the mainstream with phrases like "far out"; country pop singer B. J. Thomas employed a sitar accompaniment as he sang that he was "hooked on a feeling" (1969); and "Rowan and Martin's Laugh-In" (1967–69), a wacky comedy show featuring a rapid series of short sketches larded with counter-cultural in-jokes, became the top-rated TV program in America. In the summer of 1967, hordes of hippies migrated to San Francisco's Haight-Ashbury neighborhood wearing flowers in their hair. That reliable cultural barometer, *Mad* magazine, featured at least three psychedelic covers between 1967 and 1969 and frequently satirized the drug culture in pieces such as the "Hippie Magazine" ("Turn On, Tune In, Drop Dead Dept."), which included an ad for the exploitation film *The Wild Freakout Acid Trip at the Hippie Teeny-Bopper Love-In Orgy on the Strip* (in startling LSD-color, of course). It promised in the next issue "18 startling photos of Bad Trips—including one to Patchogue on the Long Island Railroad." While the 1960s, like every era, was the best of times and the worst of times, the decade's high points were often eight miles high.

Welcome to Hard Times

All the tensions roiling within American society were inevitably reflected in the cinema of the time even as the industry fought a rear-guard action to attract dwindling audiences. The razing of old film studios in Fort Lee, New Jersey, a town across the Hudson River from Manhattan where many early American movies, including Edwin S. Porter's *The Great Train Robbery* (1903), were made, seemed even in 1963 ominously symbolic. The decade was one of profound change and challenge for Hollywood, as it sought to adapt to both technological innovation and evolving cultural taste. Ultimately, by the end of the 1960s movies were made, distributed, and exhibited differently than when the decade began.

Many important icons of the Hollywood studio era passed away during the 1960s, beginning in the first year of the decade when Clark Gable died of a heart attack just days after completing *The Misfits* (1961). This was also the last film for Marilyn Monroe, literal embodiment of the previous decade's fixation with what Marjorie Rosen called "mammary madness"; Monroe died in 1962, an apparent victim of a drug overdose, although her death, along with that of journalist and TV personality Dorothy Kilgallen three years later, was rumored to be collateral damage in covering up the conspiracy to assassinate President Kennedy. Other Hollywood icons who died during the decade include actors Gary Cooper, Paul Muni, Spencer Tracy, Robert Taylor, Peter Lorre, Boris Karloff, Dick Powell, Harpo and Chico Marx, Charles Laughton, Buster Keaton, Alan Ladd, Stan Laurel, Clara Bow, and Judy Garland, as well as producers David O. Selznick and Walt Disney, cinematographer Karl Freund, composer Alfred Newman, and directors Mack Sennett, Frank Borzage, Anthony Mann, Leo McCarey, and Josef von Sternberg.

Some stars such as Boris Karloff continued to make movies but were trapped within their own iconographical image established in films of a previous era or, like Bette Davis and Joan Crawford, reduced to grotesquerie. Perhaps most profoundly, John Wayne, the icon of rugged American individualism and fighting grit during the 1940s and 1950s, aligned himself with Richard Nixon's right-wing Republican politics and consequently fell out of favor with a generation of filmgoers. His pro-Vietnam War position and his starring role and co-directorial credit in *The Green Berets* in 1968 turned his Davy Crockett image, fighting to the end in *The Alamo* (1960), into one associated with redneck conservatism. Replacing him in popularity were actors embodying very different images of masculinity, such as Robert Redford, Paul Newman, Dustin Hoffman, and Peter Fonda, who appealed more to the younger moviegoers dominating audiences at the time.

A few old-guard directors made their last films in the 1960s, many of them showing painful evidence of their makers' declining abilities. Howard Hawks's career was essentially over, the four films he made in the 1960s all being retreads of earlier work. *Man's Favorite Sport?* (1964), for example, starring Paula Prentiss in the Katharine Hepburn role and Rock Hudson in the Cary Grant role (which Grant declined because of his age), was noteworthy as a miscalculated attempt to recapture the charm of screwball comedy in an era of changing sexual mores. Fritz Lang made his last film, *Die 1000 Augen des Dr. Mabuse* (*The Thousand Eyes of Dr. Mabuse,* 1960), in Germany. George Cukor began the decade impressively with *Heller in Pink Tights, Let's Make Love* (both 1960) and *The Chapman Report* (1962), but then declined precipitously beginning with *My Fair Lady* in 1964. Frank Capra's career ended in 1961 with the flat *Pocketful of Miracles*, and Charlie Chaplin's with the uneven bedroom farce *A Countess from Hong Kong* in 1967. Almost alone among the great directors of the studio era, John Ford and Alfred Hitchcock continued to make interesting films.

Hollywood seemed besieged from a variety of fronts. Emblematic of the turmoil and transition the industry would face in the 1960s, the decade began with strikes in 1960 by writers and the Screen Actors Guild, led by union president Ronald Reagan, as actors successfully demanded residual payments for appearing in movies broadcast on television. With cutbacks in production, the studios abandoned the practice of signing stars to long-term contracts; as a consequence, actors gained more control over the films they appeared in, often producing them themselves. As the studios concentrated more on distribution than production (they already had been forced out of exhibition by the Supreme Court's Paramount Decision in 1948), independent producers assembled their own production "packages," including personnel. Filmmakers began to balk at the previous decade's blacklist, further eroding the studios' power: Stanley Kramer hired Nedrick Young to write *Inherit the Wind* and Dalton Trumbo wrote the screenplays for Otto Preminger's *Exodus* and Stanley Kubrick's *Spartacus* (all 1960). Exclusionary practices in Hollywood of another kind were challenged as the NAACP lobbied for the integration of Black craftsmen into Hollywood unions. The art cinema circuit was well established during the 1960s, with films like Ingmar Bergman's *The Silence* (1963) and *Persona* (1966), Federico Fellini's *La Dolce vita* (1960) and *8½* (1963), Michelangelo Antonioni's *Red Desert* (1964) and *Blowup* (1966), and François Truffaut's *Jules et Jim* (1962) and *The Bride Wore Black* (1968) playing both in major cities and college towns across the country.

The importance of television rights to the Screen Actors Guild strike was an indication of the newer medium's impact on Hollywood in the 1960s. The commercially disastrous *Cleopatra* (1963), an extravagant epic originally budgeted at $2 million but whose costs ballooned to over $44 million, almost pushing Twentieth Century Fox into bankruptcy, was one of Hollywood's overblown attempts to lure viewers off their sofas and into movie theaters. But such an approach was more typical of the previous decade, when television was regarded by Hollywood as an entertainment rival siphoning off potential audiences and profits; instead, during the 1960s the studios accepted the inevitable and reconciled with television by committing themselves to it. In 1960, commercial television had been available for only fourteen years, but already almost 90 percent of American households had a TV set. So the studios began producing series for network television, and in September 1961 NBC introduced "Saturday Night at the Movies," a regular movie night in prime time that was very successful. In early 1966 Universal took the next step, beginning production on films made directly for television.

By contrast, in the ten-year period from 1960 to 1970, the number of feature films released by the seven major film companies (Columbia, MGM, Paramount, Twentieth Century Fox, United Artists, Universal, and Warner Bros.) dropped from 184 to 151. In the same period, the number of movie theaters in the country dropped from almost 17,000 to just under 13,500 (Monaco 269–70). Most of the new theaters constructed in the decade were smaller multiplexes situated in suburban shopping centers; the demise of the sumptuous downtown movie palaces was under way, their more modest replacements bespeaking the new positioning of movies as one entertainment option among several. Studios were bought up by conglomerates—Universal (along with Decca Records) by MCA in 1964, Paramount by Gulf+Western in 1966, and Warner Bros. by Kinney National Services in 1969—whose primary interest was not movies. Overall, Americans may have spent slightly more on movies as the 1960s progressed, but the share of box office receipts in their overall recreation expenditure dwindled from 4.7 to 2.7 percent in the course of the decade (Monaco 271).

In a famous speech before the National Association of Broadcasters on 9 May 1961, Newton Minow, chairman of the Federal Communications Commission, attacked the television industry as "a vast wasteland." Popular sitcoms like "The Andy Griffith Show" (1960–68), "Car 54, Where Are You?" (1961–63), "The Beverly Hillbillies" (1962–71), "My Favorite Martian" (1963–66), "The Munsters" (1964–66), and "Gomer Pyle, USMC" (1964–69) presented escapist visions of an impossible America untroubled by real social problems. Watching a show like "Green Acres" (1965–71), with its bucolic depiction of rural America, one would never know there were political tensions troubling the country, and in the second half of the decade the surprise hit series "Hogan's Heroes" (1965–71) seemed to erase history with its portrayal of funny and incompetent German soldiers running a World War II POW camp containing irrepressible American GIs. Of course, some shows that seemed just escapist fantasy reflected real cultural tensions, such as "Bewitched" (1964–72), a sitcom about a mortal man married to a witch with supernatural powers that cleverly disguised issues of women's roles that contemporary feminists were raising. In the second half of the decade, when reality threatened to intrude on television, it was filtered, as when the Rolling Stones were forced to change their relatively innocuous "Let's Spend the Night Together" to "Let's Spend Some Time Together" on "The Ed Sullivan Show" in January 1967. The same year saw the debut of "The Smothers Brothers Comedy Hour" (1967–69), which to the surprise and chagrin of CBS evolved from hip to overtly political with appearances by antiwar performers like Pete Seeger, who had been blacklisted in the 1950s; the show was abruptly canceled in April 1969 by CBS president William S. Paley.

One of the most notable exceptions to the televisual wasteland was "The Twilight Zone" (1959–64), a nonserial program featuring stories that made intelligent use of science fiction, fantasy, and horror elements, typically with a surprise twist at the end that provided a moral lesson. Often the episodes were adaptations of stories by important writers of the fantastic such as Jerome Bixby, Damon Knight, and Ambrose Bierce. The show was produced and hosted by Rod Serling, who also wrote more than half the scripts, with others by major science fiction writers such as Charles Beaumont, Richard Matheson, and Ray Bradbury. The episodes frequently starred established movie actors and were directed by such Hollywood stalwarts of the studio era as John Brahm, Mitchell Leisen, Jacques Tourneur, and Robert Florey. Perhaps the most interesting and revealing aspect of "The Twilight Zone" was its conflicted ideology, which demonstrated the difficulty of providing any sustained social criticism on network television. While some episodes offered a pointed critique of the middle class and the status quo (perhaps most famously in the episode "The Monsters are Due on Maple Street," in which aliens conquer humankind by manipulating bourgeois Americans' innate fear of the Other so that they destroy themselves), others often showed the price to pay when someone disturbs the natural order of the universe by seeking to change the life circumstances they have been allotted.

Advances in camera and sound technology during the 1960s not only brought the era's tumultuous events into the nation's living rooms, it also brought about the demise of newsreels. Universal News outlasted the others but folded in 1967. Television news seemed more immediate and direct, as viewers learned during the Nixon-Kennedy debates in 1960 and subsequently throughout the decade in the live coverage of events following Kennedy's assassination in 1963, in footage of civil rights demonstrations and Vietnam combat, and with the televised draft lottery on 1 December 1969. Every aspect of the moon mission and landing by astronauts Buzz Aldrin and Neil Armstrong on 20 July 1969 was televised, from liftoff to recovery, with Americans the world over glued to their television sets. Technological advances also made location shooting increasingly easier. In addition, the conventions of realism established since Italian Neorealism after World War II encouraged filmmakers to work outside of Hollywood. Such "runaway" productions became a threat to the major studios, and by 1961 they were pressuring Congress to investigate the practice. According to John Baxter, Otto Preminger's *Anatomy of a Murder* (1960), shot in Michigan, was one of the films that "finally severed the studio umbilical, and by 1962 30% of Hollywood's major product was shot overseas" (Baxter 12).

The development of lightweight, portable 16 mm equipment was not only a boon to experimental cinema, but also a catalyst for significant changes in documentary film practice. Filmmakers could now shoot on location with relative ease, following events as they happened—what Stephen Mamber has called an "uncontrolled cinema." Documentary filmmakers abandoned the tripod and took the camera on their shoulders into the midst of the action. *Primary* (1960), about the Wisconsin Democratic presidential primary campaigns of Kennedy and Hubert Humphrey, showed the candidates both in public appearances and behind the scenes in the kind of moments rarely seen before. The film features a celebrated scene in which the camera follows Kennedy emerging from a car outside the hall where he is to speak to a group of local voters, and moving through the entrance and a relatively dark corridor into the large, well-lit hall crowded with people and onto the stage, changing focus and aperture as necessary.

Direct cinema filmmakers aspired to be, in Richard Leacock's phrase, "a fly on the wall," capturing truth on camera without interference and looking for "privileged moments" in which the camera is able to penetrate the surface reality that it photographs to offer a revelation about its subject. Shirley Clarke's *Portrait of Jason* (1967) consisted entirely of a series of talking-head close-ups of an unsuccessful actor who, fueled by alcohol, marijuana, and prodding questions from behind the camera over the course of an evening, lets down his smug intellectual persona and reveals his private self-pity, like a criminal confessing on the stand to Raymond Burr at the climax of every "Perry Mason" (1957–66) episode. The Drew Associates, led by producer Robert Drew and including Leacock, D. A. Pennebaker, and Albert Maysles, produced a remarkable series of nineteen pioneering films for television, beginning with *Primary* in 1960 and ending with *Crisis: Behind a Presidential Commitment* in 1963, about the integration of the University of Alabama, that brought a new intimacy to documentary journalism. Direct cinema's earnest search for truth in cinema was brilliantly satirized in 1967 with *David Holzman's Diary*, an observational mockumentary that pretends to be by a self-absorbed filmmaker about his own boring and uninteresting life.

Unlike most direct cinema filmmakers, Frederick Wiseman felt no compunction to preserve the temporality of events, relying more on rhetorical editing techniques in his remarkable series of American institutional films that began in 1967 with *Titicut Follies*, *High School* the following year, and *Law and Order* in 1969. Revealing the gaps between the purpose of public institutions like hospitals and schools and their actual functioning, these muckraking exposés were part of the decade's growing interest in bringing to light unsavory aspects of American society also manifest in nonfiction bestsellers such as Jessica Mitford's *The American Way of Death* (1962), Masters and Johnson's *Human Sexual Response* (1966), and Harold Cruse's *The Crisis of the Negro Intellectual* (1967). Revealing tensions of class, race, and gender at work in everyday life, Wiseman's documentaries questioned the platitudes and values of the American Dream as did Albert and David Maysles's *Salesman* (1969), in which even religious faith is reduced to a capitalist commodity. Using found footage rather than the observational style, Emile de Antonio similarly critiqued the status quo in documentaries that exposed government corruption (*Point of Order* [1964], about the 1954 Army-McCarthy Senate hearings) or challenged official policy *(Rush to Judgment* [1967], about the report of the Warren Commission on the assassination of JFK).

The 1960s also was the golden era of American experimental cinema, featuring some of the most important work of such filmmakers as Stan Brakhage, Andy Warhol, Jack Smith, Bruce Baillie, Ken Jacobs, Stan Vanderbeek, Robert Nelson, and Kenneth Anger. Among the many films Brakhage made in the 1960s was *Dog Star Man* (1961–64), an ambitious and lyrical four-part, seventy-five-minute mythic work that incorporated layers of superimposed images and a complex editing pattern. In 1965 Eastman Kodak introduced Super-8 home movie film in threadless cartridges, a format that would be used by several important experimental filmmakers, including Brakhage. Structural film was pioneered by Tony Conrad (*Flicker*, 1966), George Landow (*Film in Which There Appears Edge Lettering, Sprocket Holes, Dirt Particles, Etc.*, 1966), and Canadian Michael Snow, working at the time in New York City (*Wavelength*, 1967). Midnight screenings of experimental films sprang up in cities and campuses around the country. Much of the impetus for the burgeoning experimental film scene was generated by the tireless Jonas Mekas, who after founding the magazine *Film Culture*, devoted to experimental cinema, in the 1950s, generated a readership with his weekly column "Movie Journal" in New York's *Village Voice* in the 1960s. In March 1966 Mekas, Shirley Clarke, and Lionel Rogosin formed Filmmakers Distribution Center to distribute independent and experimental films (the company released Warhol's *Chelsea Girls* [1966] in commercial theaters later in the year) and on the West Coast the experimental filmmaking community formed Canyon Cinema in California, founded in 1967 by Nelson, Bruce Conner, Larry Jordan, and other underground filmmakers looking for an organizational structure to distribute their work.

Hollywood, meanwhile, struggled to remain in touch with the decade's burgeoning youth culture. In August 1965 the Beatles played before 56,000 fans at New York's Shea Stadium, the same summer that racial violence erupted in Los Angeles, Chicago, and other cities. But that year the big Oscar winner was the feel-good family film *The Sound of Music*—a work of calculated sentimental claptrap about the musical Von Trapp family that Pauline Kael almost alone disliked, referring to it as "the sound of money." Similarly, in 1968, the year of the Tet Offensive, the My Lai massacre, the

The Sound of Music (Robert Wise, Argyle Enterprises Productions—Twentieth Century Fox, 1965) was a critical and commercial success that offered escapist entertainment in a turbulent time. Personal collection of the editor.

police assaults on the Black Panthers, the assassinations of Martin Luther King and Robert F. Kennedy, the stormy Democratic National Convention in Chicago, the forcible dispersal of the residents of Resurrection City in Washington, the election of Richard Nixon, the Prague Spring, the Soviet invasion of Czechoslovakia, and of course May '68 in France, when the country experienced a general strike that led to the eventual collapse of the de Gaulle regime, the films nominated for Best Picture were Franco Zeffirelli's picturesque *Romeo and Juliet, Funny Girl, The Lion in Winter, Rachel, Rachel,* and *Oliver!* the last being the year's big winner. Clearly Hollywood needed to do more to reach the youth audience.

The studios sought to keep up, as indicated by changes in censorship during the decade. The Production Code Administration allowed onscreen depictions of homosexuality in 1961, although they were to be treated with "care, discretion, and restraint" (Benshoff 280). In 1964 the Association of Motion Picture and Television Producers (MPAA) was formed, in part to lobby for further revisions to the Production Code, particularly to end the ban on nudity, which had clearly disadvantaged American movies in comparison to the more adult sensibility of the European films showing to appreciative audiences in the United States. The following year the Production Code granted an exemption to *The Pawnbroker* (1965), despite its brief scenes of female nudity (it was still condemned by the Catholic Legion of Decency), and the year after that MGM decided to distribute Antonioni's *Blowup*, which featured a nude scene with David Hemmings and two teenage girls frolicking on rumpled purple paper, a visually bold scene that showed pubic hair and demonstrated how outdated the Code was. In 1967 the hippie musical *Hair*, which featured a quick glimpse of "the full monty" of the male and female cast, debuted off-Broadway and crossed over to the Great White Way a year later. The Production Code eventually adopted new guidelines and eliminated many specific taboos, but it was scrapped in favor of a ratings system in November 1968, the same month Nixon was elected president.

Like popular music, movies were in the process of being reconceived as art rather than entertainment. The so-called "movie brats," a young generation of Hollywood filmmakers who had studied film, some within an academic context, and who constituted what was to become known in the next decade as the New Hollywood, began to work their way into the industry. Francis Ford Coppola made *Dementia 13* (1963), *You're a Big Boy Now* (1966), *Finian's Rainbow* (1968), and *The Rain People* (1969), Brian De Palma directed *Greetings* (1968), William Friedkin made *Good Times* (1967) and *The Night They Raided Minksy's* (1968), Martin Scorsese made *Who's That Knocking at My Door* (1967), and Peter Bogdanovich crossed over from critic to director with *Targets* (1968). Like the directors of the French New Wave just before them and which in part inspired them, this generation of filmmakers was the first in the history of Hollywood to be critically aware of Hollywood history, and so inevitably made movies with a new, more self-conscious approach to traditional genres. Not coincidentally, the *New York Times* reported in 1964 that a number of U.S. colleges had been developing courses on films and filmmaking (Bart), and in 1968 the American Film Institute, a nonprofit organization with the mandate to preserve and develop America's "artistic and cultural resources in film," was established with a budget of $1.21 million as it embarked on a three-year program to collect and preserve disintegrating American classic films.

Perhaps the most significant moment in the cultural reconception of American cinema as art was the publication of Andrew Sarris's article "Notes on the Auteur Theory in 1962" in the winter 1962–63 issue of Mekas's *Film Culture*. Boldly proclaiming, "Henceforth, I will abbreviate *la politique des auteurs* as the auteur theory," he opened the floodgates of critical debate by arguing that movies, even Hollywood genre movies, may be read as expressions of a personal vision on the part of the director. In 1968 Sarris published his groundbreaking work, *The American Cinema*, which for the first time offered a critical charting of the history of Hollywood cinema, ranking all important directors to have worked in Hollywood in terms of their auteurist status, beginning with a controversial "Pantheon" and moving down to "Less Than Meets the Eye." Auteurism stimulated heated discussion, and critical barbs were slung back and forth in the pages of film journals, cultural periodicals, and the popular press. Several public feuds ensued, the most celebrated of which was the ongoing war of words between Sarris and Kael, two influential critics who developed wide, devoted readerships largely through their columns in New York's *Village Voice* and *New Yorker* magazine, respectively. Dwight Macdonald, a well-known cultural voice of the day and author of an important critical attack on the debasing nature of popular culture, parted ways with *Film Quarterly* because he refused to be associated with a magazine that included a critic (Sarris) who could be of the opinion that Hitchcock in *The Birds* (1963) was "at the summit of his artistic powers" (Magid 70). Auteurism brought directors into the cultural spotlight, and some, like Roman Polanski, Mike Nichols, and Stanley Kubrick, became celebrities themselves, sometimes more newsworthy than the actors in their films.

British critic Robin Wood began his 1965 landmark auteurist book *Hitchcock's Films* by pointedly asking, "Why should we take Hitchcock seriously?" Although no one needs to ask this question today, with Hitchcock's critical reputation well established, it was crucial at the time when auteurism was just beginning to take root in America. Noting that if the cinema were regarded as an art like the other arts the question would be unnecessary, Wood proceeded to offer an extended and convincing analogy between the films of Hitchcock, then regarded by many as but a popular Hollywood director, and the Elizabethan plays of Shakespeare. He then proposed a consistent theme in the films whereby spectators are forced to confront their own unacknowledged darker impulses and thus come to terms with them (Wood 9ff.). The proposition that a popular filmmaker, an entertainer, might express a personal vision, explore ethical and metaphysical issues as the best artists do, was almost heretical in the context of traditional aesthetics. In Hollywood, where studio mogul Samuel Goldwyn was reputed to have said that movies were for entertainment while messages should be delivered by Western Union, genre pictures were now being regarded as profound moral and metaphysical statements by their directors. Where Hollywood before had been regarded as a dream factory producing disposable entertainment, it was now seen by some as a place were artists were stamping their personalities on communal art.

"In hindsight," wrote Paul Monaco, "the Hollywood feature film appears to have been struggling throughout the 1960s with the question of how to hold its audience by creating movies that might be positioned somewhere between being 'arty' and 'conventional'" (3). In Robert Aldrich's *The Legend of Lylah Clare* (1968), the studio boss (Ernest Borgnine) explains emphatically to his son (Michael Murphy), a young idealist with visions of "cinema," "We don't make *films*, we make *movies.*" Such a distinction may be seen to inform, for example, the fate of Roman Polanski's *Dance of the Vampires*, which was recut by MGM executive producer Martin Ransohoff with cartoon fangs added to Leo the Lion to make it more palatable for mainstream audiences, and released in the United States as *The Fearless Vampire Killers or: Pardon Me, But Your Teeth Are in My Neck* in 1967. This tension—or, as they might have said in the 1960s, Catch-22—is clear throughout the decade, beginning with movies such as *Psycho, Sergeant Rutledge,* and *Spartacus* in 1960 through *Rosemary's Baby* (1968), Arthur Penn's *Bonnie and Clyde* (1968), and Sam Peckinpah's *The Wild Bunch* (1969) as it came to a close. And while various groups clamored for recognition during the 1960s, Hollywood gingerly approached such controversial issues as homosexuality in movies like *The Children's Hour* (1961) and racial discrimination in *Guess Who's Coming to Dinner* (1967). Even a more hard-hitting film like Norman Jewison's *In the Heat of the Night* (1967) needed the well-groomed presence of Sidney Poitier, an actor who would soon be rejected by more militant Blacks as an example of what Old Lodge Skins (Chief Dan George) in *Little Big Man* (1970) would sarcastically refer to as "the black white man."

After the beach and biker cycles in the first half of the decade, Hollywood made a few significant youth movies, such as *The Graduate* (1967), but it was the phenomenal success of *Easy Rider* (1969) that paved the way for the New Hollywood to follow. Made for under $400,000, the film grossed millions. A road movie with a loose, episodic structure about two guys who make a drug deal and then embark on a motorcycle trip across America, *Easy Rider* became a cult hit and made stars of Dennis Hopper, Peter Fonda, and the scene-stealing Jack Nicholson. Its success opened the doors of perception in Hollywood for the counterculture, initiating a flurry of new youth-oriented films in the next decade.

Easy Rider ends with the sudden and shocking death of its two protagonists, shot by rednecks who disapprove of their difference. The scene captures the degree to which in the 1960s the country seemed so divided. "A man went looking for America, and couldn't find it anywhere," proclaimed

The promise of freedom and its betrayal made *Easy Rider* (Dennis Hopper, Columbia, 1969) a surprise countercultural hit. Personal collection of the editor.

contemporary advertisements for the film. In a scenario that resonates with the social discord of its time, in *Fail-Safe*, both Eugene Burdick and Harvey Wheeler's best-selling novel (1962) and Sidney Lumet's 1964 film adaptation, the American president calls for a nuclear strike on New York City to compensate for an accidental American strike on Moscow in order to avoid an all-out nuclear war with the Soviet Union. Such self-destructive madness was taken to the limit in the blackest of comedies, *Dr. Strangelove or: How I Learned to Stop Worrying and Love the Bomb* (1964), written by Terry Southern and directed by Stanley Kubrick, which ends not only with the nuclear destruction of the United States but of the entire world. No wonder that in the 1960s America is imagined as an insane asylum in Ken Kesey's novel *One Flew Over the Cuckoo's Nest* (1962), Samuel Fuller's film *Shock Corridor* (1963), and Wiseman's *Titicut Follies*. Each of these works uses the metaphor of the madhouse to comment on the tensions tearing at American society. And while the cultural and political battles outside were raging across the United States, Hollywood experienced its own difficulties as it sought to adjust to the radical changes taking place within American society.

1960

Movies and Intimations of Disaster and Hope

CHRISTOPHER SHARRETT

The year seemed to look forward to a period of radical social change following a decade of repression and conformity. But this change would quickly face compromises and contradictions, emblematized in the white mainstream audience's embrace of Chubby Checker's watered-down cover version of Hank Ballard's rhythm-and-blues song "The Twist," which became an instant hit after Checker performed it on Dick Clark's whitebread television vehicle for rock 'n' roll promotion, "American Bandstand." Hugh Hefner opened his first Playboy Club in February, and in May the first birth control pill, Enovid, became commercially available, generating over a half-million prescriptions in the second half of the year. The arrival of "the pill" signaled the beginning of the sexual revolution and the feminist movement, but changes in sexual restrictions were circumscribed by male prerogatives, represented in Hefner's "playboy philosophy," the rise of skin magazines, and the continued tendency by patriarchal commercial culture to objectify and commodify the female body. Television featured some socially relevant programming, perhaps most important CBS's broadcast (on 25 November) of the powerful documentary "Harvest of Shame" with Edward R. Murrow. Exposing the impoverished and largely unacknowledged working conditions of many Americans, "Harvest of Shame" appeared within the televisual flow of popular but vapid fantasy worlds offered by such series as "The Andy Griffith Show" (1960–1968), "My Three Sons" (1960–1972), and "The Flintstones" (1960–1966), the last a family-oriented and animated version of Jackie Gleason's pioneering socially aware sitcom "The Honeymooners" (1955–1956). The activist group Students for a Democratic Society (SDS) held its first meeting in Ann Arbor, Michigan, in January, and in February a sit-in by four African Americans at a whites-only Woolworth's lunch counter in Greensboro, North Carolina, ignited dozens of similar protests across the nation over the next few months.

Diplomatic relations with Cuba became increasingly strained, emphatically with the election on 8 November of John F. Kennedy to the presidency.

The new president subscribed to the domino theory of revolution in the third world, and his so-called liberalism suggested to many the serious limitations of liberal ideology. Kennedy's perceived idealism translated into little active support of civil rights; his foreign policy was clearly pro-incursionist, if not as strident as that of his successors. During the same year, authentic social progress made significant strides, as the civil rights movement gained momentum and a crucial sit-in at Shaw College resulted in the April birth of the Student Nonviolent Coordinating Committee (SNCC), whose aim was to coordinate the use of nonviolent direct action against segregation.

These conflicting historical moments are relevant to understanding the films of the year. If the cinema as an art form is any guide, the year was a transitional moment whose contradictions reflect the conservative society shaped by the Cold War and U.S. triumphalism after World War II but also anticipate both the radical impulses of the coming years and the reaction that would close off the progressive possibilities of the decade.

There were some weak contributions from usually noteworthy directors, a few of whom conveyed the regression that accompanied the social progress symbolized by some of the more interesting films of the year. Otto Preminger's *Exodus,* often ranked high in Preminger's oeuvre, is prominent for several fine performances. But this mammoth film—enchanting for many viewers because it was shot partly on location in and around Tel Aviv—is either ignorant or disingenuous on the politics of Zionism and the role of the West in the creation and political use of the state of Israel. Vincente Minnelli's *Bells Are Ringing,* while it features a flamboyant performance by Judy Holliday, lacks the density of the director's best musicals, while Elia Kazan's *Wild River* is a flaccid, unconvincing work that probably represents the limits of the filmmaker's liberal sensibility. Robert Mulligan's *The Rat Race* repeats key ideas of much more distinguished films of the period, as does Henry Hathaway's slapstick "northern" western, *North to Alaska,* a travesty when set against the past accomplishments of the genre in the prior decade. Clearly, Hollywood was still capable of more than a few gross errors even as it exploited the collapse of the system in fostering a new creativity.

The westerns addressed the issue of race that had been tentatively broached in some movies of the 1950s, just as the previous decade's "social problem" films influenced the western's new approach toward race, producing pictures whose indictments of white society became increasingly stinging. John Ford's *Sergeant Rutledge* is one of the less remarkable of these films, in part because of a strained effort that makes Ford look less than sincere. The idealized Rutledge (Woody Strode) is another Noble Savage incarnation that protests too much Ford's late-career racial tolerance. Don Siegel's *Flaming Star* is more intriguing, mainly for the performance by Elvis Presley as Pacer Burton, a "half-breed" caught in the middle of inter-family conflict and social discord that seems more attuned to progressive contemporary activities than Ford's film. Siegel was one of the few directors to show Presley's gifts as an actor. John Huston's neglected *The Unforgiven,* the story of a Texas family repressing the secret that their adopted daughter is actually a Native American taken from a Kiowa settlement, is a remarkably pointed attack on the racism of frontier America, and by extension of bourgeois white society. If Audrey Hepburn is somewhat difficult to accept as the Kiowa foundling, the Bible-thumping Rawlins family, who turn on Ben Zachary (Burt Lancaster) and his beleaguered kin, is pointedly suggestive of the axiomatic response of white "settlers" to the native population.

In the horror genre, the year saw the inauguration of Roger Corman's cycle of adaptations of the stories of Edgar Allan Poe with *The Fall of the House of Usher.* This film, often twin-billed this year with *Psycho,* is perhaps as crucial as Hitchcock's work to the horror genre's psychological bent. *House of Usher* centers on a crazed, hysterical patriarchal figure, Roderick Usher (Vincent Price), who is himself a victim of patriarchy's oppression. Usher sees the decaying social order over which he presides—here symbolized by a crumbling mansion—collapse into ruins. Philip Winthrop (Mark Damon), betrothed to Usher's sister Madeline (Myrna Fahey), attempts to rescue her from the moribund world of her controlling brother. Philip's near-miss escape from Usher and his flight from the fire that consumes the Usher mansion have a morbid tone as the house, represented by a superb expressionist model by designer Daniel Haller, burns and then sinks into Poe's infamous tarn. Roderick succeeds only in destroying Madeline, fore-closing any hope for the future.

The tensions of the day are particularly well represented in Alfred Hitchcock's *Psycho,* perhaps the most accomplished film of a year that produced several works of distinction, and one that has since become canonical. Adapted from Robert Bloch's crude novel based on the crimes of reclusive midwestern murderer Ed Gein, *Psycho* is very much part of the climate of exploitation and sensation that had been flourishing for several years. It is also a work that captures the extreme political tensions that continued long after McCarthyism, in particular concerning "manliness" and the roles assigned to the sexes. The story of a lonely, disturbed, and dangerous young man who lives in the shadow of his deceased mother, the film has been widely interpreted as a pivotal horror film for its suggestion that monstrosity must be defined as inherent to the bourgeois family structure rather than an arcane social aberration: the crimes of Norman Bates (Anthony Perkins) can be read as the consequence of the misdeeds of a sexually rambunctious mother. The film is profoundly subversive, with its monster no longer a creature of the night, or the product of a laboratory experiment gone awry, but instead a boy next door, the logical product of a disintegrating social order. Norman's mental condition necessarily raises questions about the nature of the normal—a prescient examination of a hopelessly repressive and oppressive society on the precipice. The family violence of the Bates household is the explosion of rage against this society. That this violence could not for long be contained within the family or directed at oneself is a stunning revelation of this film, and will become obvious enough in a host of films of the following decade.

Satire as Horror

Billy Wilder's much-acclaimed *The Apartment* wants to shield its caustic aspect with comedy, largely through the performance of Jack Lemmon as C. C. Baxter, the hapless bachelor and obsequious clerk to a huge insurance firm who loans his apartment to various philandering executives in an attempt to gain favor. It is obvious that the favors have gained him little, as Wilder establishes Baxter as a go-along, get-along flunky far too narrow to understand the trap he has constructed for himself, making the upbeat moralism that Wilder finally offers as Baxter falls in love with elevator operator and boss's mistress Fran Kubelik (Shirley MacLaine) seem rather contrived.

But even with its comic shtick, the film is almost unremittingly grim in its portrayal of the workaday world of postwar Manhattan, a city festooned with the steel-and-glass skyscrapers of architects Philip Johnson and Mies van der Rohe. Baxter's employment on the central data floor of his company is depicted in a Kafkaesque image, a sea of endless, evenly spaced desks under glaring fluorescent lights populated with flannel-suited male clones and their female assistants, all miserable and resentful, all questioning in their resentment. Here, Wilder's view is cynical rather than critical. His vision of a society of dissatisfied, "cheating" husbands, for whom the family is a façade providing security and social respectability but who constantly require, for real fulfillment, access to such facilities as C.C. can provide, seems very plausible, as is the degree of predation to which men routinely subject gullible, vulnerable young women. The degree of gullibility is very much open to question—Wilder assumes that the female is simply a softheaded, easy mark. Wilder's vision is extreme, his leering executives comic grotesques close to George Grosz's expressionist sketches of Weimar Germany, best suggested in C.C.'s manipulative boss J. D. Sheldrake (Fred MacMurray). His is a character of such soulless cruelty as to place him close to film noir were he not also a perfectly representative figure of American popular culture, the TV-sitcom dad who goes to a job we never see and that has no perceivable impact on his emotional well-being. In casting Fred MacMurray in the part, Wilder took the actor from his new career as Disney icon and star of television's "My Three Sons," which debuted this same year, to return him to his prior, and more sinister, screen persona, thus subverting an image associated with the bogus tranquility of postwar life. *The Apartment* suggests what really goes on at those big-city jobs that allows dad to return apparently unruffled to his suburban comforts. Like *Psycho*, *The Apartment* raises questions as to how one defines pathology in a world that denies neurosis and unhappiness.

Jack Lemmon's distinctive comic flourishes and vocal inflections don't go far in making his C. C. Baxter entirely sympathetic; he is someone uncomfortable in his own skin, whose nervous ticks and jangled speech convey a person utterly lacking in conviction or self-possession—he simply can't be the *mensch* his neighbor, the kindly Dr. Dreyfuss (Jack Kruschen), wants him to be. C.C. is essentially a pimp, of his own self more than of the women with whom he has no association whatever (such is the degree of his alienation and worthlessness in the corporate pecking order of the Consolidated Life insurance company). Wilder's cynicism is most evident in his cop-out, boy-gets-girl ending, which seems quite capable of producing an afterstory identical to the film we have just seen. Wilder's practiced cynicism in *The Apartment* will not allow a careful look at the assumptions of gender relations in a culture predicated on heterosexual monogamy, where the extramarital relationship is perceived as a nasty transgression rather than a response to an untenable institution.

Melodrama's Summary Statements

One may argue that the pinnacle of melodrama was reached with Minnelli's *Home from the Hill,* one of the extraordinary accomplishments of the form and a representative achievement not only of this year but of the most creative and contentious phase of late Hollywood, being one of the most complex indictments of patriarchal civilization. Captain Wade Hunnicut (Robert Mitchum) is a Texas land baron presiding over a rural town and his alienated family. At the heart of the film is the question of legitimacy. The issue is most obviously manifest in the attempt by Wade's younger son to recognize his illegitimate half-brother; the more profound relates to the legitimacy of male property rights and the patriarchal capitalist order, with Theron Hunnicut (George Hamilton) representing the male child at first embracing, then rejecting, then becoming the logical consequence of patriarchy. His close connection with his half-brother Rafe (George Peppard) may suggest a homoerotic relationship, but this would appear so only to a society that cannot conceive of tenderness between two men. That this relationship comes about because Theron rebels against their monstrous father, who refuses to acknowledge the illegitimate Rafe as his lawful son, speaks to the film's profoundly radical impulses, especially as it develops the consequences of patriarchal assumptions.

Robin Wood remarks that patriarchy has as one of its victims the patriarch himself (Wood, *Hollywood* 134). The point is certainly relevant to *Home from the Hill,* since Wade Hunnicutt's need to take his son Theron from under his mother's wing and masculinize him leads to his own murder and his son's self-imposed exile. Among the film's achievements is its complex development of the complicated nature of patriarchy in modern America. Wade's attempt to shape Theron is not based simply on the overwhelming ego of the macho male trying to find an extension of his self in his male offspring. Indeed, it is Theron who feels compelled to approach Wade to learn to "be a man." He has been made into a "mama's boy" by his mother, Hannah (Eleanor Parker), as part of an agreement with Wade when she learned, returning from their honeymoon eighteen years earlier, that he had fathered the illegitimate Rafe and left destitute Rafe's mother, Ann Copley. Answering Hannah's outraged demands, Wade turned over their legitimate son entirely to her care, ostensibly so she could protect him from learning his father's sexually cavalier ways. The agreement also stipulated that Hannah would remain in Wade's house but would no longer share his bed. Their marriage is thus a sham, with Wade continuing the sexual conquests that apparently long preceded it (although he blames his behavior on Hannah). He becomes an emblem to the town both of power and depravity. By excluding the "white trash" Rafe, Hannah becomes complicit in the creation of the crisis that destroys the Hunnicutt household in order to maintain respectability, and complicit, too, in keeping Theron insulated in a situation that will backfire.

Wade arranges that Theron participate in a snipe hunt with his tenant ranchers, a necessary life lesson for the young man's growth—but the hunt is fake. The ranchers, essentially Wade's vassals, attempt to teach Theron a nasty lesson, demonstrating the pervasiveness of patriarchal assumptions and the impossibility of keeping them in check: they are a kind of gossipy, ghoulish chorus, made awful by the cruel humor Minnelli gives them. (Among them are the actors Denver Pyle, Dub Taylor, and Chuck Robertson, who filled the ranks of Hollywood westerns, often as brutes or idiots.) The tenant ranchers take Theron into the nighttime woods (the sexual connotations here hardly need Freud for explication) in search of snipes that don't exist. The ranchers giggle as Theron is left alone in the wild, blowing a whistle that he has been told will draw the snipes. The whole exercise is centered on nothing but the boy's humiliation. Their sadistic glee, which Wade doesn't chastise, flows from their enjoyment of his immaturity, his failure to know what it means to know the ways of the hunt and "being a man."

The incipient violence of the town is manifest also in Theron's would-be father-in-law, Albert Halstead (Everett Sloane), a meek figure whose notion of propriety and its violations spur the ultimate crisis of the film. Halstead is a bastion of repression, representing a town that nearly explodes, unable to maintain the façade of propriety that can be kept in place only at considerable cost. In Wade's loss of control is nothing less than the disintegration of a genre archetype. Finally Wade is shot and killed by Halstead, one of the "respectable" citizens who embodies the small-mindedness of the town and more than a little paranoia and hysteria. *Home from the Hill* conveys less a sense of timelessness in its unnamed town than the idea that time is irrelevant to long-entrenched, reactionary ideas. While the town and landscape of *Home from the Hill* clearly convey the postwar years, the cotton-pressing plant (with black workers singing field songs), the butler Chauncey, and the housemaid suggest that antebellum Texas isn't so distant, so reactionary are the town's views of race and gender. The film compares with *Psycho* for its sense of the past bearing down on the present, suffocating the possibilities represented by the young. In *Psycho*, Marion (Janet Leigh) and Sam (John Gavin) are crushed by a culture of sexual repression, represented by Marion's generalized guilt feelings and the psychological and financial burdens imposed on Sam by his late father; in *Home from the Hill*, Wade's history and the narrowness of the town prevent Theron's relationship with Libby Halstead (Luana Patten) from flourishing. For a moment, Theron, Rafe, and Libby would seem to represent a triad beyond jealousy, theirs an idyllic arrangement destroyed not by their actions but by the expectations of their society.

Rafe is perhaps the most compelling figure of the narrative. In his apparent saintliness, his affection for his half-brother (returned many times over when Theron learns of Rafe's origins and rejection), and his regular interventions, including his marriage to Libby after she becomes pregnant by Theron who is turned away by her enraged father, Rafe would seem to be almost a Dickensian character, the waif who grows to manhood on his own but accepts his lot, with his rancor largely concealed by good cheer. But as Michael Walker has noted, Rafe seems a highly complex, contradictory character who, in his marriage to Libby and ultimate embrace of Hannah, continues patriarchy even as Theron, who murders Halstead and flees from the town, portrays its fatal consequences, the notion that the sins of the fathers are not only visited on the son but destroy the very thing the patriarch is fixated on preserving. On the other hand, Rafe's ascendancy suggests that patriarchy does not need the niceties of legitimated bloodlines for its continuation. In the final scene by Wade's gravemarker, the illegitimate Rafe even dresses in Wade's style, with a new Stetson hat and a sweater not unlike the one worn by the older man (Walker 33).

Perhaps as important, Rafe seems a bit of a throwback figure, the idealized hunter Wade would like to be, or at least appear to be. He certainly adorns himself in excessive trappings and carries a personal (manufactured?) legend. Yet one could hardly imagine Wade being able to live as Rafe does in a primitive cabin. There, with his antique stone grinding wheel, Bowie knife on his belt, and easy manner, Rafe embodies a lost masculinity of myth and folklore combined with a romantic notion of the poor: his abandoned mother, Ann, buried in a pauper's grave, is at the foundation of Rafe's stolid but kind personality. Rafe is not the rebel figure one might expect, given the misdeeds done to him. On the contrary, he is present to support Wade at every turn ("I go where you go"), less to prick Wade's conscience than to move himself into place as the logic of the narrative unfolds. Rafe is the full-bodied answer to the bourgeois propriety and transparent sexual mores celebrated in the town (and demolished in the film), shouldering responsibilities as Theron flees into the wilderness, becoming the "man" Wade always wanted, if in a very fractured form. Rafe would seem the ideal answer to Arthur Schlesinger's crisis in American masculinity, since he is both the perfect postwar domesticated male and a competent hunter, a frontiersman of old quite comfortable in his own skin, good-humored, with nothing to prove. He contrasts with a collapsed image of hypermasculinity represented by Wade, one that postwar centrism viewed skeptically even as intellectuals like Schlesinger engaged in hand wringing over changes in American manliness.

It has been noted that Wade's office/den, the site of Theron's monstrous (yet commonplace) education in the masculine ways of the world, is a brilliant piece of Minnelli décor. The antithesis of Rafe's cabin, Wade's home, filled with excess, is a signal emblem of male hysteria, the domain of a man

The hypermasculine décor of the den of Capt. Wade Hunnicut (Robert Mitchum) in *Home from the Hill* (Vincente Minnelli, MGM). Digital frame enlargement.

who has little control over his life and his children, whose wife disdains him: she refers to his past legend as a "great hunter" sarcastically, as if she sees clear through the myth. With its rich wood paneling, massive red leather chairs (one of which is essentially Wade's throne, especially when he positions himself on it to give the first of Theron's lectures), refrigerator stocked with beer, and walls adorned with animal heads, fishing gear, and above all guns, Wade's den screams out a particularly threatened masculinity. His frustration with Hannah's "locked door," thus his inability to seduce his own wife and reconstruct his image in her eyes, makes the point. Wade's dwelling is no less a boy's hobby room than young Theron's, a room filled with a collection of "rocks, butterflies, and other toys" that Wade views contemptuously, snidely telling him to "come and see how a man lives." Wade's own toys replace his sex life with Hannah; his sexual exploits with other women can be read merely as the predation of a rich man who at heart is unable to sustain a relationship other than as a matter of exchange. He is no Organization Man, but one can read Wade as the perfect embodiment of the postwar Schlesinger male. In place of the big game hunting that previously defined him (and an image of an older America),

Wade's hunting, as he explicitly states, is aimed at the domestic scene itself. His predation of women highlights the nature of it. The "great hunter" Wade targets the most vulnerable: it is instructive that the two key moments featuring Wade as hunter are the goose hunt and the recounted story of Wade and the poverty-stricken "sand hill tacky" who becomes Rafe's mother. The goose hunt itself is important. Although Wade warns Theron that some of the animals decorating his den "put up a struggle before they died," it is deer and wildfowl that Wade kills, hardly the most frightening of creatures.

The central mode of exchange is involved less with money, for which Wade pretends only a passing interest (in a posture that shields the role of wealth in sustaining his power), than with gun violence and the hunt. The latter, as stated, extends to women as well as animals, the notion summed up in the goose hunt during which Wade is almost killed by a jealous husband. He later tells the admonishing doctor (Ray Teal), "I claim the right to cross any man's fences when I'm huntin.'" Theron's "education" is therefore centered very much around hunting and gun violence, while Rafe wants him to experience women (what Wade might call "another kind of huntin'"). There is no irony, of course, but a thoughtful, uncompromised logic, in the film's denouement being so involved in gun violence, with Wade murdered by the pathetic and confused Halstead in a shotgun blast that destroys part of his den, including his red chair, and Theron tracking down and killing Halstead in a replication of the hunt for the wild boar that was Theron's rite of passage. Theron's revenge killing of Halstead, father of the woman he loves, is a culmination of the lessons learned from Wade and Rafe. The killing of Halstead in a swamp both repeats and reexamines the expressionist, grotesque details of the hunt, with the marsh gas signifying the poisoned heart of the hunter and the ultimate implacability of nature. The wild boar may have functioned as a Moby Dick subdued first by Wade, then by Theron, but in this narrative the animal is clearly exposed as a metaphor for something more human. Although Wade earlier tells Theron "what every man hunts is himself," this admonition—familiar tough-guy talk of the western—is itself lacking in self-awareness, and is merely a means of instilling in Theron the notion of masculine self-discovery through specified violent acts sanctioned by patriarchal culture. The killing of the boar produces no more self-knowledge in Theron than the earlier boar hunt produced in Wade. The legend of the "great hunter" is exposed as a cover for the cruel and uncaring male.

Theron's final act of gun violence is the capstone to the near-total destruction of the bourgeois family. The killing of Albert Halstead may be seen as excessive; Theron's conversation with Libby in which he tells her of his rejection of his parents, his refusal to travel their road, makes the point efficiently enough. The final reconciliation between Rafe and Hannah, with Rafe consoling the stricken woman with an invitation to come and spoil his (actually Theron's) and Libby's son, is a happy yet melancholy ending that recognizes the fragility of bourgeois arrangements. Rafe can still offer the archetypal consolation of the homestead ("let's go home") precisely because a series of mishaps, caused by the bourgeois need to maintain appearances, has placed him in the middle class and in a position to offer solace to the very people who have offended him. Through this solace, the film offers a tentative recuperation of a manifestly irredeemable society. Patriarchy is restored, even if the patriarch isn't the one chosen for the role.

Richard Quine's *Strangers When We Meet* is another distinguished moment for the melodrama as it reaches a major key. An undervalued film, *Strangers* differs from the major accomplishments in the genre of Minnelli, Max Ophüls, and Douglas Sirk, all of whom brought to their work some degree of distanciation, either through elaborate camera technique or exaggerated mise-en-scène. Their point was usually to give the viewer some place from which to critically analyze a film without becoming removed entirely from emotional involvement. Quine's film allows no such position, but instead uses a realist dramatic mode that, heightened in the manner of the then-popular exposé—*Confidential* magazine is a representative if degraded example—is astonishing in its candid portrayal of the emptiness of marriage and postwar suburban life. The empathy allowed the spectator is disconcerting as the breadth of the film's condemnation becomes clear.

The extramarital affair of Larry Coe (Kirk Douglas) and neglected housewife Maggie Gault (Kim Novak) is a stunning and arbitrary expression of frustration with daily life, marriage in particular, its philandering couple being a kind of random sample of the bourgeois population. Larry is an architect unhappy with his work and his life; he lacks the opportunity to create the works of art he sees himself capable of, hampered by the demands of business and misunderstood by his wife, Eve (Barbara Rush), who is too concerned with economic practicalities. Larry's affair with Maggie begins with a "brief encounter" at their children's school bus stop. Although Maggie is physically very striking, Larry's pursuit of her seems undermotivated. The motivation comes into focus when Larry develops a business association, then friendship, with Roger Altar (Ernie Kovacs), a dissolute hack novelist who commissions Larry to build a new house for him. Roger's frustrations complement Larry's: he cannot write the Great American Novel that he thinks he has in him and thereby win the respect of critics who hold him in contempt. He drowns his self-disgust in alcohol, womanizing, and sardonic humor as he and Larry form a relationship of mutual support. The situation of the two male characters makes *Strangers When We Meet* among the most intelligent reflections on male anxiety and disempowerment in an era obsessed with the topic. The men's relationship reflects the film's all-encompassing sense of alienation and hopelessness, often in bleak existentialist terms suggestive of the contemporary European cinema. The relationship also reasserts the male crisis as crucial to the film: the "strangers" of the title refers as much to the Larry-Roger friendship as to the affair between Larry and Maggie. When they part company in one of the film's last scenes, Roger tells Larry: "We meet as strangers and half the time we part that way," to which Larry responds: "If we ever really get to know another human being, it's a miracle."

As Larry and Maggie proceed with their affair, Larry builds Roger's "oddball" house (Roger's term), the gradual construction of which coincides with Larry's affair, the temporary disintegration of his life, and then the ghastly, forced reaffirmation of Larry's bourgeois and suffocating routine. The two men wrangle over the details of the architecture, this wrangling an expression of Roger's insecurities, which Larry tries to assuage. The gesture is reciprocated by Roger when Larry tells him of his affair with Maggie. By film's end, Roger has written a well-received novel that brings him no consolation. He tells Larry he envies him his wife and family. Yet this is not the ultimate affirmation we may think the narrative intends. In the final scene, Larry and Maggie meet in the empty, just-completed modernist house intended for Roger, an expensive domestic domicile, a perfect emblem of upscale living but a desolate shell. (In an earlier scene, Roger's bimbo girlfriend intelligently notes that the framed-out house "looks like a prison.") It is not so much the home that Larry and Maggie *might* occupy were it not for their marital shackles and guilt as it is merely a representation of their despair and the impossibility of sexual and emotional fulfillment under bourgeois arrangements.

Strangers When We Meet consistently suggests that Larry Coe's situation is no aberration, that in fact every relationship in modern America is hopeless. That this social crisis is pervasive is best represented in the party Eve throws in an attempt to recapture Larry's attention as her suspicions mount. The conversation there, filled with banalities about the annoyances of crabgrass and self-deceptions about what qualifies as a good marriage, only furthers the tensions in Larry. (Kirk Douglas's performance is superb, his stricken facial expression well modulated to convey his character's paranoia and anguish.) Larry's good-humored neighbor Felix Anders (Walter

Matthau), a seeming prude annoyed by lurid party jokes, suddenly reveals another side of his wry, cynical wit as he starts to needle Larry with his observations, in particular a gossipy remark about infidelity, the "tramp, tramp, tramp" of what he terms the "itchy foot club," that for him shows that the desire for romance with one's neighbor is a constant of suburbia. The needling becomes vicious when Felix reveals to Larry that he knows of Larry's affair. His point is not blackmail but simply torment (Felix is an unattractive and frustrated figure who clearly wants but cannot achieve an affair), and preparation for making his own pass at Eve, whom he thinks has been emotionally abandoned by Larry.

Felix is a sinister rendition of the male's need for sexual adventure, while Larry's affair with Maggie suggests, at first glance, the "search for true love." Yet the Larry/Roger/Felix triad of male characters is in some respects a composite. Roger's pursuit of women is pathological, an addiction, like his alcoholism, to cover his deep self-loathing. His cynical humor (well done by Ernie Kovacs, a genius of early television whose famous surreal/absurd humor sent up 1950s culture) is a mask for his inability to care about anything, a problem he states explicitly to Larry. Felix wants merely to have taboo sex and transgress for its own sake; he would seem to be the most predatory and conscienceless of the trio, especially as he tries to seduce Eve Coe. These characters are contrasted to Larry as if to show that extramarital affairs can have a "pure" motivation, the pursuit of romantic love. The point would seem to be given added weight by Maggie's situation, including her frigid husband who cannot conceive that she would have an affair even as she essentially confesses it to him (so certain is he that she is his property), her at first disdainful relationship with her mother (Virginia Bruce), who had an affair that Maggie viewed with contempt, and, most especially, her surprising revelation to Larry of her brief affair with a truck driver. This revelation, which causes Larry momentary revulsion, underscores the deep dissatisfaction within the two sexes concerning marital fidelity and erases all traces of the "double standard." But Maggie's story helps to clarify Larry's; when both characters are compared to all the others and set within the fullness of the narrative, the search for true love is portrayed as a delusion, the real issue being the bankruptcy of the marital institution itself. In making such a case, *Strangers When We Meet* is an exceptionally radical gesture, a thoughtful challenge to a disintegrating Production Code. Although the film opts for the restoration of normality, with Larry and Maggie returning to their families, this is one of the bleakest restorations in late Hollywood cinema: both characters are shown alone and distraught in the final scene, Maggie in tears, Larry close to them.

When the Impossible Could Occur

As one reflects briefly on Richard Brooks's *Elmer Gantry*, perhaps the year's most controversial film, it seems extraordinary that it was made at all. Despite the lengthy disclaimers before the main title, there is no mistaking its unsparing assault not only on evangelism but on organized religion and the society that sustains it. *Elmer Gantry* represents the writers and directors of late Hollywood challenging a production and censorship system teetering at the brink, and yet the film makes significant concessions to that system. Adapted from Sinclair Lewis's 1927 novel, it retains most of Lewis's devastating vision of provincial small-town life, with its susceptibility to religious charlatans portrayed as nurtured by a cynical business culture (personified by George Babbitt, title character of another Lewis novel who reappears in the book and this film *Elmer Gantry*) that prefers an uncritical and intellectually backward public. Elmer Gantry himself, portrayed by the charismatic, larger-than-life Burt Lancaster in one of his most representative performances, is designed to elicit far more sympathetic interest than Lewis allowed his character. This Gantry is a hypocritical but big-hearted huckster, not Lewis's amoral—and rather dull—predator on the public will. He is cynical but generous and self-aware. Although he says he is a believer, he comes across as a skeptic, almost as much as the agnostic newspaper columnist Jim Lefferts (Arthur Kennedy), who is his critic and amused friend. Such alterations, combined with the gender politics of the film, hurt its contentious power.

Sharon Falconer (Jean Simmons), a young revivalist recalling Aimee Semple McPherson, is at first an ice queen totally enamored of her religious mission and immune to Gantry's charm as he joins and becomes the star of her huge evangelical enterprise. But the two develop a romance, and as Sharon falls in love with Gantry, he feels, rightly, that she is losing all touch with reality, in particular their lucrative business empire. In the film's apocalyptic ending, Sharon dies as the panicked congregation flees from a flash fire in the burning revival tent. Gantry consoles the survivors, who feel they betrayed their spiritual leader, Sharon. After his doggerel prayer, which he uses many times in the narrative (emphasizing his practiced manipulation), he gives a knowing smile to Lefferts, who says he thinks Gantry's words were "real friendly," after which the preacher again hits the road from which he came, a hero vanishing into the wilderness. In Brooks's rendering, Gantry is a relatively enlightened man for all his ruthless connivance and demagoguery, while his female counterpart is totally bemused, susceptible to beliefs that cause her downfall. Identified with the people to whom

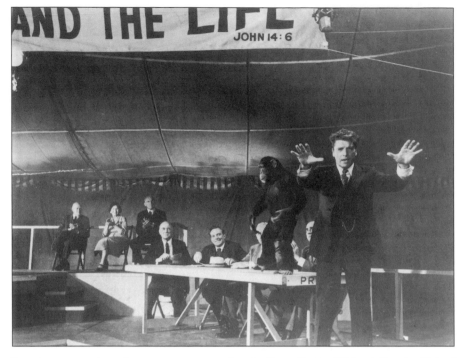

Burt Lancaster plays the eponymous preacher in *Elmer Gantry* (Richard Brooks, United Artists) as a hypocritical but big-hearted huckster. Personal collection of the editor.

she ministers, the benighted, impoverished midwestern working class, she at one point tells Gantry that she is "Katy Jones from shanty town," although this revelation does little to develop her character. The female is here portrayed as a primal force; she is linked to the people, portrayed as a mob subject to wild, uncontrollable emotions. She is therefore unlike Elmer, who is self-possessed, with a good sense of public gullibility. The notion of Sharon as irrational force, with Elmer Gantry as self-knowing, does some violence to Sinclair Lewis's criticism of America and in particular the peddlers of organized religion. As is typical of popular narrative film, the female principle is the most damaging for all the connivings of men.

If Sharon is the virgin (more or less) of the film, *Elmer Gantry* has its corresponding whore in Lulu Banes (Shirley Jones), a one-time lover of Gantry who, with the aid of her pimp, instigates a blackmail plot that temporarily brings the preacher low. Having a heart of gold, however, she refuses to follow through on her plot, invoking the wrath of the pimp. In her defense, Gantry mobilizes a brutal and righteous retaliation (convincingly enacted by Lancaster, among Hollywood's most physical, athletic actors). He is all-forgiving, still holding affection for Lulu and identifying with her hardscrabble existence. Unlike both Sharon and Lulu, Gantry is from the people but not of them. He maintains the masculine virtues of independence and rationality; he is amorous and kind-hearted yet able to keep his emotions well in check. He is a force of nature, able to survive easily on his own and take and give punishment, the latter best demonstrated when he makes short work of Lulu's pimp, throwing him down a flight of stairs in a semi-humorous scene that underscores Gantry as an archetypal, if problematic, American hero.

The Western in Transition

Elmer Gantry is a compromised work, but it nevertheless represents a significant challenge to American ideology typical of the year's films. The western, the most endemically American genre and often the most conservative, continued a process of self-evaluation. Most representative is John Sturges's The Magnificent Seven, an adaptation of Akira Kurosawa's The Seven Samurai (1954). With its stirring score by Elmer Bernstein (the main theme of which would be appropriated by Marlboro cigarettes and, typically, nearly destroyed as a work of art in its own right), a cast of actors on the cusp of stardom, and a plot that hearkens both to American folklore and ancient myth, The Magnificent Seven gained a reputation as one of the canonical "adult" westerns of the postwar period. The film is essentially a tale of redemption, as seven rootless, morally pragmatic gunfighters find meaning in their self-sacrifice to save a poor Mexican village from the savage brigand Calvera (Eli Wallach).

Each member of the Seven is an archetype from the genre. Chris (Yul Brynner) is the leader, a black-clad gunman whose outfit, deep voice, and rather sinister outward demeanor would have coded him as the "bad guy" in earlier westerns. A soulful figure, he is reflective about his wasted life and the irony of what appears to be his final mission in service of people who lack the usual treasure with which to buy his skills. Vin (Steve McQueen), who becomes a second-in-command and sounding board to Chris, is the gunfighter-as-cowboy, with a big smile, leather chaps, and sweat-stained cotton shirt and kerchief. His good nature helps form the yin-yang construct with Chris, for whom Vin also functions as conscience. Britt (James Coburn) is the gunfighter as pure professional, a lanky killer adept with knives and guns who has the least personal interactions of the film's characters, so emotionally removed is he from all concerns except perfecting his own prowess, an old notion that in this film fuses his contribution to the ultimate cause with his personal obsessions. O'Reilly (Charles Bronson) is the film's "half-breed," a legendary killer of Irish-Mexican parentage whose gruffness is softened by his deep emotional connections with the villagers, facilitated by the village children who see O'Reilly's fatherly aspect (as well as the ethnicity that O'Reilly for a time wants to hide) and eventually canonize him. O'Reilly, as much as Vin, is the conscience of the Seven, scoffing at gunplay and those who worship gunfighters as he speaks to the plight of the poor. Lee (Robert Vaughn) is a dandy, the gunfighter-as-fetishist who wears a neat three-piece suit and two sidearms. He is a man who has lost his nerve and depends on the legend constructed around men like him in order to continue. The "big reputation" of the gunfighter, a staple of the western, is another convention that the film addresses; like Britt, Lee's participation in the rescue of the village is based more in personal rather than collective, charitable concerns. Harry (Brad Dexter) is a high-rolling opportunist with a touch of happy-go-lucky shirker. He joins the Seven on the assumption that there is a hidden agenda and that the game is being played for much higher stakes than the few coins offered by the villagers. His own redemption is perhaps the most questionable; while he returns at the last moment to show solidarity with his comrades, his interest in the village is minimal, and his final words are pleas for reassurance from Chris that he was indeed playing for high stakes.

Chico (Horst Buchholz) is in many ways the film's moral center, a callow youth who overdresses the part of gunfighter as he aspires to the traditional role of acolyte, with Chris his unhappy mentor. But Chico becomes far more than this, since as the only Mexican of the group he reminds the Seven and the spectator of the dubious morality at the heart of the film. Chico at first scoffs at the peasants, refusing his own origins in a poor Mexican village "exactly like that one" (as Chris tells him before the Last Stand, not as a way of dressing him down but making him come out from beyond the dubious façade of pupil). By the end of the film, the Seven have very much debunked the romance of the gunfighter. Chris tells Chico, who says he hates the farmers, "Of course you hate them . . . because you yourself are a farmer." But Chico answers his mentor with an angry but focused retort, asking, "Who made us what we are? Men like Calvera. And men like *you*!" "What we are": the question remains as to what this implies. Chico seems to suggest that both Chris and Calvera are oppressors, forcing peaceful people to choose the way of violence or be destroyed. Such a notion has long made *The Magnificent Seven* subject to divergent interpretations that place it in a contemporary context.

The denouement of *The Magnificent Seven* is a Last Stand traditional to the western, in which all but Chris, Vin, and Chico perish fighting Calvera's bandits and restoring the village. The blood sacrifice of the men is seen as needed in order to revitalize a devastated society. The "benediction" scene of the village children visiting the graves of the dead members of the Seven makes the point easily enough. Chico decides to remain in the village, taking up farming with a young woman with whom he began a romance earlier in the narrative. He therefore acknowledges his origins and the pure life of the peasant, distancing himself from the fundamental amorality of "men like you" (Calvera and Chris). One can read this, as Richard Slotkin argues, as a valorization of American incursion into the Third World, especially as the United States embraced the "gunfighter" ethos of low-intensity counterinsurgency operations in Cuba and Vietnam (Slotkin 474–86).

If one reads *The Magnificent Seven* as an approving fable about wars of national liberation, a common question occurs: why can't the Mexican peasants free themselves? And if they really do need gunmen, aren't there plenty of these in their own nation? The film seems hugely patronizing, unless one sees the Texas border town where the peasants find Chris and Vin as a kind of evil cesspool from which the peasants need to temporarily extract some dangerous medicine. As the film suggests at the conclusion, while the villagers appreciate the good deeds of the Seven, they are happy to see them go. Chris's final line, reiterating the village wise man, is "Only the farmers won . . . we lost, we always lose." This might seem to valorize the romantic image of the gunfighter as much as suggest his essential corruption, and that of the American militarist institutions for which he acts as metaphor.

A more generous reading of *The Magnificent Seven* recognizes its deconstruction of the gunfighter mythos and takes seriously Chico's retort. Chris is certainly not as cruel as Calvera, but like Calvera he represents a way of life antithetical to humane civilization. The western has always had difficulty with the very concept of civilization, the goal that the "winning of the west" is ostensibly about. For all its high adventure, *The Magnificent Seven* would appear to answer to the domestic centrism of the postwar era, extolling domesticity as the noblest goal as Chico returns to the village.

Davy Crockett versus Spartacus

The ideological conflicts of the year are most graphically portrayed in two historical epics, John Wayne's *The Alamo* and Stanley Kubrick's *Spartacus*. The two films share much, yet no two films could be more diametrically opposed ideologically. Both are historical epics: *Spartacus* is about the slave revolt against ancient Rome, for many in the Left the originary radical rebellion; *The Alamo* is about the Texas insurrection of 1836 of Anglo-American colonizers against the army of Mexican general Antonio Lopez de Santa Ana. Each film was beset with problems that, in retrospect, underscore the ideological tensions that their narratives represent and which contained the films in their historical moment. Kubrick had "creative differences" with actor/producer Kirk Douglas, the true author of *Spartacus,* who thankfully kept Kubrick's nihilist sensibility fully in check. *The Alamo* was burdened by a terrible script—the fault entirely Wayne's, for whom the film may be his signature statement. The film's disastrous publicity campaign by Russell Birdwell contained the same clumsy, flag-waving thinking that saturated Rightist James Edward Grant's dialogue (Grant played an important role in crafting the Wayne persona through the clipped lines he wrote for Wayne in scripts dating back to the 1940s).

The Alamo, released on the eve of the election, was in many respects a Republican campaign advertisement, filled with long-winded exhortations about the need to, as Davy Crockett put it, "hit a lick for what's right." John Wayne reluctantly took the lead role as well as directed, in order to try to ensure box office grosses that didn't materialize until years of re-release. Some of the political diatribes, which often stop the film dead and detract from some interesting if formulaic battle scenes, are outrageous. For example, Alamo commander William Travis, the cannily cast Laurence Harvey, delivers a blistering tirade on the foolishness of Jeffersonian notions of equality, scoffing at "that rabble down there" (meaning his own men), extolling a Great Man view of history in which only an inspired and courageous few can step forward to hold back the barbaric hordes (in his speech, there is no mistaking the film's equation of 1836 Mexico with the Soviet Union). Travis's diction is mannered, accented by a strange mixture of Carolina drawl and Oxbridge (due in part to Wayne's hurried casting and his changing conception of Travis). By contrast, Jim Bowie (Richard Widmark) seems to represent Jacksonian populism. He despises Travis's foppishness, lying, and authoritarian view of command, preferring to talk to his own men straight and in a plain-spoken, folksy manner.

Crockett acts as mediator, a populist who tries to remind these two men of the value of compromise. In fact, Crockett, the central figure and locus for audience identification (due to the Wayne star power and the earlier, extremely popular Crockett craze brought on by Disney in the 1950s), embraces Travis's outlook but without the priggishness. Crockett isn't snooty and he appears to hold his Tennesseans in high regard, although he decides to trick them into fighting for Texas anyway. There is a moment of buffoonery when Crockett admits to his men his trickery in forging a

The populist politics of *The Alamo* (John Wayne, Batjac—United Artists) as represented by Davy Crockett (Wayne) and Jim Bowie (Richard Widmark). Personal collection of the editor.

threatening letter from Santa Ana, at which point the Tennesseans, portrayed as other than the brightest stars in the firmament, insist that Davy is right about Santa Ana's threat not only to Texas but to Tennessee. In order to convey the idea that they just talked themselves into staying in Texas and fighting, Davy gives a knowing little wink to one of his comrades. Wayne's is perhaps the screen's best representation of Davy Crockett as master of political chicanery, teller of Tall Tales, and "born liar" (Crockett's self-description during an introductory exchange with Travis). But beyond this we see a right-wing ideological view complementing that represented by Travis. Crockett may believe that the leader must retain the common touch and not be a spoiled, stuffed-shirt aristocrat (John F. Kennedy, the subject of Wayne's ire, was often portrayed as such), but he must lead nevertheless. The people cannot be trusted, especially when the nation is so obviously under siege from a ruthless foe—no film of the period ever captured Cold War paranoia better than *The Alamo*'s falsified account of the 1836 insurrection of white colonists who eventually conquered nearly half of Mexican territory.

Suffice it to say that *Spartacus* can be fairly said to be a repudiation of all that *The Alamo* stands for. While the film isn't exactly accurate on the facts of the Roman slave revolt, it doesn't show such low regard for a historical-materialist view of the world as to use history merely as a convenience for making points about contemporaneous events, which is the case with *The Alamo*. *The Alamo* pretends to uphold principles of democracy as it shows contempt for the public itself (figured first in the white Texans), while hardly representing the racial Other at all, except as frightening or "noble" stereotypes. By contrast, *Spartacus* focuses on popular struggle, delineating carefully the motives of power both in its Rightist, dictatorial mode (Laurence Olivier's oily Crassus) and bourgeois, liberal mode (Charles Laughton's overfed but sincere Gracchus). As leader of the rebellion, Spartacus (Kirk Douglas) is obviously the film's central figure, and Douglas's star power was crucial to the film's creation. Yet there is a strong sense of the collective hero (one of the most moving scenes in the film shows all the recaptured slaves standing up and proclaiming themselves to be Spartacus under pain of death), best portrayed in scenes of the slave army at rest or play, or the Eisensteinian images of the piles of the dead following the Roman victory. Such comparisons don't seem at all strained when one considers the lengths to which Douglas went to make *Spartacus* a Left statement challenging Cold War ideology. The hiring of screenwriter Dalton Trumbo, one of the blacklisted Hollywood Ten, whose name was featured prominently in the credits rather than concealed by a pseudonym as it was during the heyday of McCarthyism, was one aspect of this ambition that made *Spartacus* the target of right-wing media attack dogs such as Hedda Hopper. John Wayne not only despised the film's politics but saw it as a threat to his own historical epic, whose agenda could not be more different from that of *Spartacus*.

The Alamo and *Spartacus* represent the decade to come, with the severe reaction and retrenchment that met the most extraordinarily challenging potentials. The political-cultural divide embodied in these films suggested the potential for change. The struggle of *Spartacus*, despite the film's exceptionally downbeat ending in which the slave revolt is crushed and the participants all killed, contains an unswerving commitment to revolutionary change that also looks fondly on human beings and their failings. The despairing ending of *Strangers When We Meet*, with Larry Coe and Maggie Gault facing a return to the bleak domestic household, seems far less determined by a studio adhering to conventional mores than a recognition, in retrospect at least, that alternative sexuality and ways of living are desperately needed. Elmer Gantry can only turn his back and walk away from the hysterical middle-American population; within the decade that population would tear itself apart, literally in the context of the civil rights and antiwar movements, symbolically in the apocalyptic visions of several important films. Apocalypse versus revolutionary transformation is a dialectic clearly displayed in *Elmer Gantry*, *Spartacus*, and *The Alamo*. *Elmer Gantry* presents a situation at the precipice, with a society too circumscribed by its unthinking ideology to permit anything but a self-rending as its belief system collapses. One could make a similar case about *Home from the Hill*, where the members of the community can only re-create patriarchal structures, even as those structures have destroyed nearly everyone in the narrative, including the patriarch himself. *Spartacus* can envision a new world, one that *The Alamo*'s extreme political reaction repudiates utterly. *The Alamo* may well be the purest evocation of dominant U.S. ideology in the cinema, with its belief in sacrificial bloodshed and utter annihilation—including self-annihilation—in support of the most retrograde institutions (including slavery, despite the film's lame, mawkish, and implausible genuflections against that institution). The family, religion, charismatic male authority, property rights, and militarism are all portrayed as destroyed by an inadequately policed racial Other. The failure to be diligent about such policing, necessitating the apocalypse as the New Golden Land slips from divine grace, is among the most foundational of the poisoned narratives informing the nation's so-called civilizing experience. *The Alamo* recapitulates it with a seductive accuracy at the height of U.S. confrontation with yet another contrived foe during the peak of the Cold War. The year's films are instructive today as a foreshadowing of what was achieved and lost since, and of the awful centrality of consoling, regressive, always destructive visions to American narrative and political life.

1961

Movies and Civil Rights

ANNA EVERETT

This was a particularly notable year for Hollywood films as the so-called "turbulent decade" got under way and radically transformed many familiar social, cultural, political, and economic institutions in American civil society. It was also marked by a number of historic milestones, including the breaking off of diplomatic relations with Cuba on 3 January and the failed Bay of Pigs invasion of Cuba in April, a considerable increase in American involvement in Vietnam, Astronaut Alan B. Shepard becoming the first American successfully launched into space on 5 May, and the invention of the laser. Joseph Heller's *Catch-22* and John Howard Griffin's *Black Like Me* were published, and by the end of the year the romantic comedy *Come September* initiated the age of film exhibition on airliners. America exported the Twist dance craze to Europe, Bob Dylan made his debut in New York City, Dave Brubeck's LP *Time Out*, the first jazz album to sell over a million copies, was released, and the nation accepted the crossover appeal of African American rhythm and blues (R&B) music with songs like the Shirelles' "Will You Still Love Me Tomorrow," Ray Charles's "Hit the Road, Jack," and the Marcels' up-tempo doo-wop version of "Blue Moon" high on the charts. In fact, society's embrace of youth music culture signaled a pivotal or vanguard moment in charting visible evidence of the possibility for peaceful interracial coexistence, of sorts, as Black and white youths danced together, and sexy, alluring Black music artists were permitted to integrate the hugely popular music show "American Bandstand" (1952–1989). Clearly, this image of integration was much more palatable than televised images of the violence attending the heightening civil rights struggle. But most significant was the ratcheting up of the political stakes with regards to civil rights as the civil rights movement's Summer Freedom Rides in Montgomery, Alabama, unfolded; the inauguration of John F. Kennedy, the youngest man ever elected to the presidency; and the nation's political movement toward a "New Frontier" ethos characterized by what Douglas T. Miller calls "cautious liberalism" (78). These epochal events coincided with shifting postwar suburban and urban residential patterns based on race, the phenomenal rise of television, and its unprecedented capacity to transmit visually raw and powerfully visceral images captured from the front lines of these controversies and broadcast them live into the living rooms of the nation's incredulous TV audiences.

At the same time, Hollywood and independent filmmakers inaugurated explicit, socially relevant films addressing volatile civil rights matters for racially segregated and declining mainstream movie audiences. Most recognizable early in the decade was the film industry's production of movies that capitalized on the era's palpably changing attitudes about race, class, gender, and matters of sexuality, and other civil rights concerns. At this point, both Hollywood and independent filmmakers upped the ante in their efforts to erode the longstanding tyranny of film censorship institutionalized by the 1934 Production Code and its strictures against cinematic content potentially sympathetic to and tolerant of many of these volatile issues.

With the legislative and legal victories of the previous years, the modern civil rights movement gained new historic protections that emboldened Black activists and progressive white supporters to test the nation's resolve to dismantle racial segregation in public institutions throughout America. It was against this backdrop that two interracial groups from the Congress of Racial Equality (CORE) boarded Greyhound and Trailways buses bound for the Deep South with the intent of integrating America's public interstate travel system and procuring service accommodation at all terminal facilities en route. This strategic act of civil disobedience in May kicked off the year's spate of Summer Freedom Rides with similar sit-ins in other areas of public accommodation throughout the South, which led to the erosion of overtly racist Jim Crow segregation laws. Despite tough prison sentences, severe beatings and bombings, and other levels of violent reprisals by southern whites, including police officers and other authority figures, civil rights movement activists were not deterred. As if playing out Frederick Douglass's famous nineteenth-century aphorism that power concedes nothing without a demand, by late summer more than a thousand people had participated in the Freedom Rides (Miller 105), pushing forward their non-negotiable demands for immediate civil rights protections and equal rights. Leading this latest iteration of post-Reconstruction Black-led freedom fighting was a coterie of influential civil rights leaders including Martin Luther King Jr., James Farmer, Roy Wilkins, Whitney Young Jr., Rosa Parks, and Fannie Lou Hamer, as well as "the younger 'new abolitionists' of the Student Non-Violent Co-ordinating Committee (SNCC)," established in April, such as Stokely Carmichael. On the legal front, Thurgood Marshall and the

National Association for the Advancement of Colored People (NAACP) brought many of the landmark Supreme Court and other racial discrimination cases to bear on America's racist power structures, and thereby positioned racial equality and other social justice initiatives for all aggrieved Americans at the moral center of American life as the sixties progressed (Quart and Auster 73).

At the same time, new revelations about women's dissatisfaction with prevailing sexual attitudes and gender expectations could no longer be contained. American women had grown weary of the persistent patriarchal consensus that had relegated their social roles to happy housewives and doting mothers during the postwar boom years. Heavy governmental and public pressures led women to abandon their jobs in the workforce immediately after the war, yet, significantly, "by 1960 women constituted 40 percent of the nation's employees" (Miller 46). At the same time, however, this growing trend of female employment outside the domestic sphere conflicted with traditional values regarding gender roles. By this logic, women were expected to concede top jobs to men, gracefully. Social attitudes about sexuality and acceptable gender roles became other registers of manipulated consent or conflict for women who, at once, were expected to remain virgins until marriage and be sexually alluring to men.

As Douglas T. Miller points out, "Movies sent something of the same mixed message. Many films reflected the ideal of the meek, nurturing, domestic female. Actresses Doris Day, Debbie Reynolds, and June Allyson regularly played such roles. Yet films starring blatantly sexual stars like Marilyn Monroe, Elizabeth Taylor, and French actress Brigitte Bardot scored far more successes at the box office" (46–47). For many white, middle-class women, entrapped within what Betty Friedan called the "Feminine Mystique," the era's socially constructed and often contradictory images of women promoting domestic bliss, idealized motherhood, youthful sexual allure, and restricted educational and career opportunities masked women's deep yearning for "more freedoms and choices in their lives" (Benshoff and Griffin 272).

As the increasingly vocal civil rights movement shed light on the erasure of impoverished and oppressed Blacks from the idyllic picture of the prosperous and conformist Eisenhower 1950s, other harsh realities and disaffections came into view. Also, questions about the extent of poverty and class distinctions in America began to surface in mid-century public discourse as the 1960s got underway. Significantly, the nation's television cameras were present and captured much of the violent confrontations and social outrage attending these historic and politically transformative events.

As television covered the explosive civil rights movement the "young, articulate, and telegenic Reverend Martin Luther King, Jr., emerged from the Southern Christian Leadership conference as the movement's chief spokesman. . . . He was the perfect visual symbol for a new era of American race relations" (Everett 522). On 22 May, King flew to Montgomery, Alabama, to demonstrate support for the Freedom Riders. As he spoke at the First Baptist Church, the building was besieged by angry whites who threatened violence, prompting calls to the National Guard to disperse the crowd.

If John F. Kennedy, inaugurated on 20 January as the thirty-fifth president of the United States, was the ideal televisual president, it was also evident that television's role in diminishing Hollywood's box office bottom line motivated the film industry to tackle more controversial and relevant social themes more consistently. The film industry adopted a counter-programming strategy featuring widescreen Technicolor spectacles, adult-themed narratives, and politically charged stories designed to lure audiences away from their TV sets and back into theaters. This is a pivotal year for Hollywood's refashioning of its filmic output to compete effectively with and even surpass television's urgent and compelling coverage of the nation's violent encounters with radically shifting notions of and expectations about race, class, and gender subject positions.

Amid these spectacular social upheavals and idealistic youth-dominated movements that characterized the Camelot era of the short-lived Kennedy administration, the necessary preconditions were set for the nation to welcome and embrace a range of films keyed to contemporaneous occurrences. Moreover, films such as *The Explosive Generation, The Young Savages, The Last Sunset, Back Street, Paris Blues, Two Rode Together, Breakfast at Tiffany's, Underworld U.S.A., King of Kings, The Hustler, One-Eyed Jacks, The Misfits,* and *Return to Payton Place* were barometers of the film industry's calculated embrace of topical and controversial adult-oriented narratives involving interracial conflict, radically changing gender roles, class dynamics, and youth rebellion—narratives not likely to be included in TV's more highly sanitized, primetime flow of family programming with such shows as "Car 54, Where Are You?" (1961–1963), "Dr. Kildare" (1961–1966), and "The Bullwinkle Show" (1961–1964). Appearing as the civil rights movement gained momentum, these films reflected and refracted society's newfound willingness to confront America's complex racial politics on both the cultural and political fronts. Thus, Hollywood's bold entrance into the hyper-political fray of the day encompassed powerful cinematic treatments of racial strife and integration and cast a critical gaze on hot button issues of poverty, religion, suburbanization, the Cold War, gender, and sexuality. These movies are representative of the film industry's calculated move to reflect and contain, as only Hollywood could, America's social revolution that was televised this year.

Kennedy inspired a high level of political optimism in America, particularly among minorities and mainstream youths, that recalled Roosevelt's New Deal in the 1930s. Consequently, Kennedy's own Roosevelt-inspired "New Frontier" reform agenda for the nation's domestic affairs helped set the cultural precondition for the greenlighting of a range of Hollywood and independent film productions exploring topical issues of the period. Films such as *A Raisin in the Sun*, *West Side Story*, and *Flower Drum Song*, for example, directly addressed America's emergent multiculturalism and the upward-mobility aspirations of African Americans, Puerto Rican Americans, and Asian Americans, while *Splendor in the Grass* reminded the country that whiteness was no insulator against the debilitating economic and psychosocial ills of poverty and oppressive conformist thinking. At issue in all these films is the question of how cinema negotiated the shifting but still contentious ideas and attitudes about race and place in American society as the nation was entering a decade of profound change. In many ways these films articulate the great expectations for social transformation Kennedy engendered through his vocal criticisms of the Eisenhower administration's record on civil rights.

Narratives of Integration and Assimilation

As Kennedy put it, "If the president does not himself wage the struggle for equal rights . . . if he stands above the battle—then the battle will inevitably be lost." For his part, Kennedy pledged "that if elected he would with the 'stroke of a pen' do what Eisenhower had not done: eliminate racial discrimination in federally aided housing by executive order" (qtd. in Miller 77). This latter point is precisely what *A Raisin in the Sun*, a Columbia film adaptation of African American playwright Lorraine Hansberry's highly successful Broadway play of the same name, takes up with its focus on a Black family's struggles to integrate a white, working-class neighborhood. *Raisin*'s poignant dramatization of this volatile civil rights issue was highlighted in the film's contemporaneous newspaper reviews.

On 28 March, *Variety*'s reviewer, identified as Tube, proclaimed that *A Raisin in the Sun* would "be successful at the box-office because it is an important, worthwhile, timely social document and because, most of all, it is simply a good film, one that deals with genuine, everyday people who will be universally understood." Actually, as Mark Reid noted, "*Raisin* was neither a financial disaster nor a box-office success. *Raisin* offered studios proof that a low-budget, skillfully written Black scenario about a Black family which features well known Black performers can accrue prestige as well as return a moderate amount of money to its distributor" (60).

Raisin presents the story of a downtrodden but dignified working-class African American family from Chicago's inner city, the Youngers, who come

Lena Younger (Claudia McNeil) and her son Walter Lee (Sidney Poitier) discuss family problems in *A Raisin in the Sun* (Daniel Petrie, Columbia). Personal collection of the editor.

into a financial windfall as a result of the family patriarch's death and subsequent life insurance policy payout. Part of the film's attraction for the studio was the cast's collective star power, beginning with the phenomenally successful crossover star Sidney Poitier (as the male lead, Walter), Claudia McNeil (as Lena, the family matriarch), Diana Sands (as the sister bound for medical school), and Ruby Dee (as Walter's long-suffering wife). Much of *Raisin*'s narrative conflict revolves around differing views on religion and other key matters in the Younger family household (Reid 61). These familial tensions erupt when Lena decides to use a portion of the money to purchase a home in a white, working-class suburban neighborhood—a decision met with strong anti-integration resistance from the neighborhood's homeowners' association.

Whereas *Raisin*, a small Hollywood studio drama featuring an urban, working-class African American family, failed to "equal the play's critical acclaim and popularity" (Reid 60), the situation for the more lavishly produced film adaptation of the popular stage musical *West Side Story* (itself adapted from Arthur Laurents's book) was completely different. *West Side Story* is a film about star-crossed, interracial young lovers torn apart by racial hatred between Puerto Rican and white American youth gangs. It cost approximately $6 million to make, compared with *Raisin*'s more modest budget for Columbia Pictures of $1.5 million, and unlike *Raisin* it won enormous critical acclaim, ten Academy Awards, and staggering box office success. The difference is telling. While Reid attributes the imbalance between *Raisin*'s film and theatrical successes to "different expectations of theater and film audiences," whereby "theater productions like *Raisin* can attract an interracial audience and still focus on topics that would offend a mainstream film audience . . . the first priority of the film industry is to avoid products that threaten its major markets" (60–61).

Reid's observation that film critics' also played a role in *Raisin*'s disappointing box office performance by ignoring its importance (61) seems validated especially given *New York Times*' film critic Bosley Crowther's mixed review that manages, on one hand, to applaud the performances of the key players while, on the other hand, to reduce the film's larger social critique to merely a "drama that takes place mainly in the hearts of its people . . . and what they say of themselves, of each other and their views of the society in which they live." Such a reductive description betrays his own, and by extension, the nation's reluctance to acknowledge what George Lipsitz calls its ingrained "possessive investment in whiteness." Most telling is Crowther's complete dismissal of the pivotal narrative emphasis on the film's representative white male character, Karl Linder, the housing association agent, portrayed convincingly and tellingly by John Fiedler. Reid understands Linder's narrative function as signifier of "the intra-class racial hostility of working-class American ethnics" (63) when he is dispatched to the Younger family's ghetto apartment to prevent their undesired integration by buying out their housing contract at a tidy profit. For Crowther, this crucial discursive element fails to register and is hostilely rejected. As he wrote on 30 May:

> Least valid is the stereotyped, if not downright caricatured role of the one white person in the drama, a deceitful segregationist. This man . . . sounds a false and irrelevant note of anti-white agitation in what is essentially a drama of Negroes becoming adjusted among themselves. . . . For this, as we say, is a drama of troubled and hungry hearts confused by many indigenous factors besides the passing social snobbery of some whites.   *("A Raisin in the Sun")*

Would that America's endemic racism were only a "passing social snobbery of some whites" that the newly aroused nation and the Kennedy-era New Frontier ethos might overcome. This seems to be the larger message of *Raisin* that apparently escapes Crowther completely. Apparently America's resistant mainstream film audiences were not quite ready either for such an in-your-face cinematic indictment of racism and the benefits of white privilege.

West Side Story, even with its similar interrogation of American racism as advanced by *Raisin*, fared much better among both mainstream critics and film audiences. Like *Raisin*, *West Side Story* was a film adaptation of a successful stage production, with a presumed built-in audience base. Unlike *Raisin*, *West Side Story* opened to unqualified raves from film critics from the *New York Times* to *Variety* and to wide acceptance from mainstream film audiences. If *Raisin*'s gritty, visceral, black-and-white dramatic realism proved too off-putting for the nation's traumatized body politic (vis-à-vis TV news coverage of the growing and increasingly confrontational Black civil rights struggle), evidently *West Side Story*'s lush, Technicolor musical treatment of racial conflagration better suited both audiences and critics' willing suspensions of disbelief. Upon the film's release, *Variety*'s critic, named Whit, wrote on 27 September:

> *West Side Story* is a beautifully-mounted, impressive, emotion-ridden and violent musical which, in its stark approach to a raging social problem and realism of unfoldment, may set a pattern for future musical presentations. Screen takes on a new dimension in this powerful and sometimes fascinating translation of the Broadway musical to the greater scope of motion pictures. The Robert Wise production, said to cost $6,000,000, should pile up

handsome returns, first on a roadshow basis and later in general runs. . . . It is a preachment against j.d. [juvenile delinquency] even more potent than . . . a "message picture" and in a sense may lack popular appeal, but in the final analysis the over-all structure is so superior that it should deliver mass impact.

It is interesting that *Variety*'s critic offers more effusive praise for the costly *West Side Story*, even though it too was designated a "message picture," than for the favorably reviewed *Raisin*. Similarly, Bosley Crowther's glowing review for the *New York Times* was filled with accolades:

What they have done with *West Side Story* in knocking it down and moving it from stage to screen is to reconstruct its fine material into nothing short of a cinema masterpiece. In every respect, the recreation of the Arthur Laurents–Leonard Bernstein musical in the dynamic forms of motion pictures is superbly and appropriately achieved. . . . Against, or within, this flow of rhythm is played the tender drama of two nice kids, a Puerto Rican girl and a Polish boy, who meet and fall in love, despite the hatred and rivalry of their respective ethnic groups, and are plunged to an end that is tragic, just like Romeo and Juliet. . . . It is a cry that should be heard by thoughtful people— sympathetic people—all over the land.

It is striking that both the *New York Times* and *Variety*'s critics championed *West Side Story* and not *A Raisin in the Sun*, given that both films were set in big city urban ghettoes and featured themes of economic conflict between different working-class racial and ethnic groups. Whether or not *West Side Story* would have been as successful with both audiences and critics had it made the conflict revolve around a Black/Puerto Rican, or a Jewish/Anglo American couple, is arguable. Perhaps the production design and aesthetic choices for *Raisin* contributed to the critics and audiences' discomfiture with this already threatening topic; *West Side Story*, by contrast, featured wonderful music and dance, despite its tragic end. Following closely its theatrical production and limited by its spartan budget, *Raisin* was shot largely in close-up and in the cramped, claustrophobic quarters of the Younger family's tiny ghetto apartment.

An "assimilation narrative" provides a rich and useful framework for how these two films represented the nation's efforts to achieve racial integration of diverse ethnic and racial groups into mainstream society during Kennedy's so-called "Camelot" era. Charles Ramirez Berg critiques the power of the assimilation narrative in Chicano films:

This familiar formula dramatizes the trade-offs involved when first- or second-generation immigrant protagonists (or sometimes class, race, or gender Others) set out to better themselves in the American system. In this formula, success is defined in upwardly mobile, professional, and socioeconomic terms and goes hand in hand with mainstream assimilation. (There is no success outside the dominant.) . . . Since mainstream success requires compromise and the loss of identity—giving up who you are for what you want to become—few protagonists from the margin ever really achieve success *and* assimilation [original emphasis]. Trying to have it both ways exacts a high price, resulting in a tragedy of some kind, often involving the protagonist's death. (31–32)

Ramirez Berg's observations are clearly relevant to a consideration of *West Side Story*'s assimilationist narrative and to *A Raisin in the Sun*'s integrationist agenda. Besides the primary plot line involving the budding interracial or interethnic romance between the Latina and Polish teens caught up in the eye of the gang-war storm, several of *West Side Story*'s other assimilationist tropes are the song lyrics of "America" and the subplot centering on the pro-America attitude of Puerto Rican character Anita's eventual awakening to the limits of the assimilation or melting pot ideal in the United States. In terms of the assimilationist imaginary shared by would-be lovers Maria and Tony, the film poses the naive desire for interracial romance against intractable racial intolerance, which is eloquently expressed in the lyrics of "Somewhere" ("There's a place for us"): while embracing, the young lovers sing, "We'll find a new way of living/ We'll find a new way of loving, some-where, somehow, someday." The updated Romeo and Juliet theme suggests that the optimistic youths' "someday" remains elusive and untenable for themselves and metaphorically for the nation as a whole at this historic juncture.

Underscoring the film's assimilationist pessimism that captures actual social conditions is the exuberant musical number "America." The song fea-tures the existentialist, intra-group gender conflict wherein the young Puerto Ricans espouse the American assimilationist dream in oppositional terms: for the girls, "Life is all right in America," while for the boys, this is true only "if you're all white in America." The girls' pro-America stance affirms, "Here [in America] you are free and you have pride," but the boys' counter, "Free to wait tables and shine shoes." The film's lyrical address to American realities likely contributed to its mass appeal for both main-stream and racial minority audiences, attracting a white mainstream audi-ence through its pro-immigration narrative and appealing to audiences of color whose experiences of racism have them disinclined to buy into the melting pot ideal. And when Anita (Rita Moreno)—functioning as a sign of pro-American, immigrant assimilation—is assaulted by the rival white gang, the Jets, after reluctantly agreeing to assist Tony and Maria's romantic union, she ultimately adopts the cynical perspective of her dead fiancé, Bernardo (George Chakiris), on American pluralism. At its conclusion, the film enacts Ramirez Berg's punitive assimilation narrative predicated on the immigrant protagonist's death and in keeping with the overall Romeo and Juliet theme of mutual demise for intolerance (in this case, on both sides of the racial divide). The tragedy is compounded to the extent that not only does Tony suffer the ultimate punishment of death for transgressing the miscegenation taboo, but his best friend, Riff, the emblem of second- or third-generation Polish immigrant aspiration, also dies.

The colorful musical film *Flower Drum Song*, based on Rodgers and Hammerstein's 1958 Broadway show about first-generation, earlier period Chinese American immigrants, projects the narrative assimilation discourse from a different, nontragic perspective on racial integration that, similar to *Raisin*, is in keeping with the more optimistic, post–Jim Crow era political logic associated with the Kennedy administration's New Frontier agenda. Upon its release in early November, the film received mixed reviews from both Tube at *Variety* and Crowther at the *New York Times*. Crowther surmises, "In short, there's nothing subtle or fragile about this *Flower Drum Song*," but instead, "It is gaudy and gaggy and quite melodic. Along these lines it is quite a show." According to Tube's more caustic assessment: "As a film, it emerges as a curiously unaffecting, unstable and rather undistinguished experience. Lavishly produced but only sporadically rewarding . . . while hardly an overpowering box office contender, the Universal release is certainly a safe commercial risk." These dismissals aside, *Flower Drum Song*'s importance lies in its lighthearted but groundbreaking address to the bifurcated stereotypes of Asians as model minority and yellow peril that informed film discourse and social views at large. Additionally, as in the case of *West Side Story*, *Flower Drum Song* reframes America's racial integration problematic in ways not easily or literally reducible to terms of a Black and white binarism. Whereas *Raisin* and *West Side Story* convey their melodramatic assimilation narratives via the generic intensity of drama and musical-drama, respectively, *Flower Drum Song* deploys comedy's more disarming generic powers to engage with otherwise difficult topics. *Flower Drum Song* thus crafts a seemingly depoliticized or alternative cinematic vision about locating and recognizing the Americanness of the nation's racial Others, or what some term hyphenated Americans (e.g., African Americans, Asian Americans, and Latino/a Americans).

Flower Drum Song is about a series of inevitable cultural clashes between East and West, denoted here as China and America. Here traditional or old Eastern world Chinese societal practices are counterposed to its modern or new Western world Chinese American counterpart. The cultural differences become manifest through a series of comedic misadventures involving a Chinese immigrant father's efforts to arrange the marriage of his dilettant-ish, eldest son, Wang Ta (James Shigeta), a first-generation Chinese Ameri-can college student, to a suitable picture bride (Miyoshi Umeki) smuggled in from Hong Kong. The plot turns on the humorous escapades that ensue when the son resists his father's plan and pursues instead a modern, con-niving, and aggressive new woman (Nancy Kwan).

Through an assortment of key song lyrics, costume changes, speech patterns, and ethnically informed character delineations that frequently juxtapose traditional Chinese to contemporary American cultural tropes, the film exemplifies for a mass audience the cultural hybridity and linguis-tic heteroglossia underpinning aspects of the Chinese American experience. This idea is explicitly addressed in a revealing moment of dialogue between Wang Ta and his Chinese-American girlfriend of the moment, Linda Low, as they confront Wang Ta's expected submission to his father's will. What follows is a timely and revelatory exchange on this hyphenated identity problematic. Responding to Linda's comment that his immigrant father "sounds very Chinese," Wang Ta agrees that "he is completely Chinese," but hastens to add, "and that's good, because my [younger] brother is com-pletely American. *I am both* [emphasis added]. And sometimes the Ameri-can half shocks the Oriental half, and sometimes the Oriental half keeps me from showing a girl what is on my mind." Linda quickly retorts, "Well, let's start working on the American half." At this point, *Flower Drum Song*, like *Raisin* and *West Side Story*, seems progressive in speaking to the essential Americanness of the nation's racial minority groups, about which the bur-geoning civil rights movement of the day was so insistent.

Peter Feng's consideration of cinematic constructions addressing post-modern hyphenated identity or subjectivity as it pertains to Chinese Ameri-cans specifically and Asian Americans generally is revealing in the context of *Flower Drum Song*'s particular address to Asian American assimilation nar-ratives. Feng points out the contested nature of the term "Asian American," due, in large measure, to its capacity and impulse to collapse the diverse cultures and traditions of peoples of Chinese, Japanese, Korean, Filipino, Vietnamese, Indian, Pakistani, and Arab origins into a homogeneous racial-ized identity category. Despite the hyphenated identity rubric's inadequate lumping of "Asians together," Feng concedes, "it does so in the service of a racial rather than a racist logic, unlike the term 'oriental'" ("Being" 187). "Being Chinese American," he writes, "is not a matter of resolving a dual-ity, for proposing to draw from two cultures inevitably results in not

In the genre of the musical, *Flower Drum Song* (Henry Koster, Universal International) addresses questions of Asian American cultural assimilation.

belonging to either culture. . . . The challenge of the hyphenated reality lies in the hyphen itself: the becoming Asian American" (192).

Where *Flower Drum Song*'s representational economy departs from Hollywood's stock Chinese stereotypes and Orientalist imaginings is in its refashioning of Asian characters as fully assimilated if not fully integrated Americans. *Flower Drum Song*, after all, occupies a racially segregated diegetic space of modern San Francisco's Chinatown. Although Feng, Maxine Hong Kingston, and other cultural critics today reject the hyphenated identity and its liminal subject formations, particularly for Chinese Americans, it is important to bear in mind that *Flower Drum Song* was among the first major Hollywood studio films about Chinese Americans qua Americans in lead roles beyond what Darrell Hamamoto calls the usual "Chinese bachelor character" (7) and other stereotypical Asian sidekick roles.

For Hamamoto, *Flower Drum Song*'s "sappy and sentimental" adaptation of Chin Yang Lee's 1957 novel "was nonetheless the first commercial film to feature Asian Americans exclusively in singing, acting, and dancing roles. If nothing else," Hamamoto adds, "*Flower Drum Song* showcased the talents of Asian American performing artists who were otherwise consigned to less-than-glamorous, unchallenging positions within the entertainment field" (11). The film's version of Chinatown is one of palpably obvious sets, and although the *Times*' Crowther regards the film similarly as "gaudy and gaggy" and "quite a show," he affirms the essential Americanness (albeit it hyphenated) of *Flower Drum Song*'s Chinese characters when he writes of the film's "prefabricated world":

> Don't get the idea, however, that the characters and comedy put forth in this fable of Chinese-Americans residing in San Francisco's Chinatown are in any way basically different from the characters and comedy that used to bloom in any number of plays about German or Swedish or Jewish immigrants coming from the old to the new country (via the comedy route) in years gone by.

However, in his review for *Variety*, Tube expresses profound misgivings about this musical's comedic function, particularly its primary "joke," which to his dismay is predicated on the humorous "spectacle of observing Orientals 'adjusting to' or 'adopting American customs.'" Like Crowther, Tube also recognizes the need to acknowledge within the nation's multicultural and multiracial composition the existence of a Chinese American subject. Taking issue with the comedic inscription of these characters as "darling" or "precocious" fish-out-of-water subjects humorously grappling with "U.S. idioms such as 'American plan' or 'filter flavor, flip top box' or 'that's bop, pop,'" Tube finds such stereotypical renderings "hollow" and "occasionally distasteful." As he puts it, "Chinese-Americans do not figure to be very amused." Whether or not Tube or Crowther got it right in their reviews, their respective acknowledgments of the Chinese American subject position within America's melting pot ideal cannot be underestimated, nor separated from new thinking about race, identity politics, and the broader civil rights struggles for racial justice just getting under way.

Troubled Waters

Among other vitally important civil rights concerns appearing in films this year were women's and minority men's changing social roles, an emergent radicalism in youth culture, and even the homosexuality taboo in American society. The year's film crop did not espouse a monolithic message on the range of novel and persistent social complexities confronting the nation, although, in keeping with hegemonic norms and expectations for aggrieved racial minorities, women, youth, and homosexual constituencies, most narrative resolutions in these films affirmed traditional, white patriarchal values even as they gestured toward eminent social changes blowing in the wind. Still, the fact that a film such as *The Children's Hour* was produced in the same year as *A Raisin in the Sun, West Side Story,* and *Flower Drum Song,* and likewise engages several civil rights issues explicitly, signals an important first step in the American film industry's move toward what has been called "New Hollywood Cinema." If these films betray Hollywood's opportunistic, albeit delayed, notice of the longstanding struggle for racial justice at the epicenter of the growing civil rights movement, then the ailing film industry's related cognition this year of America's seething gender troubles is hardly surprising.

Emblematic of Hollywood's output of films dealing with the nation's emerging gender problematic was United Artists' release of *The Children's Hour* as the year came to a close. *The Children's Hour* is a cinematic distillation of a number of the era's social contradictions involving generational, gender, and class conflicts. It is an interesting coincidence that both the release of *The Children's Hour* and the initiation of President Kennedy's Commission on the Status of Women occurred in December. In his discussion of the widespread and persistent legal discrimination against women, Douglas T. Miller writes:

> Established by executive order in December 1961, the President's Commission on the Status of Women was authorized to examine "the story of women's progress in a free democratic society" and to recommend remedies to combat the "prejudices and outmoded customs [that] act as barriers to the full realization of women's basic rights. . . ." Several states, for example, prohibited women from serving on juries, and numerous state laws interfered with a married woman's rights to own property, enter into business, sign contracts, or even control her own wages. . . . Many prestigious universities excluded women altogether; professional schools of law, medicine, and business routinely admitted only a tiny quota of women.   (308–09)

Given such Draconian denials of women's basic civil rights, the fact that Samuel Goldwyn and United Artists dared to produce and distribute a film addressing the topic of lesbian sexuality for a mainstream audience clearly signals an important element in what Miller describes as the nation's "radical awakening" (49). *The Children's Hour* was director William Wyler's remake of *These Three* (1936), his film adaptation of Lillian Hellman's wildly popular 1934 Broadway play of the same name. This iteration of *The Children's Hour* saw the light of day against strong opposition from the Motion Picture Association of America and its fear of violating the Production Code because Arthur Krim, president of United Artists, was willing to release *The Children's Hour* without the seal of approval from the Production Code office (Westbrook). Nonetheless, when provided the opportunity to rectify the earlier film's censorious erasure of the lesbian coupling plot complication replaced by a heterosexual love triangle, Wyler's remake, twenty-five years later, was still compromised by lingering social taboos against explicitly naming homosexuality and lesbianism. Thus Wyler's updated film capitulated to the still influential but weakened Production Code through prudent metaphoric allusions to the restored lesbian plot complication such as "Karen and Martha's 'sinful sexual knowledge' of each other" (Westbrook), and the characters' ascribed unnatural emotional attachment. In fact, by the time of its release, *The Children's Hour* had received the Production Code seal.

Shot in black-and-white, *The Children's Hour* featured the stellar casting of Audrey Hepburn, Shirley MacLaine, and James Garner. The plot concerns the plight of two young, independent women proprietors of a successful boarding school for adolescent girls who are ultimately ostracized and ruined by mean-spirited rumors about their unnatural devotion to each other. In typical melodramatic fashion, Karen Wright (Hepburn), Martha Dobie (MacLaine), and Joe Cardin (Garner) find themselves in the midst of a tragic, unconventional love triangle of sorts that is divulged when Joe's spoiled, troublemaking young niece, Mary Tilford (Karen Balkin), spreads a lie about a lesbian relationship between Karen and Martha that ultimately devastates the lives of all involved and leads to Martha's suicide. As competent and committed career women, rather than loving mothers and adoring wives, Karen and Martha's strong professional and personal partnership is represented as a threat to traditional family values. For example, the bond between Karen and Martha comes at the expense of the women's assumption of their expected gender roles as Karen and Joe are engaged for two long years, and Martha confesses that "she never loved a man" but did in fact love Karen. The fact that the single young professional women live together in the school provides the willful child Mary the opportunity to accuse the women of scandalous conduct that the well-to-do parents believe too readily. The wealthy community thus takes sides against the working-class teachers as one by one the girls are yanked from the Wright-Dobie School for Girls.

Cinematographer Franz Planer worked well with Wyler to render the film's provocative melodramatic shifts and turns through dramatic lighting, expressive framing, and shot composition. When the film opens, the optimism of life at the Wright-Dobie School is conveyed through bright lighting, quick-paced edits, and a general adherence to the conventions of realism. But as the town turns on the women, the lighting and mood become much darker, Karen and Martha converse in low-lit scenes, and the pacing of the narrative slows until the tragic scene of Martha's suicide. This pivotal scene of Martha's hanging is shot in shadows and injects a horror-film element to underscore the frightful nature of Martha's gender transgression and the town's complicity in her unwarranted death.

For Bosley Crowther, the film had not caught up with the changing times but was "socially absurd" ("The Screen"). As with his incredulity about *Raisin*'s indictment of Americans' persistent racial intolerance, Crowther again fails to recognize the nation's endemic prejudices, which clearly included homophobia. However, he does rightfully challenge the film's anachronistic treatment of the volatile topic given the dated nature of the original source material. Be that as it may, *The Children's Hour's* bold broaching of the civil rights predicament of lesbians marked a radical awakening for the times and reverberated with the inquiry of the Kennedy Commission on the Status of Women.

If a pivotal failure of *The Children's Hour* (in both film iterations) hinged on an avoidance of the issue of "unchecked" power, as Brett Elizabeth Westbrook argues, the fact that "power is constructed, not inherent in a righteous moral position," then *Splendor in the Grass*'s direct engagement with the vicissitudes of power engendered by wealth presents an important contrast. Poverty and class concerns are also featured prominently in *A Raisin in the Sun* and *West Side Story*, but it is in addressing the often underrepresented reality of white poverty that *Splendor in the Grass* gains its powerful resonance. A period film about tragic young lovers from different class backgrounds in the 1920s and 1930s caught up in the financial vicissitudes and disastrous reversals of fortune caused by the Great Depression, Elia Kazan's *Splendor* is a melodramatic, cautionary tale with certain parallels to the transformative social changes taking shape by this year. As with *Raisin* and *West Side Story, Splendor* centers its assimilation narrative and class critique on the devastating consequences wrought by class differences and parental pressures on youth, whose changing social and political consciousness encompassed repressive sexuality and other gender norms. Set in Kansas on the eve of the 1929 stock market crash, *Splendor* tells the tender but tragic love story of working-class teen beauty Wilma Dean ("Deanie") Loomis (Natalie Wood) and her boyfriend, oil-company heir and Commerce High School football hero Arthur ("Bud") Stamper (Warren Beatty). Deanie follows her mother's advice to resist her desire to have sex with Bud.

As the story unfolds, Deanie edges toward insanity and is institutionalized, while Bud's family loses its fortune in the Great Depression. At the end of the film, Deanie returns home after more than two years in a sanitarium; she meets Bud, who is now married and has a child, and both of them accept the fact that their lives have gone in separate directions. As with his earlier films *On the Waterfront* (1954) and *East of Eden* (1955), Kazan infuses *Splendor* with a scathing condemnation of bourgeois society's repressions and hypocrisies, particularly in the policing of teen sexuality and generally unmitigated social conformism. The championing of unpopular political causes and socially ostracized characters, as happens in these films, is indicative of Kazan's auteurist point of view forged from his own painful outsider status in Hollywood as an unrepentant informer during the controversial hearings of the House Un-American Activities Committee into alleged communist infiltration in Hollywood the decade before. But more to the point, Kazan's redemptive assimilation narrative in *Splendor* succeeds by his skillful representational displacement of volatile and controversial social conflicts onto the troubled, though safely removed, recent history of the Depression era.

Deanie's psychological meltdown, induced by her inability to come to terms with the period's punitive double standard regarding premarital sex and for transgressing accepted gender roles, articulates well the nation's unchanged, everyday schizophrenic sexual values and biased gender norms reflected on the one hand in teen exploitation films such as Elvis Presley's *Blue Hawaii* and Sandra Dee's *Gidget Goes Hawaiian*, featuring hormone-raging, swimsuit-clad youths, and women's magazines like *Vogue, Cosmopolitan, Family Circle, Good Housekeeping, McCalls,* and *Redbook*; and, on the other, the flourishing of women's intellectual circles. As Ann Medina notes, women's intellectual circles flourished—on 1 November, for example, some fifty thousand women in sixty cities, mobilized by Women Strike for Peace, engaged in protests against above-ground testing of nuclear bombs and tainted milk. Still, the pressures on women to conform to established feminine behavior was great. The deep structural gender troubles of the era, then, are referenced in Deanie's failed attempt to sacrifice her virginal, good-girl innocence to secure Bud's affections, and Bud's unexpected rejection of his heterosexual masculine prerogative to unfettered sexual freedom signified by his father's gift of a prostitute. Deanie and Bud's uncharacteristic actions are more in keeping with the independent spirits of contemporary youth than with the film's 1930s setting.

Judith Butler reminds us of an essential tenet in Simone de Beauvoir's germinal book *The Second Sex*, which suggests that "only the feminine gender is marked, that the universal person and the masculine gender are conflated, thereby defining women in terms of their sex and [especially crucial here] extolling men as the bearers of a body-transcendent universal personhood" (13–14). It is precisely Deanie's sex or gender that convinces

Bud's father that the showgirl he has procured for the night is "the same damn thing" and thus is indistinguishable from Deanie. According to this logic, the attractive stand-in should satisfy completely his son's sexual if not emotional longing. Of course, neither the working-class Deanie nor her white-trash showgirl counterpart are suitable marriage material in the elder Stamper's class-oriented worldview. As a self-made rich man, Stamper is emblematic of the Horatio Alger rags-to-riches mythos that ascribes wealth and privilege to individual initiative and not to institutional deep structures. Both Deanie's and Bud's rejection of these untenable assumptions parallel much of the ideological and spiritual motivations behind the burgeoning youth culture's rejection of bourgeois materialism, and their prominent participation in the period's civil rights movement. Additionally, white youths willingly relinquished for a time their middle-class comforts to heed Kennedy's call for self-sacrifice as many joined the Peace Corps, established by the president this year.

▌ Cold War Rhetoric

Films of the year also served up politically pointed messages dealing with the Cold War in both a serious and a comedic vein. On the one hand, in *Judgment at Nuremberg* Hollywood delivered a searing indictment against the politics of hate that engendered World War II. The film's dramatic message of necessary punishment and accountability for Nazi hate crimes also contained a conciliatory and politically expedient message of tolerance and forgiveness for the guilty. On the other hand, the Cold War's dangerous absurdity was soft-pedaled in the political comedy *One, Two, Three*, a farce that opposes hyperbolic U.S.-style capitalism to equally exaggerated Soviet-style communism in the battle for ideological supremacy in postwar Germany.

By the time of *Judgment* and *One, Two, Three*'s theatrical releases in October and November, respectively, the new Kennedy administration's hawkish military policies had "plunged the world into [two] crises that threatened nuclear holocaust" (Miller 86). In April, Kennedy sought to overthrow Fidel Castro's Soviet Union-backed revolutionary communist government in Cuba by authorizing a CIA-led invasion on Cuba's beach of Playa Giron. "Claiming that Castro represented 'a clear and present danger to the authentic and autonomous revolution of the Americas'" (84), Kennedy accepted the CIA's contention that the Cuban people would welcome and fully support "an uprising against Castro." It took only three days for Castro's army to kill or capture all fourteen hundred American-trained and -supplied

One, Two, Three (Billy Wilder, Mirisch—Pyramid, United Artists) opposes capitalism and communism in a political comedy about a Coca-Cola executive (James Cagney) in West Berlin. Personal collection of the editor.

Cuban exiles in the humiliating and apocalyptically dangerous Bay of Pigs incident (84–85). And in June occurred his confrontation with Soviet leader Nikita Khrushchev at a summit conference in Vienna. For Kennedy and Khrushchev the meeting was essential, as each wanted high-value political concessions from the other, Kennedy looking to ensure that important access routes to Berlin did not fall into communist hands, and Khrushchev hoping to prevent the embarrassing spectacle of hordes of East German refugees seeking capitalist freedoms in the West (86). The leaders failed to reach consensus at the failed summit, and Kennedy escalated the Cold War by calling up "reserve units of the army and rushed a $3.2 billion supplemental military appropriation through Congress." Subsequently, the Soviets and East Germans built the Berlin Wall to stop the exodus (86–87).

It was this real-life political crisis that informs the humor of *One, Two Three,* an important star vehicle for the venerable James Cagney, brilliantly cast against the familiar gangster type that catapulted him to fame during Hollywood's Golden Age. In this updated tale about psychosocial dynamics engulfing the repressed, obedient, and rebellious corporate man popularized in films of the previous decade, *One, Two, Three* resituates this antihero figure into a highly politicized but comedic rendering of the contemporary and volatile Cold War business environment. *One, Two, Three* tells the farcical story of a scheming American Coca-Cola executive in Germany, McNamara, who endeavors to thwart the marriage of his capitalist boss's naive but headstrong daughter Scarlet "to a communistic East Berlin boy" (Crowther). As the story plays out in an eerie anticipation of the actual collapse of the Soviet Union decades later, the communist boy (Horst Buchholtz) marries the boss's daughter (Pamela Tiffen), renounces his errant communist ways amid his profitable conversion to the ideology of capitalism, and ultimately captures the highly coveted executive job at Coca-Cola sought by McNamara himself.

The film's pace is fast and furious, playing on the iconic Cagney's frenetic energy. In the opening scene, for example, McNamara enters his office in the morning and has to deal with his German employees, who all rise in military fashion; arranges for his wife and children to leave on a trip to Venice so that he can spend the evening "studying his umlauts" with his sexy blonde secretary, Fraulein Ingeborg (Lilo Pulver); tries to train his assistant Schlemmer (Hans Lothar) not to click his heels when responding to McNamara ("Adolph who?" Schlemmer wonders when McNamara asks him what he did during the war); brokers a deal with a Russian trade commission to distribute Coke behind the Iron Curtain; and agrees to host his stateside boss's daughter, who is arriving at the airport later that day. McNamara moves through it all pacing around his office and barking orders loudly, frequently punctuated with the word "next," whether he is dictating a letter to Fraulein Ingeborg or talking with his wife on the telephone about their son, who wants to pack roller skates and a snorkel for their Venice trip.

Among *One, Two, Three*'s more familiar Kennedyesque Cold War referents are opening images and voiceover narration explaining the postwar partitioning of Germany into a capitalist West and communist East; mass protest marches in the streets with East Germans carrying signs and placards reading "Kennedy, Nein, Castro, Ya" and "Vas ist los in Little Rock" ("Kennedy, No, Castro, Yes" and "What is going on" or "What is wrong in Little Rock") and crowds singing political songs with banners and balloons with signs in English that read "Yankee Go Home." These anti-American icons and slogans are deliberately contrasted with pro-American images of Coca-Cola advertisements featuring bathing beauties enjoying bottles of Coke, which together encapsulate Germany's geopolitical attitudinal split on Western hegemony and ideologies of global consumer culture. Cultural signs conjoined in this way throughout the film construct powerful intertextual messages about American film culture and the congealing Cold War rhetoric.

It is particularly striking that the American civil rights movement, indicated by the political march noted above, should loom noticeably throughout *One, Two, Three*, for a "sign" of the visual economy referencing the civil rights movement is also featured in *Judgment at Nuremberg*, the politically more serious of the two films. In *Judgment* there are two Black (presumably African American) military police officers prominently positioned as witnesses to and putative enforcers of racial justice in the complex mise-en-scène of the highly charged courtroom sequences. Both films eschew the likely narrative complications posed by embracing a Black speaking subject. Yet *Judgment*'s dramatic utterances clearly deploy mute but strategically visible Black male bodies to reject simultaneously anti-Black and anti-Jewish racist oppression. By contrast, *One, Two, Three* relays its antiracist message through comedic inference and narrative indirection, as there are no Black bodies in it; but the Black racial problematic is evoked through several of the film's intertextual references to the 1939 film *Gone with the Wind*. For example, the boss's daughter is named Scarlet, and the character of Mrs. McNamara remarks on her disappearance, "Who knows where Scarlet is? She's gone with the wind, maybe kidnapped by white slave traders." Such dialogue in *One, Two, Three* speaks differently to the era's civil rights movement than the iconic function of the Black military policemen along with the anti-genocide rhetoric in *Judgment*; nonetheless, both films make use of the panoply of aesthetic signifiers readily available in American culture's "metalanguage" on racial difference. As Umberto Eco notes, "Common artistic experience also teaches us that art not only elicits feelings but *also produces further knowledge* [emphasis in the original]. The moment that the game of intertwined interpretations gets under way, the text compels one to reconsider the usual codes and their possibilities" (qtd. in Hawkes 142). The usual codes and their possibilities being recoded in *One, Two, Three* and *Judgment* are the changing societal, political, and economic positions and civil rights demands of African Americans that dominated mainstream news and culture at this historical juncture.

On the surface, though, *Judgment* casts its courtroom drama based on the Nuremberg war trials of top-ranking Nazis in 1945 and 1946. Significantly, although the actual trials were conducted by American, French, Russian, and British authorities, in the film the proceedings are conducted solely by U.S. judges. Representing the film's (and the American) perspective is

Hollywood icon Spencer Tracy as Chief Judge Dan Haywood, who struggles to understand how such horrors can take place. An answer of sorts comes in a climactic speech from Dr. Ernst Janning (Burt Lancaster), who in a voluble outburst lays the blame on all those who permitted it to happen. Shot in the restricted space of a courtroom, producer/director Stanley Kramer makes imaginative use of the moving camera, zooming in for dramatic facial close-ups or tracking around the room to connect testimony with the reactions of the characters. Boldly, the film includes as evidence documentary footage of actual Nazi atrocities.

Judgment is a docudrama that, like *One, Two, Three*, is shot in black-and-white and avails itself of the documentary look and mimetic effect that Paul Arthur (following Adorno) terms "Jargons of Authenticity." Whereas *One, Two, Three* is a purely fictional Hollywood product, *Judgment* is a docudrama that follows more along the Griersonian model of the creative treatment of actuality. But as Arthur reminds us, "Documentaries and Hollywood narratives do not issue from separate and pristine worlds but have over the course of their histories maintained a tangled reciprocity" (108). This productive tension between cinematic fact and fiction is clearly at work in the films of the year, in which both mainstream and independent filmmakers became interpreters of the emergent civil rights movement as it took root in the Camelot of the Kennedy era.

1962

Movies and Deterioration

ERIC SCHAEFER

By any measure it was a dreadful year. In the United States and abroad, events seemed to be marked by a steady spiral of deterioration. Certainly, there was some positive news. New Frontier optimism began to see results in the heavens as John Glenn became the first American to orbit the Earth in February. After a number of frustrating postponements, Glenn's flight "put the U.S. back in the space race with a vengeance, and gave the morale of the U.S. and the entire free world a huge and badly needed boost" ("New Ocean" 11). And AT&T's Telstar became the first commercial communications satellite to be launched in July. However, for those who cast their gaze toward more earthly matters, events were troubling. In April the United States resumed atmospheric nuclear testing. The following month the stock market convulsed through its worst week since 1950. The U.S. Supreme Court decided, to the chagrin of many Americans, that prayer in public school conflicted with the First Amendment guarantee of the separation of church and state, and June saw the Students for a Democratic Society (SDS) issue the Port Huron Statement, the manifesto that signaled the start of the student protest movement. Helen Gurley Brown published *Sex and the Single Girl,* a significant milestone of second wave feminism, and for some yet another step down the road to perdition because it told single women to find fulfillment in careers and that premarital sex was all right. In *Silent Spring,* which arrived in bookstores in September, Rachel Carson wrote, "For the first time in the history of the world, every human being is now subjected to contact with dangerous chemicals, from the moment of conception until death" (15). Carson ominously chronicled the decaying quality of the air and water and in doing so gave birth to the modern environmental movement. Other books of the year included Ken Kesey's *One Flew Over the Cuckoo's Nest* and Katherine Anne Porter's *Ship of Fools,* both of which offer negative views of the body politic. Racial integration received serious setbacks that were marked by increased violence throughout the South.

The United States was drawn more deeply into the conflict in Vietnam, a move that Senate Majority Leader Mike Mansfield questioned, making him the first political leader to express doubts about America's Vietnam policy.

Most significant, already strained relations between the United States and the Soviet Union rapidly degenerated as the Cuban missile crisis unfolded in the autumn. The globe braced for a third world war and the possibility of an atomic apocalypse. In mid-October American U-2 spy planes compiled photographic evidence that indicated the Soviets were preparing to install nuclear missiles in Cuba, less than one hundred miles from U.S. soil. Although some hawks pushed President Kennedy toward direct confrontation, on 22 October he went on television to announce that the socialist island nation was being "quarantined" with a naval blockade to stop further shipments of Soviet missiles. On 25 October the U.S. ambassador to the United Nations, Adlai Stevenson, displayed photographs of the missile sites in a tense emergency session of the Security Council. As Soviet ships neared the blockade on 27 October, an American U-2 was shot down over Cuba, killing the pilot. The following day a headline in the *New York Times* anxiously queried, "Will There Be War? The Question the World Is Asking." The United States was making preparations to bomb the Cuban sites when Soviet premier Nikita Khrushchev suddenly backed down, offering to dismantle the missiles in exchange for a promise that the Americans would not invade Cuba. Kennedy agreed and also quietly acquiesced to the Soviet demand that a small number of American missiles in Turkey be removed. The immediate crisis was over, yet as historian Walter LaFeber observes, "The aftershocks of the near-tragedy rippled on. The possible horrors of nuclear war overhung the lifetime of the generation that lived through those days of October 1962" (228).

Deterioration seemed to plague the American motion picture industry as well. It may be an overstatement to call this the worst year in American film history, but by any measure it was a dreadful one. Box office receipts hit their lowest point since the start of World War II, coming in at a miserly $903 million. Weekly movie attendance continued its drop, with 25 million buying tickets every week, down 2 million from the previous year, a trend that would continue through the decade. Employment in the motion picture industry fell to 174,000, the lowest numbers since the Great Depression (Finler 288). But statistics tell only one part of the story. While some good motion pictures were released—from blockbusters such as *The Longest Day* to intimate independent films like *David and Lisa*—even the most cursory evaluation reveals that the year represented a low-water mark in creativity in the American film industry. It was dominated by films that can best be described as workmanlike (*Billy Rose's Jumbo, Sergeants 3, Tender Is the Night*), if not downright indifferent (*Five Weeks in a Balloon, The Horizontal Lieutenant, Mr. Hobbs Takes a Vacation*). Many of the movies cranked out by the industry would barely have qualified for programmer status a decade earlier.

Casting about for inspiration, Hollywood turned to its past. Some features, such as *The Great Chase,* raided the archives to compile footage from silent action and comedy films featuring the likes of Buster Keaton, Lillian Gish, and Douglas Fairbanks, while other films attempted to revive successful old franchises. Columbia, which had underpaid and exploited the Three Stooges in short subjects for years, capitalized on the success their two-reelers had found on television by trotting out two new but tired productions, *The Three Stooges Meet Hercules* and *The Three Stooges in Orbit.* Bing Crosby and Bob Hope were given their marching orders for the first time in more than a decade as they set off on *The Road to Hong Kong,* the last—and least—of their seven "Road" pictures. Bette Davis and Joan Crawford, two of the most dazzling stars of the Golden Age, found their fading careers getting a bounce when they teamed as a latter-day Boris Karloff and Bela Lugosi in the fascinating thriller *What Ever Happened to Baby Jane?* There were tepid remakes: Elvis starred in yet another recapitulation of *Kid Galahad,* originally a 1937 Edward G. Robinson–Humphrey Bogart boxing drama, and bland crooner Pat Boone led a cast in the third incarnation of *State Fair.* That three of the year's better movies were big-screen versions of live television dramas (*Days of Wine and Roses, The Miracle Worker, Requiem for a Heavyweight*) is indicative of the industry's lassitude.

At the end of the year the *New York Times'* veteran film critic Bosley Crowther observed "the widening divergence in the nature and quality of the best American films and the nature and quality of the best films that are coming to us from abroad" ("Theirs" X5). Indeed, the most exciting releases on American screens during the year were films made in Asia and Europe. Even the year's most popular and potent box office hits had a British pedigree. *Lawrence of Arabia* became the most lauded picture of the year and *Dr. No* kicked off the hugely successful James Bond series. Crowther despaired that the "scarcity of distinguished or praiseworthy films from Hollywood" would probably prevent him from finding ten worthy of inclusion for his annual "10 best" list (X5). In a year of memorable events, any survey of American film releases continually leads one back to the same word: forgettable.

▮▮▮▮▮▮ Cold War Hysterics

The atmosphere of deterioration that characterized U.S.-Soviet relations and the Cuban missile crisis—the sense that things could go from bad to worse—was a dominant theme in the most interesting American film productions released during the year. Even if nuclear annihilation was not its subject, the anxiety bred by the Cold War found its most jittery and paranoid evocation in *The Manchurian Candidate*—perhaps the year's most memorable film. While the film was generally appreciated during its initial release, its withdrawal from distribution following the Kennedy assassination and its subsequent re-release and reappraisal have positioned it as one of the greatest political thrillers ever made. Based on Richard Condon's 1959 novel, *The Manchurian Candidate* opens in semi-documentary fashion as an American army patrol is ambushed in Korea in 1952. Flash forward to Sgt. Raymond Shaw (Laurence Harvey) arriving by plane in Washington to be awarded a Medal of Honor for saving the lives of his patrol, lost for several days behind enemy lines. However, Shaw is no ordinary army grunt: his stepfather is Sen. John Iselin (James Gregory), a right-wing politician cast in the mold of Joseph McCarthy and married to Raymond's power-hungry mother, Eleanor (Angela Lansbury). Some time later Shaw's commanding officer in Korea, Major Bennett Marco (Frank Sinatra), suffers from a recurring nightmare. A disorienting dream sequence finds the patrol waiting out a storm in a hotel lobby, listening to a talk being delivered to a ladies' garden society. As the camera pans 360 degrees around the room and the speaker drones on, the ladies become communist agents, and the hotel lobby transforms into a lecture hall in Manchuria and back again all within the same shot. Yen Lo (Khigh Dhiegh), a pudgy psychologist, explains his techniques in brainwashing to the assembled functionaries and instructs Shaw to strangle the member of the patrol he considers his closest friend. Shaw dispassionately follows orders while the other members of the outfit sit by, oblivious to his act. Marco wakes from his dream, screaming.

In many ways *The Manchurian Candidate* is a startling film. The figures in Marco's dream shift, their initial identities peeling away to reveal their true nature. This holds true in the "reality" of the film as well, as nothing is as it initially appears to be. Raymond, the Medal of Honor winner, is actually a remote-control killer. He has been programmed to return to the States as a sleeper assassin, triggered by the suggestion that he play a game of solitaire. Raymond's stepfather, the seemingly powerful Red-baiting senator, is merely a buffoonish marionette whose strings are pulled by Raymond's mother, Eleanor. And Eleanor, a rabid anticommunist on the surface, is in

Eleanor Iselin (Angela Lansbury), the ultimate smothering mother, betrays her son (Laurence Harvey) in *The Manchurian Candidate* (John Frankenheimer, United Artists). Digital frame enlargement.

fact a Red agent who plans to use her trained killer to assassinate her party's presidential nominee so that her husband, the vice presidential candidate, will be elected by default.

Male privilege and power are also an illusion, as the film presents a picture of American masculinity in crisis. When we first meet Major Marco, he is a basket case, waking from his nightmare, shaking, in a flop sweat. He is unable to concentrate, unable to carry out his job effectively. After being relieved of his duties, Marco travels to New York to confront Raymond. In the train's club car he quails as he tries to light his cigarette. A stranger, Rosie (Janet Leigh), takes an improbable interest in him. She helps him light his smoke and then tries to draw him into conversation as one would with a frightened child. Her motherly ministrations are combined with a direct romantic bid as she presses upon him her telephone number and address—a vaguely incestuous posture echoed later in the film.

The other major male characters in the film are just as fragile as Marco. Raymond is portrayed as an effete prig. During the opening of the film it is established that he is not "one of the boys," as he rousts the patrol from a Korean whorehouse, then looks down his nose at the hostess's invitation to come in and enjoy himself. Later, in a drunken moment of candor, he confesses to Marco, "I'm not very loveable." No wonder: Raymond is marked as a spineless mama's boy, admitting that he signed a "Dear Jane" letter to the love of his life based on the dictates of his mother. The brainwashing plot device, and Raymond's susceptibility to it, also connote weakness, a failure of will, and a lack of mastery over self. The depleted masculinity embodied in Marco and Raymond is evident in the supporting characters as well. Senator Iselin—always referred to by the diminutive "Johnny"—is incapable of acting on his own behalf, his every move choreographed, his every word fed to him, by Eleanor. She berates him, insults his intelligence, and Johnny affably swallows it all, like a cat drinking cream. Even Raymond's employer, columnist Holborn Gaines (Lloyd Corrigan), wears his late wife's frilly dressing gown in bed—protesting to Raymond that it's the only thing he has that keeps him warm.

American masculinity is threatened by women who have turned men into quivering children, doing violence to the psyche of the "average Joe" as well as to the foundations of democracy. Eleanor Iselin serves as the personification of Philip Wylie's concept of "momism." In his infamous postwar book *Generation of Vipers*, Wylie excoriated the smothering mother figure, singling her out for all that was wrong with American society. His description of "Mom" could have served as blueprint for Lansbury's performance:

> She is a middle-aged puffin with an eye like a hawk that has just seen a rabbit twitch far below. She is about twenty-five pounds overweight, with no sprint, but sharp heels and a hard backhand which she does not regard as a foul but a womanly defense. In a thousand of her there is not sex appeal enough to budge a hermit ten paces off a rock ledge. . . . Mom is organization-minded. Organizations, she has happily discovered, are intimidating to all men, not just to mere men. They frighten politicians to sniveling servility and they terrify pastors; they bother bank presidents and they pulverize school boards. Mom has many such organizations, the real purpose of which is to compel an abject compliance of her environs to her personal desires.   (201–03)

Wylie's misogyny found lunatic form in Eleanor Iselin. We are even left with the impression that the mothering, assertive Rosie may be another Eleanor-in-the-making.

When a vice-presidential candidate is a communist plant, when that all-American symbol, Mom, trades in her apple pie for brainwashed zombie assassins, we see a state of affairs in which rationality and reasoned political discourse have been replaced by absurdity. And the film is one that, as critic Greil Marcus suggests, "revels in absurdity" (45), a condition amusingly apparent when Johnny Iselin complains to his wife that she hasn't given him a firm number of communists to cite in his trumped-up allegations that the State Department has been infiltrated. She tells him to pick any number and, glancing at a bottle of Heinz ketchup, he proudly selects 57. It is more shockingly illustrated when Eleanor, explaining her motivations to the catatonic Raymond as she sends him off to assassinate the presidential candidate, kisses him on the mouth—a betrayal of biblical proportions and a literal kiss-off.

The Manchurian Candidate is ultimately less about left and right, communism and capitalism (or even momism), than it is about extremism. Upon its release it was attacked by the fringes of both ends of the political spectrum (Monaco 170–71), indicating just how prickly the extremes had become, as well as how true believers are inevitably blind to parody. In *The Manchurian Candidate* political extremism was taken to seemingly outlandish proportions, becoming an object of ridicule.

America's "Others" on Film

During the postwar economic boom fueled by home building and eager consumer spending, the problem of poverty in the United States had largely been ignored. In the spring the issue received its most wide-ranging and passionate treatment with the publication of Michael Harrington's *The Other America: Poverty in the United States*. Starting from the premise that "the millions who are poor in the United States tend to become increasingly invisible" (2), Harrington set out to open the eyes of "every well-fed and optimistic American" to those who had been "maimed in body and spirit" (18). The book was widely reviewed, read by President Kennedy, and is largely credited with inspiring the Johnson administration's program of social and economic initiatives that came to be known as the War on Poverty.

Unlike *The Other America, Strangers in the City* is all but forgotten. Yet stills from the low-budget film, featuring a cast of unknowns (virtually all of whom would remain unknown), could have served as a series of illustrations for Harrington's book. Produced, co-written, and directed by Rick Carrier, who had worked in commercials and industrial films, *Strangers in the City* was perched somewhere between the independent, New York–based "New American Cinema" of John Cassavetes and Shirley Clarke and the cheap sexploitation productions that were proliferating in Gotham. A review in *Time* magazine acknowledged the film's dramatic flaws but praised it as a "brilliantly abrasive" work that "takes moviegoers where many Manhattanites themselves fear to go, into the rat-infested tenement hovels of the bruisingly poor, the lower depths of the richest city on earth" ("Manhattan's Lower Depths" 69).

The *Strangers in the City* are the Alvarez family, Puerto Rican immigrants who live in a one-room tenement on the Upper East Side of Manhattan.

José, the father (Camilo Delgado), is a guitarist who refuses to hold menial jobs that might damage his hands and interfere with his ability to play his beloved instrument. He also refuses to let his wife, Antonia (Rosita De Triano), work, and so their two teenage children, Filipé (Robert Gentile) and Elena (Greta Margos), are forced to find employment to support the family. Filipé gets a job as a delivery boy at a local market but becomes the constant target of a street gang led by a dandified hood named Caddie. Elena turns to sweatshop work but discovers that the foreman expects her to put in "overtime." He passes her along to Mr. Lou (Kenny Delmar), a paternal pimp who takes Elena to his "den of antiquity" where he introduces her to martinis and dresses her in the swank clothing she has always dreamed of wearing. Defying her husband, Antonia finds a job in another sweatshop, where she learns of Elena's fate from a co-worker. She tracks down the drunken foreman who took advantage of her daughter, stabbing him with a pair of scissors when he tries to assault her. The bruised woman returns home and is questioned by her jealous husband. In their altercation she falls backward into the bathtub, clutching for a naked light bulb that hangs above it and is electrocuted. Distraught, José eats rat poison and stumbles out onto the stoop to die. Filipé tracks his sister to Coney Island, where he pulls her from a sedan in which she is plying her trade with another prostitute. The final shots of the film show the siblings making their way to the elevated train. Filipé has rescued Elena from a life of exploitation, but whatever solace may be found there is undercut by the last shot of the train heading back into the city and the knowledge that the two are returning not to a family but to a tragedy.

At times raw and overly melodramatic, *Strangers in the City* successfully conveyed the essence of the "new poverty" Harrington said was constructed to destroy aspiration: "It is a system designed to be impervious to hope. The other America does not contain the adventurous seeking a new life and land. It is populated by failures, by those driven from the land and bewildered by the city, by old people suddenly confronted with the torments of loneliness and poverty, and by minorities facing a wall of prejudice" (10). The Alvarez family struggles with inveterate poverty. Hunger and privation are a part of their daily experience. Prejudice is casual, and street crime is prevalent. Even as members of the family attempt to improve their lot, they are constrained by substandard wages and demeaning working conditions. Failure for the Alvarez family is, as Harrington suggests, chronic, starting with a lack of opportunity that is compounded by burdens placed on them by the city.

Carrier stated that he wanted to show "the city as the dominating factor in people's lives" (Alpert, "Anglicized" 31). Despite the film's other shortcomings, in this quest he fully succeeded. The largest presence in *Strangers in the City* is New York City itself, a gray fabric that stretches out in all directions, frayed at its edges and worn thin in the center, a place where a milky sun casts failed shadows the color of dust. Following the initial cityscapes that open the film, dramatic sequences are punctuated several times with pans of anonymous blocks, sagging tenements, and grimy streets. The typical postcard views of the Empire State Building or the Brooklyn Bridge of most New York–based films are replaced with shots of tumble-down structures and rubble-strewn lots; the hustle of the Great White Way is substituted with a collection of dour faces in a crowded market. *Strangers in the City* offers a vision of a metropolitan wasteland that victimizes its most vulnerable inhabitants. It provides a picture of an economic system that fails to offer any escape from poverty, vividly depicting what Harrington called "the most distinguishing mark of the other America: its common sense of hopelessness" (161).

Hopelessness marked the civil rights movement during the year as well, as it appeared to lose ground to the strident challenges that segregationists mounted to integration. George Wallace won the Democratic primary for the governor's race in Alabama in the spring, pledging to "stand in the schoolhouse door" to prevent integration of the state's educational institutions ("What You Believe In" 25–26). Tensions increased in the South through the summer, culminating in the fall when Supreme Court justice Hugo Black ruled that the University of Mississippi had to admit a Black Air Force veteran, James Meredith. Governor Ross Barnett vowed to block Meredith's admission to Ole Miss, declaring "there is no case in history where the Caucasian race has survived social integration. . . . We will not drink from the cup of genocide" ("This Righteous Cause"). Backed by a phalanx of Justice Department lawyers and federal marshals, Meredith tried to register three times, only to be rebuffed, sparking what *Time* magazine called "the gravest conflict between federal and state authority since the Civil War" ("The Edge of Violence" 15). The campus erupted in hostility as surly mobs attacked the marshals and the federalized Mississippi National Guard troops with rocks, pipes, and gasoline bombs. When the tear gas cleared, two bystanders were dead and dozens of troops were injured, but Meredith was attending classes—albeit with several armed marshals hovering in the background.

Hollywood began to deal with the subject of race relations more directly but most often tentatively and with caution. *To Kill a Mockingbird,* the adaptation of Harper Lee's 1960 Pulitzer Prize–winning novel, was among the year's most successful pictures and it remains one of its most fondly remembered. Set in the Deep South during the Great Depression, the film is narrated by the adult Scout Finch (the uncredited voice of Kim Stanley) recalling her small-town childhood. Scout (Mary Badham) and her brother Jem (Phillip Alford) live with their widowed father, lawyer Atticus Finch (Gregory Peck). The first portion of the movie focuses on the Finch children's adventures with their new friend, Dill (John Megna), whom they meet over the chicken-wire fence surrounding the lush cabbage patch planted by Dill's aunt. They play on a tire swing in front of the small white-washed clapboard houses, in a ramshackle tree house, and in the dusty, sun-baked streets. While the life of the Finch children and Dill is hardly ideal, it is suffused with a golden glow of nostalgia, all lemonade and sponge cake. Peck towers over the movie as the idealized father figure: loving yet stern, capable of dispatching threats (such as a rabid dog) with calm strength, all the while dispensing homey homilies about poverty and justice as if he were handing out pecan pralines. *To Kill a Mockingbird*'s depiction of childhood is warm and comforting—even the boogey man who haunts the story, Boo Radley (Robert Duvall), turns out to be Caspar the Friendly Ghost—and this is clearly one of the reasons the movie continues to be embraced by new generations of viewers.

Courtroom drama dominates the second half of the film as Atticus valiantly defends Tom Robinson (Brock Peters), a black sharecropper who is falsely accused of raping a white woman, despite a foregone outcome at the hands of an all-white jury. *To Kill a Mockingbird* is earnest in its depiction of bigotry, but the characters in the film are quite literally black or white: drooling, prejudiced hayseeds or tolerant, understanding souls. Atticus appears to be motivated by noblesse oblige as much as a belief in racial equality. A fact seldom acknowledged is that the fatherly authority he exercises with family takes on a paternalistic tenor in his dealings with others because of his status as an elite within the community. Furthermore, the film's retrospective structure gives the impression that racial division is a relic of the past, an artifact as old-fashioned as Atticus's ice cream suit and horn-rimmed glasses. As a drama of childhood *To Kill a Mockingbird* is unquestionably a piece of superior craftsmanship. The intimate opening titles, designed by Stephen Frankfurt, plunge the viewer into a child's world with a montage of close-ups of a cigar box filled with marbles and jacks and a child's hands drawing a bird with stubby crayons. The screenplay by Horton Foote, hewing closely to the original novel, also succeeds in maintaining the children's point of view. Robert Mulligan's direction is as unhurried as a walk on a summer day, and he extracted excellent performances from Peck and his young actors. Russell Harlan's black-and-white cinematography shifts between a hard-edged realism, reminiscent of Walker Evans's Depression photographs, and an expressionist sensibility that imbues the Radley house and the lonely nighttime gardens with menace. Even Elmer Bernstein's tender score evokes both joy and a sense of loss. But as a statement on race, it was clearly not Hollywood's most potent offering during the year. The movie that qualifies for that title, *The Intruder*, had many discomforting parallels with the situation at Ole Miss. It was also a box office flop that came from a most unlikely source: Roger Corman, the director of such titles as *Attack of the Crab Monsters* (1957) and *The Little Shop of Horrors* (1960).

Corman had become aware of Charles Beaumont's 1959 novel of the same name, which in turn was based on a 1956 integration standoff in Clinton, Tennessee, engineered by segregationist John Kasper (Graham 165). Unable to find financing for the potentially volatile project, Corman and his brother Gene were forced to produce the film with their own money. They eventually arranged a release through Pathé Labs, which was attempting to get a foothold in distribution (Corman 98). Shot largely on location in Sikeston, Missouri, and using only a handful of professional actors, the movie's supporting roles and crowd scenes were filled with local townspeople who were kept in the dark about the details of the script. As word began to leak out about the true nature of *The Intruder*, threats and intimidation against the crew increased and the last of the shooting was conducted in guerrilla fashion. The finished film benefits tremendously from a sense of authenticity of place and of the people, described by Corman as "old, toothless, lined, weary rural American faces" (100).

Adam Cramer (William Shatner) arrives by bus in Caxton, a small town in an unnamed southern state. He heads to the town's hotel where he books a room with Mrs. Lambert, the elderly desk clerk. She orders the equally aged white bellhop to air out a room, berating him for his slow reaction. "I swear," she confides in Cramer, "I believe that boy's got nigger blood in him somewhere." He picks up on her racism and tells her that he's in Caxton to help with the town's integration problem. "Oh that," Mrs. Lambert sighs, "that's all over. I mean they've got ten niggers enrolled already in the school. And they're startin' Monday." She admits she doesn't like it but says that it's now the law. Thus, within the first several minutes of *The Intruder*, Corman establishes the matter-of-factness of racism as well as the resigned recognition among some that times and the laws are changing. As a representative of a shadowy Washington-based group, the Patrick Henry Society, Cramer is part traveling snake-oil salesman and part rabble-rouser. He is there to fan the smoldering resentments of Caxton's white residents into flames of rage. The town's patriarch explains that they've fought and lost, conceding, like Mrs. Lambert, "It's a law now." Cramer challenges, "Whose law? Is it the collective will of the people that Negroes should be allowed to mix with whites, right under the same roof? Study with them, eat with them, maybe even sleep with them? Is it the collective will of the people that niggers should be allowed to take over the whole world?"

On the first day of school Cramer arranges to have several whites picket with signs filled with racial epithets and veiled threats. Later that night at a rally in the town square he speaks to the throng, playing on their fears with claims that integration is part of a communist plot. Shots of the enthralled crowd watching Cramer cannot help but call to mind the rapt faces that gaze up at Adolf Hitler in *Triumph of the Will* (1935). As the agitated group disperses, a pack sets upon a Black family driving down the street. Tom McDaniel (Frank Maxwell), the editor of the local newspaper, tries to get the sheriff to intervene, but he merely laughs the newsman off by saying, "You want me to arrest everybody, Tom?" The situation in Caxton deteriorates as Cramer rides through the Black neighborhood at night with four Klansmen in a convertible, leading a parade that ignites a cross in front of the Black church. Later, two of the local rednecks bomb the church, killing its pastor. When McDaniel, realizing that integration is both right and necessary, accompanies the Black children to school, he is savagely beaten by white rabble, losing an eye. Cramer is able to convince McDaniel's daughter Ella that the only way to keep her father from being killed in the hospital is to accuse Joey Green, one of the young Black men attending her school, of attempted rape. Cramer sees to it that word gets out, and the mob sets upon the school. As he had been warned earlier, Cramer loses control of the seething mob and they almost lynch Joey on the playground before Ella is brought forward to confess that the intruder persuaded her to lie about the attempted assault. Cramer's deception and manipulation are exposed and the crowd disperses in shame.

The *deus ex machina* conclusion of *The Intruder* may have sounded a tinny note, but it did not diminish Corman's precise depiction of the violent irrationality of racism and mob psychology. Ultimately, the movie proved to be a bitter experience for the director, for whom this was the first film he made "from a deep political and social conviction" (Corman 97). It won an award at the Venice Film Festival but the MPAA refused to give it a Production Code seal because of the use of the word "nigger"—even though the same word is uttered in the big-budget, studio-produced *To Kill a Mockingbird*. Once Corman was finally able to convince the organization to

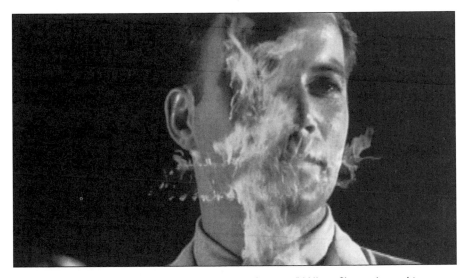

A dramatic dissolve in *The Intruder* shows Adam Cramer (William Shatner) watching some of his handiwork (Roger Corman, Filmgroup). Digital frame enlargement.

award *The Intruder* a seal, he found that the picture was withdrawn from Cannes following the rioting on the Ole Miss campus after Meredith's registration. Then Pathé pulled out of the distribution business, leaving Corman and his brother to continue the release through their own company, Filmgroup. The film's tortuous history clearly was due to its depiction of racial bigotry in contemporary America, which simply hit too close to home for audiences who were forced to confront their own attitudes, whether those of active racism or simple indifference. The film died at the box office. "This was—and remains to this day," wrote Corman in his 1990 memoir, "the greatest disappointment of my career" (103). Nevertheless, despite some dramatic shortcomings, *The Intruder* stands as the most honest and unflinching statement about American race relations to come out of Hollywood during the period.

The Production Code's Last Stand

Corman's run-in with the MPAA over a seal for *The Intruder* was becoming an increasingly common experience for filmmakers. Throughout the 1950s censorship and self-regulation of the movies had undergone steady erosion, and during the early 1960s a growing chorus chided the film industry for its "sickening exploitation of sex" (Wharton 37). While some ire was directed at frank foreign imports and the growing number of "nudie-cuties," cheap independent films that swaddled their moving pin-ups with a thin veil of comedy, the bulk of the criticism was directed at mainstream movies such as *Walk on the Wild Side*. Projects that in years past would have been vetoed outright by Code enforcement officials were now being massaged through the system. The Code may have been crumbling due to its age and failure to keep up with changing attitudes, but columnist John Crosby borrowed the Cold War rhetoric of "escalation" when he wrote about a rise in adult themes such as adultery and rape. As part of his call for a ratings system—something that would become a reality in six years—Crosby railed against *Cape Fear* as "the most sordid, vicious and utterly depraved movie I have ever seen. . . . It literally makes you sick" (8). At the same time he described *Lolita* ("the very word is almost synonymous with salaciousness") as "one of the finest movies I have ever seen" (10). The two films signaled how hobbled the Production Code had become, and each had its own unique take on the theme of deterioration.

Cape Fear has all the marks of a conventional thriller. Based on John D. MacDonald's 1958 pulp novel *The Executioners,* the film opens with Max Cady (Robert Mitchum), just released from prison, sliding through the central square of a small Georgia city. He enters the courthouse and watches lawyer Sam Bowden (Gregory Peck) arguing before the court. Sam leaves court and as he prepares to drive home, the ex-con confronts him, reminding Sam that he testified against him in an assault case in Baltimore eight years earlier and indicating that he holds Sam responsible for his prison term. Sam drives away, merely annoyed, but starts worrying when Cady shows up later that evening at the local bowling alley, casting his sleepy leer on his wife, Peggy (Polly Bergen), and teenage daughter, Nancy (Lori Martin). It dawns on Sam that the vengeful hood is engaging him in a battle of nerves and that the safety of his family is at stake.

From the start the vindictive and calculating Cady is presented as a predatory beast, whether in his studied regard of a pedestrian's posterior as she crosses the street or through his suggestive questions to a waitress in the bowling alley bar. Later, he drives through town with the attractive but damaged drifter (Barrie Chase) he has picked up in a bar. She tells him he is an animal: "I wouldn't expect you to understand this, but it's a great comfort for a girl to know that she could not possibly sink any lower." She soon discovers the depths of his brutality when he beats and rapes her. The private detective (Telly Savalas) Bowden hires to help protect his family suggests that the only way to get rid of Cady is to hire some muscle to give him a thrashing: "A type like that is an animal, so you've gotta fight him like an animal." Indeed, much of the film's power comes from Mitchum's performance. His Max Cady takes on the dimensions of a mythological creature, part reptile, part big cat. His commanding size and slow, languid movements are those of a man capable of dominating his surroundings with mere physical presence. This, combined with Cady's internal reserve, suggests a power that can lash out at any moment with deadly force.

If Cady is characterized as an animal from the outset, the dramatic core of *Cape Fear* is Sam Bowden's slide into savagery. As a lawyer, he takes for granted that the law will protect his family and that Cady will be contained. He slowly comes to realize, however, that this is not the case. Cady, who has used his time in prison to become a jailbird lawyer, ramps up his threats against the family while always remaining just within the law. As the Bowdens prepare for a day of boating, Cady leers at Nancy, smacks his lips, and drawls to Sam, "Say, she's getting to be almost as juicy as your wife, ain't she?" Bowden takes a swing at Cady in front of witnesses on the crowded dock. Sam then sinks to hiring three thugs to work over his adversary. The attackers end up hospitalized as a result of their encounter with Cady, who, bloodied, calls the Bowden home and tells Sam, "You just put the law in my hands and I'm gonna break your heart with it. Ain't nothing can stop me." His intimidation becomes more explicit: "I got something planned for your wife and kid that they ain't never gonna forget." With Sam facing disbarment for his actions, he conspires with his wife, the private eye, and the local police chief to lure Cady to a secluded houseboat on the Cape Fear River where he can be killed in "self-defense." The plan almost backfires and Sam, forced to confront Cady alone, nearly dies along the banks of the river before finally getting the upper hand. Ready to murder his injured foe, Sam backs off, telling him, "We're gonna take good care of you, nurse you back to health. You're strong, Cady. You're going to live a long life. In a cage! That's where you belong." Bowden is able to stop his personal slide into savagery in the film's final moments, but not out of a humanitarian impulse. Sam puts aside any thoughts that the justice system might fail him again and refrains from killing Cady because he hopes that years behind bars will ultimately be a more brutal punishment than death.

As the camera cranes up over Sam and Cady at the end of *Cape Fear,* Sam's victory is undermined by a series of troubling realizations. Among these is the facility with which Cady skirts the edges of the law to achieve his retribution against Sam. Even more disturbing is Sam's readiness to undermine the law that he has taken an oath to uphold. Beyond this, Sam and Peggy do not fear so much for their daughter's life as for her virginity and her reputation. They despair over the fact that Nancy might have to testify in public if she is violated by Cady. "It's the clinical reports, and questions, and the detailed answers that she'd have to give," whines Sam, his sense of bourgeois propriety undermined. Though Cady faces a life behind bars, he has, on some level, gotten his revenge against Sam, for the Bowden family is effectively shattered. Nancy has been sent into hysterics repeatedly by her encounters with Cady and by the climate of fear that her parents have introduced into her life; by the end of the film she appears to be irreversibly traumatized. Moreover, Sam and Peggy must live with the knowledge that they conspired to kill a man, and Sam faces an ethics committee inquiry that could deprive him of his livelihood. In a year when large issues like nuclear war and racial strife threatened to send human progress spiraling backward, *Cape Fear* intimately demonstrated just how fragile basic institutions like law and family are. The middle-class comfort and privilege enjoyed by the Bowdens—and by extension, every middle-class family—is shown to be held together by the slenderest of threads, threads that can snap when outside pressure is brought to bear upon them.

The distasteful elements of *Cape Fear* were enough to convince some that movies were taking a turn for the worse in showing the seamier aspects of life. News that Vladimir Nabokov's notorious novel *Lolita* was to be made into a movie was taken as proof positive of Hollywood's slide into a "preoccupation with sex, and particularly its aberrations" (Bunzel 90). Told in the first person, the novel chronicles the life of Humbert Humbert, a well-educated but none-too-successful European scholar pushing middle age. Humbert's infatuation with twelve-year-old "nymphet" Dolores "Lolita" Haze drives him to obsession, paranoia, and eventually murder, as he kills his nemesis—and Lolita's first lover—playwright Clare Quilty. Praised as brilliant by some, panned as pornography by others, *Lolita* became a controversial best seller when it was published in the United States in 1958. Director Stanley Kubrick and producer James B. Harris optioned the rights to the book and began negotiating with the Production Code Administration to find a way to get the film made with an eye toward reaching the widest possible audience. Initial plans were to have the pre-teen and her older lover secretly marry in Appalachia; later the idea was to bump Lo's age to fifteen (Leff and Simmons 221–22). That Code chief Geoffrey Shurlock was even willing to discuss ways that the film might be made to conform to the Code was something of a victory for Kubrick and Harris.

Once the film was completed, Kubrick made some requested cuts and *Lolita* received Code approval based on liberalized provisions regarding "sex perversion" that had been passed in October 1961 (Leff and Simmons 235). The resulting film was far from the masterpiece that Nabokov's novel is now considered. Critic Richard Corliss has observed:

It happens that Nabokov wrote *Lolita* at exactly the right moment for its artistic and commercial success. Within a few years of his completing it, the Supreme Court in the US and Parliament in the UK had liberalized statutes protecting the written word. It happens that Kubrick directed *Lolita* at just the wrong moment. Within a few years of his completing it, American filmmakers would take their cue from Europeans and force an "adult" cinema on their sponsors and their audience.   (13)

MGM, the film's distributor, provocatively asked in its advertising, "How did they ever make a movie of *Lolita*?" The answer was, by being considerably tamer and reducing the erotic elements of the story, something Kubrick regretted in later years (Corliss 12). Still, some of the satiric sting remained and it is there that the theme of deterioration remains most evident.

Although the film makes occasional use of voiceover narration by Humbert (James Mason), it ultimately does not convey the corrosive sense of self-delusion that underlies the novel. In the film Humbert's enchantment with his twisted personal aesthetic is suppressed and replaced with a broader statement about cultural decline. Mason's Humbert stands in for a cultural elite—more sophisticated, more accomplished, and considerably less threadbare than his literary counterpart. He is undone not so much by his sexual peccadilloes as by his susceptibility to a mass culture that caters to youth and middlebrow taste. The beginning of the film (chronologically the end of the tale) finds Humbert tracking down Quilty (Peter Sellers)—a television writer in the movie—to his mansion. The sybaritic Quilty, nursing a hangover, realizes that Humbert plans to murder him and stalls for time. He barrages Humbert with a series of impressions of pop culture archetypes—a grizzled B-western sidekick, a down-and-out boxer looking for a last shot. Unloading his revolver into the writer puts an end to Humbert's affair with a degraded American culture.

A lengthy flashback charts Humbert's immersion in cultural banality. The moment he sets foot in the Haze home in Ramsdale, New Hampshire, in search of a room he is assaulted with mediocrity. Charlotte (Shelley Winters) shows him around the house, babbling with affected sophistication about the cultural advancement of Ramsdale. She notes that as chair of the Great Books Committee she brought in Clare Quilty as a speaker. Humbert, the lover of great books, admits to the disappointed Charlotte that he has never heard of the TV writer. Charlotte's verbal barrage, as well as the kitsch of the Haze household, appears to overwhelm the aesthete. As he stares, bewildered, at a ceramic dog covered with a floral pattern, Charlotte exclaims, "I see you're interested in art! In that case you really must see the collection of reproductions I have in my bedroom." Although he feigns

Charlotte Haze (Shelley Winters) introduces Humbert Humbert (James Mason) to a culture of mediocrity in *Lolita* (Stanley Kubrick, MGM). Personal collection of the author.

polite interest in the prints, once Humbert sees Charlotte's most accomplished reproduction—Lolita—sunbathing in a bikini in the backyard, he's hooked. From there it's a steady diet of drive-in movies, pink champagne, the cha-cha, and TV. Televisions appear in many of the rooms in the film. Although never turned on, they sit conspicuously in the background, like gaping black holes.

As played by Sue Lyon, Lolita is a far cry from the "little deadly demon" nymphet of Nabokov's novel, and is instead more the Madison Avenue ideal of vanilla youth and beauty. Similarly, Humbert is less the Epicurean pedophile exalting in his deviant tastes than he is a run-of-the-mill dirty old man who succumbs to Lolita's banal charms as if she were a model selling new cars or cigarettes in magazine advertisements. At one point Humbert eagerly makes Lo a sandwich on white bread, "loaded," he enthuses, "with mayonnaise, just the way you like it." Lolita is all mayo and white bread, a bland sylph who becomes Humbert's new ideal, for whom he willingly throws aside his taste and prunes his intellectual capacity in exchange for suburban torpor and, eventually, a string of blank motel rooms along miles of anonymous highways. Even stripped of his sophistication, Humbert is still unable to compete with Quilty, the media-made celebrity and writer of jejune television dramas whom Lolita and all her friends find so "dreamy." In Kubrick's *Lolita*, sophistication and seriousness are dead, victims of a society enamored with mass culture and middlebrow taste. The irony, of course, was that in making a statement about the bland state of American culture, Nabokov and Kubrick concocted a middling entertainment that was a pale imitation of the original.

A Genre in Twilight

If the erosion of the Production Code was seen by some as a sign of Hollywood's decay, the slow death of its most enduring genre, the western, was perhaps the clearest indication of the fading fortunes of the American film industry. The number of primetime network television western series declined during the year, although fifteen still commanded primetime slots at the start of the fall season. The glut of small-screen westerns, compounded by popular culture's growing love affair with spies and spacemen, led to a general decline in the quantity and quality of the genre's theatrical form. The movie cowboy seemed to be an anachronism, a one-horsepower hero in a new jet-fueled age. This attitude was contained in two key westerns: *The Man Who Shot Liberty Valance* was arguably the last great western made by the director who created its most enduring classics, John Ford; and *Ride the High Country* was the second film made by Sam Peckinpah, who honed his skills directing episodes of small-screen oaters and would spend his career redefining the genre. The films are united in their elegiac quality, a doleful view of modernization, and their unsentimental portrait of aging.

Ride the High Country finds one-time federal marshal Steve Judd (Joel McCrea) reduced to accepting a job guarding a quarter-million-dollar gold shipment being transported to a bank from the remote mining town of Coarsegold. Judd hires his former deputy, Gil Westrum (Randolph Scott), and Westrum's young sidekick, Heck Longtree (Ron Starr), to help in the task, unaware that they plan to steal the money if they fail to convince Steve to join them in their plot. *The Man Who Shot Liberty Valance* concerns the aging Senator Ransom Stoddard (James Stewart) returning to the town of Shinbone with his wife, Hallie (Vera Miles), to attend the funeral of their old friend Tom Doniphon (John Wayne). Many years earlier Stoddard became renowned as "the man who shot Liberty Valance" (Lee Marvin), the vicious gunslinger hired by the cattle interests to block the cause of statehood. As Stoddard reveals in the lengthy flashback that makes up the bulk of the film, it was Tom Doniphon who actually shot Valance from the shadows on the streets of Shinbone. As a result, Stoddard gained wealth, had a long career in politics, and won the heart of Hallie from Tom, who died poor and forgotten.

A sense of loss and resignation pervades both films. Upon arriving in Shinbone, Hallie comments on how much things have changed with the building of a school, churches, and shops. Yet all the progress is tinged with sadness. Hallie's delivery is flat and matter-of-fact, recognition that Shinbone no longer possesses the coarse energy that made it both dangerous and alive in the past. Youth and vitality are also lost, as expressed by *Liberty Valance*'s flashback structure. The major portion of the film, dealing with Shinbone's lawless history, features Ranse, Hallie, Tom, and the other characters in their prime. This is contrasted with the framing story, as the characters return for Tom's funeral. Not only is Tom dead, but those who remain have aged some thirty years. Ranse, Hallie, and Tom's right-hand man Pompey (Woody Strode) move like ghosts. Even Link Appleyard (Andy Devine), the lily-livered marshal, no longer has the energy to put into his whining. Similarly, in *Ride the High Country,* Steve and Gil pass the time reminiscing about bygone days, the people they knew and the experiences they shared. They miss their vigor and ruefully joke about sore feet, rheumatism, and their lack of agility. Steve wears reading glasses, a fact he hides from the bankers who hire him, for fear he will not secure the job. The quiet longing that Steve and Gil express for lost youth is made all the more poignant by the presence of Heck and Elsa (Mariette Hartley), the young woman who travels to the mining camp with them to marry her boyfriend. Their fresh, unlined skin can barely contain their stirring hormones. Watching both films, it is almost impossible not to recall the stars in earlier roles: Wayne as the agile Ringo Kid in *Stagecoach* (1939), the boyish Stewart in *Destry Rides Again* (1939), Scott in *Belle Starr* (1941), or McCrea as *Buffalo Bill* (1944), for example.

In both films the arrival of the law and the process of civilization marginalize and diminish the western hero. *The Man Who Shot Liberty Valance* is perhaps Ford's most interior western. The majority of the scenes take place indoors: the backroom at the undertaker's, the office of the *Shinbone Star,* the kitchen and dining room of Peter's Place restaurant, the saloon, and the hall where the statehood convention takes place. The exteriors that are featured are largely studio backlots and, in some instances, stage sets. In this film, the frontier has been walled off and clapboarded over. Tom won't propose to Hallie until he finishes building an addition to his house—a chore he can't seem to bring himself to complete, realizing it would bring about an end to his freedom. Tom's frontier skills, his gut instinct, his ability with a gun are being displaced by Stoddard's knowledge of the law, his logic, his capacity to use words and to teach. Indeed, it is these civilized traits that gradually shift Hallie's affections to Ranse, leaving Tom alone.

Ride the High Country positions Judd and Westrum as men who are trapped in the past, who have outlived their usefulness. When Steve arrives in town to take his job guarding the gold shipment, he is almost run over by a sputtering automobile and told to "watch out, old timer" by a passing cop. His wizened employers tell him they expected a much younger man. Steve replies, "I used to be . . . We all used to be." He finds his old pal Gil operating a shooting gallery in a sideshow, complete with a crepe hair Buffalo Bill wig and moustache. The frontier is now only to be found in dime novels and cheap entertainment; the expansive possibilities once before them have been replaced by steadily diminishing expectations. Steve learns that the gold shipment he is to guard is not $250,000 but a mere $20,000, and in the mining camp the final tally comes to just over $11,000—"A far cry from a quarter million," complains Gil. Old doctrines, whether Steve's hidebound code of honor or the fundamentalist faith practiced by Elsa's father that drives her from home, are no longer operable in the changing west. Elsa tells Steve that her father says there is only right and wrong, good and evil, and asks him, "It isn't that simple, is it?" Recognizing that the old ways are dying, he wistfully replies, "No, it isn't. It should be, but it isn't."

Ford biographer Joseph McBride writes of *The Man Who Shot Liberty Valance*, "The wilderness may have become a garden, but it has become poisoned at its heart. Ford strikes this theme from the opening shot of the train bearing the Stoddards back to Shinbone: as the train leaves the frame, Ford lingers a moment on its black smoke hovering over the otherwise pristine landscape, visually showing that 'progress' is a polluting force" (632). *Liberty Valance* and *Ride the High Country* provide implicit critiques of modernity and the dissipation of the passion and energy that helped build the frontier. The present of both films has become a place of lawyers, politicians, bureaucrats, greedy bankers, and even a press that is more staid and businesslike compared to the florid proclamations of Dutton Peabody (Edmund O'Brien), the editor of the *Shinbone Star* in its pre-statehood days. Ranse has lived a lie for years as "the man who shot Liberty Valance," an act that propelled him to fame, power, and wealth. When he finally confesses the truth to the newspaper reporters, the *Star*'s current editor responds with one of the most famous lines from the Ford canon: "When the legend becomes fact, print the legend." Although said in deference to the past, by denying the truth the editor and the audience are forced to consider the degree to which truth has suffered at the hands of progress.

Progress inevitably comes with a price. It took a heavy toll during the year. U.S.-Soviet relations deteriorated to a point where confrontation and a nuclear war appeared to be inevitable. The American economy struggled, and the plight of the big cities along with the poor who lived in them worsened. The cause of civil rights took a step backward in the face of challenges from segregationists. It is understandable, and perhaps it was inevitable, that decay and decline became a central theme in many of the year's movies. Even the best westerns of the year were homages, weighted with age and infused with resignation. But when you hit bottom there is only one way to go. The United States and the Soviet Union stepped back from the brink of mutual destruction. The American people were awakened to the plight of the poor and began a war on poverty. Segregationists became increasingly isolated in the face of civil rights legislation.

Things gradually got better—and they gradually got better for the American film industry as well. The decline of the Production Code and the embrace of increasingly adult material in films such as *Cape Fear* and *Lolita* paved the way for the aesthetic revitalization of the American motion picture industry at the end of the decade. Independent productions—whether large star vehicles such as *The Manchurian Candidate*, or small ones like *Strangers in the City*—would generate new enthusiasm and imagination by decade's end. The political commitment evident in movies like *The Intruder* would eventually be embraced by audiences rather than snubbed. And even if the western appeared to be headed toward that last sunset, films like *The Man Who Shot Liberty Valance* and *Ride the High Country* would signal the genre's developing reinvigoration through a combination of overt political commentary and historical revisionism. While this may have been a fairly dismal year for American film production, it signaled a tipping point between the old Hollywood and the new, between convention and innovation, and between stagnation and recovery.

1963

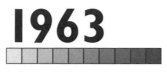

Movies and the Little Soldiers
of the New Frontier

JOE McELHANEY

This is a pivotal year in the history of civil rights: among the most important events were the highly contested first registration of Black students at the University of Alabama, the shooting death of Medgar Evers by white segregationist Byron de la Beckwith, and President John F. Kennedy's submitting of a civil rights bill to Congress, all in June; the March on Washington culminating with Martin Luther King Jr.'s "I Have a Dream" speech in August; and the explosion of a Ku Klux Klan bomb at a church in Birmingham, Alabama, killing four girls on 15 September. It is also the year in which Sidney Poitier became the first Black actor to win an Academy Award for a leading role (for *Lilies of the Field*). But African Americans were not the only ones engaged in ideological and political struggle. The same year that saw Gloria Steinem publish an exposé of her experiences working as a bunny at the Playboy Club in New York gave birth to an epochal moment in feminist history with the publication of Betty Friedan's *The Feminine Mystique*. And in the most scandalous (if ultimately rather chaste and sentimental) best-selling novel of the year, John Rechy's *City of Night,* a gay hustler begins his career by working in Times Square.

Nevertheless, if we are to isolate one event in American history which marks that entire year, symbolically destroying the mythology of the early 1960s and laying the foundation for the years to follow, it would certainly be the Kennedy assassination on 22 November. The exhaustively analyzed 8 mm film of that assassination, captured by Abraham Zapruder, has assumed an extraordinary status, not so much for the power of the motion picture camera to bear witness to a cataclysmic historical event (it had been doing that since its invention) as for the source of the images themselves: the amateur. However, there is another image from the Kennedy assassination that is almost as powerful and perhaps even more iconic: that of the three-year-old John F. Kennedy Jr. saluting his father's coffin as it is carried through the streets of Washington. While frequently reproduced as both a still photograph and documentary film image, the film image of this moment makes clear what the still photograph does not: that his mother is clearly stage-managing this gesture of her son as she whispers instructions to him and then gently prods him forward to perform the rehearsed salute. That it does not diminish the emotional impact of this gesture as we see the strings being pulled here by Jacqueline Kennedy (if anything, it intensifies the gesture's emotional power) may be seen as a touchstone for some possible ways for thinking about American cinema of the year.

The Kennedy administration was strongly defined by images of not only the youthful glamour of a young president and first lady, but also by images of two very young (and frequently photographed) children, Caroline and John Jr. This was the first White House in modern American history in which preschool children played a major literal and symbolic role, particularly for an administration self-consciously proclaiming that it embodied the vision of a New Frontier. (The president's brother, Attorney General Robert Kennedy, had eight children.) The administration's official historian, Arthur Schlesinger Jr., would later write that Kennedy was the first president since Franklin Roosevelt "who had anything to say to men and women under twenty-five, perhaps the only President with whom youth could thoroughly identify itself" (Schlesinger, *Thousand* 740). Furthermore, and in marked distinction to the Eisenhower years, this was a highly theatrical White House in which the Kennedys assumed movie-star like status and in which there were also strong ties to the world of Hollywood and show business. *PT 109*, a film about Kennedy's World War II adventures, starred Cliff Robertson as Kennedy; movie star Peter Lawford was the president's brother-in-law; another star, Gene Tierney, had been a former girlfriend of Kennedy; and Frank Sinatra, Sammy Davis Jr., Angie Dickinson, Marilyn Monroe, and Judy Garland likewise had strong personal connections with the Kennedys. But this was also an administration that forged ties with the world of "high" art: the Kennedys publicly expressed their devotion to art and invited artists and writers to the White House. According to Schlesinger, Kennedy believed that "the health of the arts was vitally related to the health of a society" (Schlesinger, *Thousand* 731).

There is no indication that the cinema was ever part of this widespread presidential interest in art. Still, the general atmosphere within America was of a certain cautious optimism in art's transformative capacities, and the cinema inevitably picked up on some of this. It was not so much Hollywood, though, that seemed to be at the forefront of this potential renaissance as it was the avant-garde and underground cinema, particularly as it was being practiced in New York, with Jonas Mekas's column in the *Village*

Voice serving as a major pulpit. The teenage George and Mike Kuchar continued to produce their Hollywood-on-the-Bronx super-8 mm epics, casting friends and relatives in hilarious reworkings of the clichés of Hollywood melodramas and horror films: *A Town Called Tempest, Confessions of Babette, Anita Needs Me, Tootsies in Autumn*. After viewing a number of these Kuchar films, Mekas would write that "Hollywood keeps complaining that there are no new faces. They are searching in the wrong places, that's their trouble. The underground is full of new faces and bodies" (Mekas 122–23). And if the Zapruder film showed that a motion picture camera in the hands of an amateur could pose one significant challenge to the professional, Andy Warhol would take up this challenge in another way. By stripping the cinema to its essence in a series of films shot with a primitive, silent 16 mm camera, Warhol was able to capture the most banal of activities with a wide-eyed (albeit slightly decadent and ironic) wonder unmatched since the Lumière brothers and in films whose titles announce their mesmerizing simplicity, at once epic and minimalist: *Kiss, Eat, Haircut, Blow Job*.

Hollywood, by contrast, appeared to be losing its widespread cultural hold. For the second year in a row, it was a British film (in this case, *Tom Jones*) that won the Best Picture Oscar and not an American. Few major new filmmaking talents were emerging out of Hollywood and its most interesting films that year were directed by veterans. Elia Kazan would make his most personal work, *America, America;* but this film, seemingly so much about America that the country's name is repeated in its title, was shot largely on location in Greece and Turkey. America is the great destination for its protagonist, but once he arrives in America the film concludes. The biggest hit of the year, Joseph L. Mankiewicz's *Cleopatra,* was also (given its monumental budget) the biggest flop of the year, its catastrophic expense the result of a network of factors relating to the breakdown of the old studio system. Near the end of the first half of this epic, a political assassination takes place, that of Julius Caesar (Rex Harrison). Witnessing the assassination through the telepathic powers of a medium, Cleopatra (the former child star Elizabeth Taylor) cries out, "My son!" The son she is referring to is the offspring of her relationship with Caesar, and the child's line to political power is now in jeopardy with the death of his father. Earlier in the film, in what was clearly its most expensive sequence, Cleopatra is paraded through the streets of Rome, her child directly at her side and serving as an emblem of her power as both politician and woman. For Taylor's Cleopatra, politics is nothing less than a type of aristocratic street theater in which a young male child is both co-star and infantile ornament.

For Friedan, much of the feminine mystique of the postwar period was constructed upon mothers subordinating their own dreams and desires to those of their children. The dreams of the child became absorbed by the mother and a cult of the child emerged, leading to children who were increasingly marked by passivity as well as a "dreamlike unreality" (Friedan 288). If the nurturing mother who lives her life through her children is one impossible ideal of the postwar period, we find numerous variations on and responses to this ideal in American films this year. Beverly Boyer (Doris Day) in Norman Jewison's *The Thrill of It All* (written by Carl Reiner) represents the purest extension of a certain 1950s ideal of the housewife and mother. Boyer, bored by a life as a housewife whose primary fulfillment is making ketchup in her basement, briefly finds fame (as well as satisfaction) by starring in a series of television commercials. This fame, however, threatens her ability to be an effective mother to her two children and a devoted wife to her pediatrician husband (James Garner). The resolution to this dilemma takes place when Beverly assists her husband in the delivery of a child in the backseat of a limousine, a sight so miraculous to Beverly that she resolves to be nothing more than a wife and mother after this. "A woman that cannot bear children is like a river that is dry," says Taylor's Cleopatra. Billy Wilder's *Irma la Douce* ends with a sequence unimaginable under the old Production Code as pregnant prostitute Irma (Shirley MacLaine) weds a policeman played by Jack Lemmon and immediately gives birth to their child in a church vestibule. Shortly before this sequence, her future husband (who will soon return to his original job as the policeman on a children's playground) tells her, "When I first met you, you were a street walker and now you're going to be a wife and mother. Isn't that a miracle?" In these films, the act of childbirth itself constitutes the "miracle" that transforms these problematic or recalcitrant women, absorbing them back into the family.

At the Kennedy funeral, it is not Caroline (also standing at her mother's side) who is asked to perform the salute to her father's coffin but the younger John, a gesture at once personal (a farewell salute from son to father) and public (a farewell salute from one "soldier" to another). While this same year Andrew Sarris would claim that he did not believe in women directors, surely this magnificently staged moment by Jacqueline Kennedy is proof of a highly gifted metteur en scène, one with a sure command of costuming and gesture and a finely tuned sense of scale. John F. Kennedy Jr. not only salutes his father, but with this salute go the dashed hopes of his father's administration, a gesture of resignation and profound mourning as much as one of strength and resilience, all of this encased in the body of a three-year-old boy. Nicholas Ray's final Hollywood film, *55 Days at Peking*, takes the symbolism of a male child caught up in a violent political situation one step further by having the young son of David Niven's British diplomat shot by a stray bullet (while playing soldier) in the midst of the Boxer Rebellion.

The children in American films of the year intersect with a number of issues emerging from the final year of the New Frontier. A year earlier, the English translation of Philippe Ariès's *Centuries of Childhood* (originally published in France in 1960) appeared, effectively launching the field of child studies. Fundamental to Ariès's thesis is that the concept of childhood we accept today was formed during the Renaissance. Prior to this, the world of the child was less distinct from the world of the adult, and once this separation of childhood and adulthood was put into place, the child began to assume major mythic and symbolic functions. For Leslie Fiedler, like Ariès, childhood is less a biological fact than a myth with definite historical and cultural contours. Fiedler sees this obsession with childhood as something essentially connected to modern thought which, for a variety of reasons, moves the child from the periphery of life and art to the center of it (Fiedler 255). Children stand at the center of much of American cinema this year, their mythic and symbolic function assuming a particular force within the context of American cultural life poised at a moment of uncertain transition.

Indeed, children dominated the movie screens even when they were not visible. In the opening sequence of Robert Mulligan's *Love with the Proper Stranger* a defensive Macy's shop girl (Natalie Wood) tells a one-night stand (Steve McQueen) who barely remembers her, "I'm going to have a baby." The entire narrative situation of the film subsequently revolves around this unborn child. In *The Cardinal,* Tom Tryon's priest faces his first major theological and personal crisis when he is forced to choose between allowing a hospital to save the life of his sister (who is about to be wheeled into the delivery room to give birth to an illegitimate child whose father is Jewish) or save the life of the unborn child. In the end, the priest's inflexible Roman Catholicism only allows him to choose the latter. In August, only three months before the assassination, Jacqueline Kennedy would prematurely give birth to a third child, a boy, who would not survive, the demise of the child all too ominously portending the more cataclysmic death of his father shortly afterward.

But it is ultimately the visibility and active presence of the child that is of concern here. In the Robert Drew–produced *Crisis: Behind a Presidential Commitment,* a documentary about the confrontation between George Wallace and two Black students attempting to register at the University of

Alabama, both Wallace and Robert Kennedy are surrounded by their children: Kennedy is shown breakfasting with his many, many children and Wallace's little girl plays the piano for him. While Wallace's interactions with his daughter undoubtedly serve to humanize him, Kennedy's enormous brood already seems to stack the deck in Kennedy's favor: Wallace is simply outnumbered, facing a far more fertile, Roman Catholic opponent who appears to have taken the biblical edict to be fruitful and multiply quite literally. At a pivotal moment in the film, when Kennedy must decide whether to intervene in the situation or not, he allows his young daughter Kerry to talk on the telephone with Deputy Attorney General Nicholas Katzenbach. While Kerry talks to Katzenbach, Kennedy makes his decision to have the federal government step in. As the film presents this moment, it is almost as though Kerry's innocent chatter with Katzenbach has indirectly willed her father into making this historic decision. In *Cleopatra*, Julius Caesar speaks of a dream he has in which "strange and solitary birds were seen in the Forum. They said one flew into the Senate itself, carrying a sprig of laurel which it dropped at the base of Pompey's statue." Like the children in so much of American cinema this year, the birds in *Cleopatra* are caught up in ambivalent associations, at once images of peace and violence: the dream is a premonition of Julius Caesar's assassination.

These Kids Today

A Child Is Waiting (written by Abby Mann) is a film in which a large group of children not only dominate the narrative world but do so as a result of their mental "retardation." In the film, a thirty-something music teacher, Jean Hansen (Judy Garland), begins working at the school and develops a special interest in a young boy named Reuben (Bruce Ritchey). But her favoritism toward the boy causes friction with the head of the school, Dr. Matthew Clark (Burt Lancaster), and intensifies an already difficult relationship the boy has with his parents (Gena Rowlands and Steven Hill). While director John Cassavetes would disown the film after it was recut by its producer, Stanley Kramer, it is a far more interesting work than its reputation would indicate. On paper, the film's subject matter might suggest a work of sincere and liberal humanism, especially given so many of Kramer's other projects. And the film undoubtedly retains some links with this tradition. But *A Child Is Waiting* is a fascinating hybrid, part earnest Hollywood problem film (and with two Hollywood stars, Burt Lancaster and Judy Garland, at the center of it) but also part of another tradition of American cinema: the low-budget, American independent cinema of the late fifties and early sixties, of which Cassavetes's first film, *Shadows* (1961), is a primary example. These films are predicated upon their refusal of the more polished ideal of Hollywood craftsmanship and in which the actors are given both greater physical improvisational space and greater demands to enact a certain kind of post-Method behavior that, at times, uncannily evokes the behavior of children.

A Child Is Waiting relativizes the distinction between the normal and the abnormal, taking the form of a didactic social problem film, a form the film also struggles against. "Normality is relative," Dr. Clark explicitly states, arguing with a stubborn board of directors that they would all seem comparatively retarded in a room full of Einsteins. In *A Child Is Waiting*, the "normal" world and the world of mental retardation are not opposed to but instead mirror one another. Dr. Clark tells Jean that the secret to having an effect on the children is not for the teacher to believe in her own transformative powers but for the teacher to see herself *in* the child. In a line of dialogue with a clear connection to Kennedy's famous inaugural speech, Clark says, "It's not what you can do for these children, but what they can do for you." And the mental retardation of Kennedy's sister Rosemary is one the film brandishes at one point when Clark (again on his soapbox) proclaims, "It happened to a sister of the President of the United States." The problem here is less an internal one between doctors and patients (or children and their teachers) as between the children and their parents, most of these parents refusing to understand the specific nature of the problems that beset their own children. As Clark says, "Sometimes we should be treating the parents rather than the kids." For *A Child Is Waiting*, a crisis is clearly affecting the American family.

George Sidney's *Bye Bye Birdie* pushes this possibility of a crisis to brilliant, farcical extremes. The family here is equated with both death and excrement. Harry McAfee (Paul Lynde) runs a fertilizer business ("Been in it for twenty years") and his daughter Kim (Ann-Margret) is dating a boy whose father is an undertaker. Devotion to God and country has been replaced by devotion to mass media and popular culture. The sexual mania the teenage girls in the film have toward the Elvis Presley–inspired Conrad Birdie (Jesse Pearson) leads them to replace the words to the Pledge of Allegiance with a pledge to the rock star. The American family here is both linked and shattered by the mass media and other kinds of modern communication that form an alternate community. In the opening montage, images of both John F. Kennedy and Frank Sinatra are used to show their disapproval at the image of Birdie, who dominates more of the airwaves than they do. The blatantly erotic image of Birdie has marginalized the charismatic image of the president. Political awareness is utterly secondary to a culture that feasts on eroticized images of male spectacle. Birdie sings in the town square of Sweet Apple, Ohio, with such sexual force that the entire population of the town (male and female) passes out in a kind of sexual frenzy, their bodies scattered everywhere like corpses, as the sound track plays "The Battle Hymn of the Republic."

While Harry will scream, "I don't know what's wrong with these kids today," he is not immune to this passionate attraction for popular culture either: the McAfees, led by Harry, sing a hymn not to God but to Ed Sullivan, lined up across a wide Panavision frame, wearing matching choir robes. The hymn reaches its near-conclusion with Harry's passionate declaration, "Ed, I love you!" delivered into the camera in close-up. Lynde's performance turns the cantankerous middle-American stereotype of the father he is portraying inside out. Lynde's quivering body, snarling line readings, and general hysteria suggest a nervous, barely repressed homosexual trapped within a middle-class American family situation that both defines and oppresses him: "The next time I have a daughter, I hope it's a boy," he says.

In contrast to all of this, *A Child Is Waiting* seems almost puritanical. Within the logic of the film, it is the social institution and the social group (however flawed) that forms a substitute for the shattered American family—although in a gesture that picks up on burgeoning sentiments of the civil rights movement, it is the working-class Black mother who "understands her son better" than any other parent who has a child at the school. The film stresses the importance of integration, discipline, and of achieving happiness by being what Clark terms "part of the whole." According to Ariès, our contemporary concepts of childhood began to emerge when the child's natural exuberance and energy were increasingly seen as a negative force. Importance was then given to institutional forms of education in which the child must be, as Suzanne Pleshette's schoolteacher Annie Hayworth instructs her students in Alfred Hitchcock's *The Birds,* "quiet and obedient." The family, no longer solely concerned with lineage and estate, performs a similar repressive function, molding future citizens: "The solicitude of family, Church, moralists and administrators deprived the child of the freedom he had hitherto enjoyed among adults" (Ariès 413). Within this context, the integration and discipline that Dr. Clark so strongly insists upon has a slightly chilling tone for, in spite of the doctor's resistance to discourses of normality, he also is part of a long history that sees childhood in fundamentally negative terms, as something to be controlled. What do these mentally retarded children represent but "unruly" childhood at its most spontaneous and least able to easily submit to the needs of the family and social institutions?

Garland's entire presence in *A Child Is Waiting*, though, complicates the film's more comfortable attempts at didactic clarity. Garland, another former child star, brings to her role a strange physicality that the film cannot completely accommodate. Garland is unable to comfortably insinuate herself into the fabric of the Hollywood/Stanley Kramer problem film. She is too nervous in the part, constantly interrupting her own delivery of the written lines with breaks, hesitations, unfinished sentences, as though there is a short in the connection between her brain and her command of language, and in ways that completely override the logic of the character she is portraying. But Garland does not easily adapt to Cassavetes's cinema either, a cinema seemingly "freer" for the actor but, in fact, more oppressive in its relentless drive toward authenticity in performance. In Cassavetes's world, Garland is too stylized and artificial, too much the show business personality and not "real" enough. She sometimes stands with her legs slightly apart, as though she is about to burst into a song but one with which the film cannot supply her. As a child performer, Garland was unusually sophisticated in her demeanor ("The Little Girl with the Big Voice" as she was sometimes billed), but in *A Child Is Waiting*, at every turn, her presence speaks to some kind of deep need that is not being met by the film.

Throughout Kennedy's presidency, Garland and JFK often spoke on the telephone at night and the call would always ritualistically end with the president's request that Garland sing "Over the Rainbow" to him (Frank 516–17). After the assassination, and on her weekly television variety series, Garland sang her final song to JFK, not "Over the Rainbow" this time but "The Battle Hymn of the Republic," giving special emphasis to the lyrics "His truth is marching on." As an adult, though, Garland's relationship to "maturity" reverses itself. If John F. Kennedy Jr.'s three-year-old body as he salutes his dead father speaks to an impossible collective American longing, Garland's forty-one-year-old body in *A Child Is Waiting* is that of a ravaged and wasted child/woman, someone who has grown up too fast and yet not grown up at all, with her heavy makeup, teased hair, and the false eyelashes that seem to weigh her lids down, all of this suggesting an adolescent girl who has not yet mastered the art of adult female "sophistication." Garland becomes a ruin of her former Hollywood self but without completely losing her mythic innocence.

At the beginning of *A Child Is Waiting*, the mildly retarded Reuben sits in a car waiting for a visit from his mother, Sophie, a visit that never transpires. Sophie avoids visits with Reuben because she claims that her love for

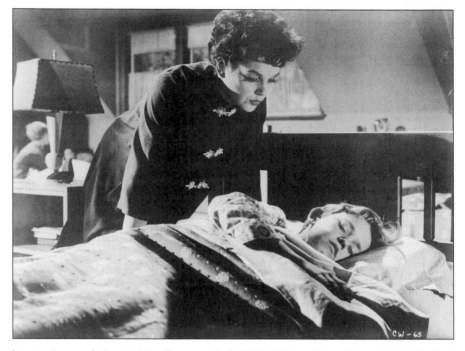

Seemingly out of place in John Cassavetes's *A Child is Waiting* (United Artists), Judy Garland embodies the transitional period of Hollywood itself. Personal collection of the editor.

him is so intense she cannot bear to face him, either in his mentally retarded state or in this institutionalized environment. An issue the film does not explicitly raise but which is suggested in the sequences involving this mother (emerging particularly in Gena Rowlands's brittle performance) is the strong narcissistic component to her love for the boy. She cannot bear to face Reuben because he represents a breakdown and failure of her own self and her own value as a mother. Her attachment to her son, according to Dr. Clark, "de-natures" the boy. Maternal love here becomes something counterproductive, not useful to the social institution. This thread in the film picks up on another thesis of Friedan's, that within a world dominated by a cult of the child, and in which the mother herself has become increasingly infantile, the pathology of the frustrated mother is transferred over to the child. For Friedan, the "pathological retreat" the child inherits is even more apparent in boys than in girls since boys are more expected "to commit themselves to tests of reality which the feminine mystique permits the girls to evade in sexual phantasy" (290). Reuben's mental retardation becomes the most extreme symptom of this pathological retreat since his ability to grow up and become a productive citizen—to "be a man"—will always be compromised or limited in some manner.

American democratic ideals of transparency and directness continue to be expressed in films of this year and often assume the form of the theatrical. At the end of *A Child Is Waiting*, Reuben's father shows up at the school in order to have his son transferred. But as he arrives, a Thanksgiving pageant, staged by Jean, is underway. The father arrives just in time to observe Reuben's recitation as an American Indian, a sight that not only profoundly moves him but causes father and son to tentatively connect with one another afterward. The show, if it does not resolve all differences, allows for a temporary healing and bringing together of seemingly opposed elements. "What a pageant!" is Clark's disgusted response earlier in the film at the various idiotic notes the parents have sent him; by the end of the film, it is precisely a pageant that attempts to resolve some of these problems. That it is a Thanksgiving pageant, performed by a racially mixed group of mentally retarded children who must learn to memorize their lines, perform the songs in unison, and stand where they are supposed to stand, connects this theatrical enterprise to American democratic ideals. As in so many Hollywood musicals, the show becomes an example of a diverse collective working successfully together, overcoming various differences for the good of the show. That the show in this case is staged by one of the great stars of the Hollywood musical only reinforces this point.

The one major Hollywood musical of the year, *Bye Bye Birdie*, likewise ends with a show, in this case a live telecast of "The Ed Sullivan Show." But what we get in this instance is not an example of collective joy but one of social and political disorder, as Russian ballet dancers hog the spotlight from Birdie and the residents of Sweet Apple. The solution to getting the Russians off the air sooner involves lacing the ballet conductor's pre-broadcast glass of milk with amphetamine so that he will conduct at a manic rate. This strange resolution (not present in the original Broadway production on which the film is based) reverses the implications of the end of *A Child Is Waiting* by having the protagonists ultimately walk away from show business. Birdie's appearance on Sullivan's show is ruined by Kim's boyfriend punching Birdie as he kisses her, and the film ends with all of the protagonists forming (or solidifying) as romantic couples, turning their backs on their show business goals to go into another type of business: peddling amphetamine to the rest of America in a concoction devised by soon-to-be-ex-songwriter Albert (Dick Van Dyke) and given the name of Speed Up! Nevertheless, Sidney delivers this rejection of show business on the stage and in the seating area of a large, empty outdoor arena, as though the protagonists will continue to turn their private lives into some form of public performance.

■■■■■■■■ **Worse Than a Couple of Kids**

The American obsession with youth has so often played itself out in a fascination with celebrities and fictional characters who, in their refusal or inability to completely sever their relationship to adolescence, retain links to the world of childhood, a state inevitably understood as more spontaneous, uncensored, and natural. The children (and adults) of the year's movies articulate this paradox with a particular acuteness. The constant comic brawling of Donovan (John Wayne) and Gilhooley (Lee Marvin) in John Ford's *Donovan's Reef* is completely devoid of genuine physical violence or anger but is understood by the film as a form of adolescent roughhousing—"You're worse than a couple of kids," Dr. Dedham (Jack Warden) tells Donovan and Gilhooley in the midst of one of their fights. In *The Birds*, both the eleven-year-old Cathy (Veronica Cartwright) and her thirty-something brother Mitch (Rod Taylor) are referred to as "the two kids" by a local general store owner, while the sophisticated Melanie Daniels (Tippi Hedren) retains strong ties to adolescent behavior, being fond of pranks and practical jokes. In this film about a small town in northern California besieged by an inexplicable series of massed bird attacks, Melanie, the "outsider" from San Francisco, comes to the town on a lark but finds herself caught up in situations that repeatedly test her moral strength. Indeed, much of the second half of the film is driven toward breaking down the shell of sophistication that she has built up around herself, not in order for her to "grow up" but to allow her to become the child she fundamentally wishes to be. Hedren's voice is ideal for capturing this quality of a modern, seemingly adult woman: as she gets excited, her voice becomes high-pitched, like a little girl's. At the end of the film, after Melanie has been brutally attacked by birds within the space of the adolescent Cathy's bedroom, she is finally dependent upon a substitute mother, the rather chilly Lydia Brenner (Jessica Tandy), who is fleetingly shown to offer Melanie the kind of maternal nurturing that Melanie never received from her own mother.

Melanie Daniels in *The Birds* and Amelia Dedham (Elizabeth Allen) in *Donovan's Reef* are single women in their thirties, drifting, who must undergo symbolic trials by fire in which they suffer or are humiliated or lectured to, their defenses lowered. In this manner, they are descendants from comic heroines such as Tracy Lord (Katharine Hepburn) in *The Philadelphia Story* (1940). The banter and comic misunderstandings between Mitch and Melanie in the first hour or so of *The Birds* often deliberately play like the bickering, erotically charged exchanges between couples in Hollywood romantic comedies of earlier decades. Unlike Tracy, though, for whom romance and a second marriage are enough for an ostensible humanizing to take place as part of that film's resolution, these women must first be integrated into a new type of community in which their connection to children becomes fundamental to this process of integration. The sense of the close ties between the formation of the couple, the presence of children, and integration into community is especially strong with Amelia, and Melanie's romance with Mitch is secondary to her effectively becoming a third child to Lydia at the end of *The Birds*.

In *Donovan's Reef*, Amelia Dedham is, like the Kennedys, a Bostonian Irish Catholic and deeply connected to the founding of the United States (her family established a shipping company in 1763). The film invites an allegorical reading of America during a year in which the nation struggled to move toward a more racially integrated culture. But its setting is a fictional utopian South Pacific island, far removed from American soil, with no Blacks in sight. Amelia finds romance with an ex-sailor named Donovan (John Wayne)—and in the process discovers that her young half-brother and two half-sisters are racially mixed, "little half-castes," as she calls them. Amelia's siblings are half-Asian, the result of her father's second marriage to a woman from the island (now deceased). The children are not actively searching for a substitute mother (although that is what they end up with), and instead the narrative partially concerns itself with Amelia's search for her biological father, whom she has never met. By the resolution of the film, a successful reunion with the father has been achieved; but such a happy ending also involves Amelia becoming at once the sister to her "half-caste" siblings *and* their mother, as she marries Donovan and all of them go off to live together in the film's final shot.

Ford ends *Donovan's Reef* with a long shot in which the major characters walk, either in small groups or single file, back toward the Dedham home from which the children were banished at the start of the film for the sake of Amelia. The image suggests that everything is in place here for an ideal community: at the head of the line, a jeep carrying a doctor (Dedham), a French priest (holding a book of Chopin scores), and two French nuns, followed by Donovan carrying all of Amelia's luggage, followed by Amelia holding the hand of her sister, the younger sister holding a doll, the boy holding a baseball bat, the military police holding up a piano, and with Gilhooley holding up the end of the line with the piano stool. Religion, medicine, family, culture, law and order, and the military are all combined in one graceful, concise image, the impulses of the children contained within this unit with the boys and girls carrying out their carefully assigned gender roles.

For the resolution to *The Birds,* though, Hitchcock reverses this basic structure. Instead of a reconceived family moving back into the home, a reconceived family moves away *from* it, as Lydia and her "children" get into Melanie's convertible and drive away from the devastation wrought by the bird attacks. The birds themselves in this sequence have massed in an image of staggering profusion, filling almost every inch of the frame, as Melanie's car slowly snakes its way through the birds before the car eventually disappears into the horizon. It is an apocalyptic image, confirming the Irish drunk's speech at the Tides restaurant earlier in the film, that the bird attacks represent the Old Testament prophecy of "the end of the world." In the sky, however, the clouds are separating and a ray of sunlight is breaking through. Is this an image of hope, of a God alternately destructive and benevolent, now looking down on this world and halting the tide of destruction, like the Old Testament God after the flood? The film invites such interpretations but does not confirm them. Instead, the final shot derives its force from the sense of suspended meaning. The film has nowhere to send this strange family, made out of rags and patches of old myths about fathers, mothers, and children. Instead it can only place them within this image that implies both hope and destruction.

The Birds is an extreme instance of how social behavior in the films of the year often becomes physically agonized, borderline if not literally insane, and linked with the nonhuman. The brain itself often appears to be slightly disconnected from the body in these films, malfunctioning or behaving in ways that seem "abnormal." Hitchcock's linkage of bird behavior with human behavior is the most obvious instance of the introduction of a nonhuman element into an examination of human behavior, and vice versa. As the children in that film attempt to escape from the attacking birds outside of their school, their screams of terror and the screams of the birds as they attack form one sound fabric, as though the false innocence of the birds and the children are profoundly tied together. Although the ornithologist, Mrs. Bundy (Ethel Griffies), initially refuses to believe that the brainpans of birds are capable of organizing such massive attacks on humans, it is exactly this kind of overriding of the usual structure and function of the brain that she and everyone else in the film must ultimately confront. While the film contains a number of ancient Greek citations (from Oedipus to archaeopteryx to Pandora), it is as though Hitchcock wants to invert the desire so central to the culture of fifth-century Athens in which birds represent the desire for flight, for escape and transcendence from the tragic nature of existence. In Hitchcock's film, the birds become savage and destructive—imitating mankind—and cause the film's human subjects to alternately flee in states of utter confusion or to hide inside cramped, bar-ricaded spaces. The human brain in the film (including, ultimately, Mrs. Bundy's) cannot process this irrational shock to the system. After Melanie has been brutally attacked by the birds near the end of the film, she becomes virtually catatonic, her brain unable to fully comprehend the events sur-rounding her.

Flaming Youth

Vincente Minnelli's *The Courtship of Eddie's Father* places the search for a new, substitute mother at the very center of its narrative situ-ation. The film splits the possibilities for a new mother for Eddie (Ronny Howard) into four distinct parts, revisiting stereotypes but also rethinking them: Elizabeth (Shirley Jones), obviously the most maternal of the four but a slightly melancholic divorcee whose career as a nurse is a volunteer one, connected to nurturing, and thereby more easily allowing for immedi-ate passage into substitute motherhood; Rita (Dina Merrill), the fashion consultant whom Tom (Glen Ford) refers to as "the efficient, self-possessed American career woman," a label Rita refuses, claiming that she's seen "too many Rosalind Russell pictures" to fall into that trap; Mrs. Livingston (Roberta Sherwood), the housekeeper hired immediately after the death of Eddie's biological mother, performing domestic duties in the absence of the mother; and Dollye (Stella Stevens), a revisionist thirties bombshell, with all of the trappings of a "floozy" (Mrs. Livingston's term) but who remains fundamentally a "good" woman, fully capable of taking care of Eddie, who adores her. Of these women, only Elizabeth and Rita are serious contenders for replacing the mother. There is no indication that there was the slightest tension in the marriage between Tom and Eddie's mother or that she was anything less than an ideal mother and housewife. Nevertheless, her death, like the death of the mother in *Donovan's Reef,* suggests that there is some-thing fundamentally unrepresentable about her, that the very impulse toward idealization of the mother (the mother in *Donovan's Reef* was a princess on the island) also results in her erasure from the narrative worlds of the films (the princess dies giving birth to her third child). This mother, as Tom tells Eddie, is "right smack dab in the middle of Heaven."

In *The Courtship of Eddie's Father,* unlike *Donovan's Reef,* in which the chil-dren assume a more ornamental function, Eddie has a more disruptive and active presence. The choice for a new mother creates a major conflict between Eddie and his father. Eddie wants his father to marry Elizabeth, who makes brownies for Eddie, was the best friend of Eddie's mother, and slightly resembles his late mother as well. Tom, though, wants to marry Rita, who, while doing her best, has no particular rapport with children, certainly not with Eddie, who dislikes her because she resembles the big-busted and small-eyed villainesses of his comic books. The film's sympathetic portrayal of Rita, however, allows for the comic possibilities offered by Eddie's dislike of her to have a slightly bitter tone since Eddie is being patently unfair to Rita. He runs away from his summer camp in protest over the impending marriage, throwing his father into an emotional tailspin. But Eddie ultimately gets what he wants. Rita, while not banished, is marginalized (she and Tom remain friends, we are told, in the film's final sequence). In an earlier sequence set in a bowling alley, Rita declares to Tom that she has no interest in being the little woman behind the big man and that her ideal marriage partner is one with whom she is on equal terms. His response is "Well, I'm afraid you're going to have to be satisfied with the vote right now. I don't think that that'll ever become a national movement." While the line is always certain to get a laugh from contemporary viewers (and its appearance in a film that was released in the same year in which *The Feminine Mystique* was published only intensifies the irony here), this moment in the film is also extremely poignant. If Amelia Dedham and Melanie Daniels are descendants of forties romantic comedy heroines, "tamed" 1960s-fashion through their contact with children, Rita (linked with Rosalind Russell, regardless of her protestations) escapes from the connection with children and mothering central to Amelia and Melanie's "maturation." At the end of the film, she remains what she was at its beginning. But it's not just Eddie who has no real use for Rita. Rita is also a romantic heroine in the "wrong" film, a comic melodrama centering around middle-class family life, a film about fathers and sons in which women (whatever guises they assume) must always have some kind of linkage to the maternal.

The Courtship of Eddie's Father was released by MGM, once the most glamorous of all Hollywood studios and one that boasted to possess "more stars than there are in Heaven." By this year, though, this reputation had evaporated and *The Courtship of Eddie's Father* was another financial failure for the studio. Minnelli, who had directed some of MGM's most important and successful films of the 1940s and 1950s (including several with his first wife, Judy Garland), was near the end of his tenure there. (He would make only one other film for the studio.) In *The Courtship of Eddie's Father*, his mastery at cinematic staging, his direction of actors, and his use of color and widescreen are at their most accomplished. But the film, a very sad comedy about death and loss, also seems to be bidding a gentle, melancholic farewell to this type of cinema. While Hollywood continued to serve as a

Eddie (Ronny Howard, center) takes control of the narrative quest to find a new wife for his father (Glenn Ford) to marry in *The Courtship of Eddie's Father* (Vincente Minnelli, MGM). Personal collection of the editor.

repository of dreams, the dreams it now tapped into are more closely tied to a collective unconscious, Its "latent" content and repressions increasingly exposed through a variety of means, including camp. Hollywood is lovingly perceived as a rotting organism, now available for plundering and appropriation, in which the child (or the childlike) is part of this process of re-reading Hollywood.

In the winter issue of *Film Culture,* Jack Smith published his legendary essay "The Perfect Filmic Appositeness of Maria Montez," ostensibly a celebration of Montez's long (and, for Smith, unfairly) derided Technicolor adventure films of the 1940s but which is also a polemic for the kind of cinema Smith elevates above all others and for the kind of cinema that Smith himself put into practice with *Flaming Creatures.* For Smith, Montez is an "imaginator/believer/child" whose star persona is made up of disparate elements of "fantasy—beauty" and "child—siren" that no longer exist in cinema (Smith 28). Montez's often mocked Venezuelan accent ("Geef me that Coprha chewel!") for Smith transcends traditional distinctions between good and bad acting. Montez's films, simultaneously lavish and cheap-looking, are dominated by the star's grandiose and narcissistic vision of herself, and their appeal has little to do with the confines of a traditional narrative. Both in this essay and in another one published later this year on Josef von Sternberg, Smith puts forth an ideal of cinema in which the image assumes precedence over not only traditional narrative but language as well. *Flaming Creatures*, shot on washed out black-and-white film stock, is assembled through a series of sequences that, while sometimes individualized, ultimately give the impression of blending together, as we observe transvestites and various androgynous male and female bodies in states of undress, engaging in almost indescribable activities of movement, movements at once animated and listless.

In *Flaming Creatures*, synchronization between sound and image, between actor and dialogue, is about as far from a professional ideal as one could imagine. Language is not banished from this world but instead is treated as a free-floating element of the sound track's texture, never synchronized with the body and not always intelligible. When language does emerge clearly it often sounds as though it were emerging from the mouths of foul-mouthed adolescents who have only just discovered (and only par-

Theatrical play and childhood regression in Jack Smith's experimental film *Flaming Creatures*. Personal collection of the editor.

tially understand) the specifics of sexuality. "Is there a lipstick that doesn't come off when you suck cock?" Smith's voice asks on the sound track to *Flaming Creatures,* interrupting what at first appears to be a radio commercial for an indelible lipstick. After his first viewing of *Flaming Creatures,* Mekas wrote that "American movie audiences today are being deprived of the best of the new cinema" (83). And Susan Sontag would see in the sexual activities of Smith's subjects "something alternately childlike and witty" (Sontag 227). But the release of *Flaming Creatures* culminated with an obscenity verdict passed down the following year by the New York Criminal Court, banning all public and private screenings. If the behavior of the women, transvestites, and homosexuals who inhabit this film seemed shocking to viewers at the time, it may have had less to do with its exposed breasts and limp penises than with the manner in which Smith's camera subjects evoke a state somewhere between a thoroughly adult and decadent sexuality and the world of childhood.

Whereas *Flaming Creatures* achieved some of its notoriety by its conjoining of homosexuality, transvestism, and a type of innocence linked to childhood, the end of *The Courtship of Eddie's Father* enacts some of the same issues but masked within the form of a mainstream "family" entertainment and a "classical" Hollywood film. Smith and Minnelli are both filmmakers for whom the image not only assumes precedence over all other forms of expression; they are also filmmakers for whom the act of creating images and staging scenes becomes a way of crossing or blurring gender lines. Eddie belongs to a long line of Minnelli characters who serve as doubles for Minnelli's own function as a director-figure. Eddie's mastery at staging action and controlling narrative development occurs during a sequence near the end of the film. Throughout the film, Tom and Elizabeth conclude almost every encounter they have with a fight, and by the end they are no longer speaking. Eddie maneuvers this apparent impasse to his advantage when he begins to instruct his father on the proper mating ritual to employ with Elizabeth. He constructs a hypothetical scenario in which Tom calls Elizabeth on the telephone and asks her for a date. This scenario involves Eddie playing the role of Elizabeth to his father, using various terms of endearment to speak to Tom: "My darling man" or "My sugar man" or "My future husband."

This sequence is interesting for several reasons. One is the element of playful seduction of the son toward the father, lightly touching upon incest and homosexuality before just as quickly swerving away from it as Eddie pulls his father toward the telephone to call Elizabeth in her apartment across the hall. The seduction is ultimately directed not toward the father but rather becomes a strategy Eddie uses to lure his father into calling Elizabeth. Nevertheless, the startling moment when Eddie segues into his language of seduction is not easily forgotten, as though an incest taboo has been violated before we have the chance to absorb its full implication. The second and third elements of interest here are closely linked: Eddie is at once an "actress," performing a scene in the kitchen with his father, and a metteur en scène, directing his father and Elizabeth in a scenario of his own making. While John F. Kennedy Jr. becomes the primary performer in a scenario staged by his mother for the symbolic benefit of the entire country, Eddie reverses this role. Here, it is the child who stages a scene in a domestic space involving adults and strictly for his own personal needs: he finally gets the substitute mother he has been longing for, regardless of whether she is the ideal partner for his father or not.

Minnelli ends his film with a wide, Panavision image of the child alone, a slow forward tracking shot into Eddie. He stands in the hallway looking back and forth from Elizabeth's apartment to his own, as Elizabeth and Tom speak to one another on the phone, their voices not heard as music plays over them on the sound track. Have they finally resolved all their differences, and are they about to embark on a compatible marriage? Is it the child who possesses the ultimate wisdom here, seeing the genuine love the two of them have for each other behind all the bickering? Or is this a moot point within the context of the film's basic drive to allow Eddie to get what he wants, the child's will and desire overriding all else, even if this occurs at the expense of the happiness of the adults? The child here is a potential agent of both chaos and order, a figure at once of innocence and destruction. As Fiedler writes, "'Satanic' is merely another word for the impulsive, unconscious life otherwise called 'innocent'" (288).

At the conclusion of *Flaming Creatures*, the title characters engage in a series of solo and ensemble dances. These dances follow far more cataclysmic events, including a rape, several deaths, and an earthquake. In a year in American history dominated by dramatic transformations and upheavals, concluding with the assassination of the president, *Flaming Creatures* both picks up on some of this violent uncertainty and then (literally and symbolically) dances around it. Smith passes through gothic and apocalyptic possibilities for bringing his film to a head before concluding everything on a note of theatrical play.

As with the Thanksgiving pageant at the end of *A Child Is Waiting*, the show biz turns that conclude *Flaming Creatures* are done not by polished professionals. But unlike the performers in the Cassavetes film, Smith's performers (which include the transvestite performer Mario Montez and

Judith Malina) blur and indeed transcend the conventional boundaries between the professional and the amateur and, by extension, the boundaries between male and female, between adult and child, just as Smith's film transcends the boundaries between documentary and fiction, the avant-garde and the entertainment film, and between the obscene and the innocent. Fiedler writes: "The child remains still, what he has been since the beginnings of Romanticism, a surrogate for our unconscious, impulsive lives" (293). For the American cinema this year, these surrogates for our collective unconscious signify in ways that are, like the culture and history from which they emerge, at once traditional and explosively new.

1964

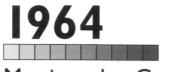

Movies, the Great Society, and the New Sensibility

JAMES MORRISON

Armageddon was cinematically forecast this year in *On the Beach,* based on Nevil Shute's 1957 novel about nuclear holocaust. But aside from the cool, sly fantasy of annihilation at the climax of Stanley Kubrick's *Dr. Strangelove,* the year passed without the arrival of the impending apocalypse. Instead, as Andy Warhol declared, "Everything went young in 1964" (Warhol 69). This pronouncement coincided with the release in January of Bob Dylan's epochal record *The Times They Are a'Changin.'* That elegiac folk anthem would become an all-purpose evocation of the era ever after, but it was not until later the same year that Dylan produced *Another Side of Bob Dylan,* his "first cool album" (MacAdams 260). Dylan may have heralded the rise of the first full-fledged "age" of the cool, but it was only after cool as style had begun an irrevocable decline, when its best-known paragons were already, in Lewis MacAdams's words, "struggling to remain cool" (223). Maybe that conflict was what made Dylan's off-center elegies edge into wistful paradox: "Ah, but I was so much older then," as he sings in "My Back Pages" on *Another Side,* "I'm younger than that now."

American movies had never really been cool in this sense, and their earlier, tentative efforts to claim that mantle only showed, for the most part, how inimical their sensibilities were to the free-wheeling pop avant-gardism of postwar hipster culture. Even so, despite the continued insularity of Hollywood filmmaking, American movies of the year are largely about Hollywood's responses to the shock of the new, the same clash of generational styles, of young and old, the novel and the entrenched, that shaped the wider culture of that time.

The assassination of President Kennedy produced a malaise that initiated the year, squelching many of the new hopes of the decade's beginning but giving rise to a restless agitation that only further stimulated the cult of the new, while infusing it with the kind of melancholy strain heard in Dylan's dirges. Kennedy's successor, Lyndon Johnson, was eager to build on the sense of novelty energizing the Democratic platform and to forestall fears, fostered by his own more advanced age, of reversion to an Eisenhower-like paternalism. This led to an unusual emphasis on social change and innovation in his public address. The quintessential policy of the Johnson administration, the Great Society, was framed as something like a new New Deal, and when Johnson unveiled this program in a famous speech in May, he adopted a style of millennial oratory in a timely dedication to a new age.

In this speech, Johnson adapted the frontier metaphor of his predecessor to more progressive uses in turning it to the question of domestic crisis rather than to that of global conquest: "Today the frontier of imagination and innovation is inside [our] cities and not beyond their borders." In its sense of crisis, the Great Society speech is nearly unprecedented in peacetime American oratory—and, though the conflicts in Vietnam were escalating, it *was* peacetime if only in the sense that no wars had been officially declared. Yet Johnson speaks to his audience of "the turmoil of your capital" and salutes public "indignation" as a source of positive change. He cites a "catalog of ills" that includes poverty, racial injustice, economic overexpansion, urban decay, suburban sprawl, and pollution. Where previous generations might have counseled a conservative retreat to older values in the face of such problems, Johnson appealed to the force of the new as the means to move beyond them, reciting a litany of its potential forms: "new visions," "renew[ed] contact with nature," "new techniques of teaching, to find new ways to stimulate the love of learning," "new concepts of cooperation," "new country," "new world."

Johnson's forward-looking mix of moderation and progressiveness in the Great Society speech, reacting against an increasingly radical Republican conservatism, enabled the quick accomplishment of key domestic initiatives in the course of the year, including the War on Poverty with its subtending social programs, the consolidation of Housing and Urban Development as a cabinet department, and the passage of the Civil Rights Act, one month after the speech. Johnson's vision of the new was hardly identical to the sensibility of cool, and in fact, when Johnson warns that the loss of community "breeds loneliness and boredom and indifference," he may well have been implicitly invoking the defiant alienation, splenetic ennui, and calculated detachment of the Beats and their spiritual, cultural, or aesthetic compatriots in the new sensibility. But neither was his vision incompatible with that sensibility, dependent as it was on a cult of the new, and addressing the same social issues that culture had been highlighting for years.

The year provided a virtual parade of films that illustrated the utterly distinctive tenor, at once ripened and stunted, of films by aging auteurs trying to appear up to date, their work now marked by a sort of elegiac clumsiness—despite the evident quality of many of their later films by past standards—a fully wrought sensibility daunted by a theoretical modishness, an ungainly straining for newfangled effects that remain in view but beyond reach, a near-hysterical effort to appear *current*—or at least remotely timely. Some of the older directors had major hits in the course of the year, as in the case of George Cukor's *My Fair Lady*, in many ways a nostalgic throwback to the ever-declining studio era. Others were treated with unprecedented abuse, as if their efforts to conform to the latest fashions only amplified the scorn heaped upon them. Vincente Minnelli's *Goodbye Charlie* and Howard Hawks's *Man's Favorite Sport?* seemed like fairly innocuous sex comedies, but the degree of the critics' derision implied they were sins on a cosmic scale. This exaggerated vitriol may have indicated, in turn, aging critics' efforts to keep up with the shifting fashions: they tended to give the benefit of the doubt to even slightly younger directors, like Richard Quine or David Swift, whose respective films in the same genre, *Sex and the Single Girl* and *Good Neighbor Sam*, though scarcely less offensive in their innuendo or their chi-chi lasciviousness, were not subject to anything like the same ridicule. In general, younger directors fared much better in the year's critical vocabulary, often being praised for a putative avant-gardism even in the cases of relatively unadventurous films, such as Sidney Lumet's *Fail-Safe* or John Frankenheimer's *Seven Days in May*. The touchstone of the year was clearly Stanley Kubrick's effortlessly hip *Dr. Strangelove*, an object of nearly universal praise and admiration—often in the name of this new valuation of cool.

"Cool" took on new meaning with the publication of Marshall McLuhan's *Understanding Media*. In McLuhan's terms, "hot" media were those with a high definition that promoted low participation, while "cool" ones were those with low definition that promoted high participation. Though McLuhan maintained a hipster's neutrality on the ultimate desirability or meaning of participation itself—advising a strategic playfulness as the best bet in most cases—it was no accident that the hot medium of film was a blast from the past, the cool one of TV the wave of the future. McLuhan's model was easy to read as an update of the aesthetics of cool, privileging a disdainfully nonchalant antagonism toward the status quo, or an insouciant refusal to participate in a corrupted order. What McLuhan brought to the idea of cool was a new sense of an all-embracing euphoric apathy, and *Time* predicted that soon McLuhan's categories would "be used to classify everything" (Hoberman 111).

For many in the cultural sphere, the rise of consumerism threatened the power of the new. In July, two months after Johnson's speech, *Esquire* published an influential anatomy of current cultural trends under the title "The New Sentimentality," in which Johnson's commitment to community, despite his progressive rhetoric, earned him a place as a holdover (along with Pete Seeger, Jackie Robinson, and Rodgers and Hammerstein) from the *old* sentimentality. This New Sentimentality entailed nostalgia not for old values and real histories but for the pop referents of recently past culture. "The New Sentimentality" was the work of Robert Benton and David Newman, who would soon parlay this idea into the New Hollywood as coauthors of the screenplay for *Bonnie and Clyde* (1967).

Amid this tumult of newness, Hollywood went on plying a stability that had in fact departed, went on waging its localized in-fights—against television, against runaway production, against expansions of star power (Monaco 16–39). But it did not do so in complete heedlessness. Even the best films of the year were mostly either failed efforts to capture the new sensibility or failed efforts to restore the old order, in the throes of a sentimentality so entrenched and stultified that it could really be called neither old nor new. Perhaps no other year is so crucial in the run up to the New Hollywood, revealing the spectacle of a still-powerful institution, so recently new but quite suddenly old, trying to confront unprecedented social and cultural pressures while struggling perversely to maintain an equilibrium that was clearly already gone.

Old Hollywood and the New Sensibility

Susan Sontag may be the last person one would think of to initiate a discussion of Hollywood, the Great Society, and the New Sensibility, especially one that begins with John Ford's *Cheyenne Autumn*. Yet in essays like "Notes on 'Camp,'" Sontag emerged as the principal spokesperson for this new sensibility, defending sensibility itself as an idea whose time has come. No longer viewed strictly in "the realm of purely subjective preferences" (Sontag 276), sensibility is conceived in her work as a structure of aesthetic, moral, or intellectual taste that has "not yet been brought under the sovereignty of reason" (276), and it becomes Sontag's main tool in her quest to revamp American culture toward international counterculture, because it combines social and cultural standpoints and elides establishmentarian rationalism. Though Sontag never retreats from a modernist emphasis on aesthetic form as the defining object of cultural renewal, she also rarely doubts that a revived attention to dynamics of form can revitalize mass sensibility, to bring American culture at large into alignment with the advances of contemporary art. Under Sontag's aegis, the new sensibility does not just embrace the aesthetic of cool, with its exuberant anomie, casual radicalism, playful iconoclasm, off-handed anger, and laidback provocation, but also reconciles with a formerly derided mass culture, rendering modernism itself as something of a rearguard attitude, and making it possible to celebrate all at once a song by the Beatles, a painting by Jasper Johns, a film by Jean-Luc Godard, and a movie by Budd Boetticher.

In commercial, popular art, if the new sensibility appeared at all, it emerged in the form of a newly explicit liberalism, an avenue Sontag rejected vehemently as an expression of its energies. This rejection appears most clearly in a series of theater reviews she wrote in the course of the year for *Partisan Review,* and what Sontag saw happening on the Broadway stage—a sort of pale, toothless simulation of the new sensibility, albeit without the sensibility—was appearing at the same time in Hollywood. *Cheyenne Autumn* is a prototype of the shift: while not the first Hollywood western claiming to present a sympathetic portrayal of Native Americans, it was directed by the filmmaker whose work had perhaps done the most to establish the genre's conventional vilification of the Indian. When characters in earlier Ford westerns spoke of Indians as "savages," they were usually meant to be taken seriously; when a cavalry officer in this film refers to the Cheyenne as "bloodthirsty savages," the audience is supposed to see him as contemptible. The change was drastic, and palpable: Native Americans who had been demonized as barbarians incessantly on the warpath would now be viewed through the lens of a makeshift liberalism, as beset populations displaced from their land.

The challenge to sustain this altered viewpoint exerts unusual pressure on Ford's methods, conferring a troubled self-consciousness that plays out in the film most often as a stodgy, processional atmosphere. The first third of the film unfolds in an ambience of breathless, arrested suspension, as the displaced Cheyenne, with white functionaries of an Interior Department outpost, await a dispatch from the East of food and medicine. The tone is earnest, solemn, cautious, stilled, but when the dispatch fails to come, and the Cheyenne respond to the settlers' broken promises by trekking across the continent to return to their Dakotan homeland, the scene shifts abruptly to a raucous Dodge City, and the tone converts into insolent burlesque. Where formerly Ford's buoyant folk comedy was integrated effortlessly into his ritual melodrama, here the stoical prudence of his approach insulates these tones and drives them to extremes. The ritual takes on a fey reverence, while the comedy broadens into slapstick, complete with a vaudeville turn by James Stewart as Wyatt Earp. Losing sight altogether, during this interlude, of the plight of the Cheyenne, the film turns to farce, in a mode that prefigures the cycle of western parodies of a few years later. When the film bids to revert to its dominant mode of high dudgeon, it turns out that this righteous indignation is not so easily regained.

Part of this problem derives from an absence of contrition. To be a serious moral document, *Cheyenne Autumn* would need to have acknowledged the legacy of racism in which its maker was complicit. Its failure to do so places it in the same bind of doublethink Sontag identifies in "liberal" Broadway, portraying American society as "*both* guilty and innocent, responsible and not responsible" (Sontag 143). Publicity surrounding *Cheyenne Autumn* remarked on the high regard Navajos had for Ford; cast as extras in his films since *Stagecoach* (1939), they dubbed him "Tall Soldier." Ford professed a mutual respect, but Native Americans do not appear in any leading role in *Cheyenne Autumn*, where they are enacted instead by performers such as Ricardo Montalban, Dolores Del Rio, and Sal Mineo. Indian relocation is seen not as American policy, but as the scheme of a few bad-apple senators, or a renegade German captain, played by Karl Malden as a quasi-Nazi who, against the objections of noble whites, inters the Cheyenne in prisons that explicitly recall the Third Reich's death camps. The effect, paradoxically, is to *dis*avow the genocidal implications of American treatment of the Indians,

Cheyenne Autumn (John Ford, Warner Bros.) is a western that reveals the difficulty of fitting new problems to old myths. Personal collection of the author.

by mythically associating it with past foreign threats. The Great Society platform strived for a liberal consensus based on acknowledging a legacy of injustice, but in allegorizing this new social wrinkle, *Cheyenne Autumn* underlines the difficulty of submitting the "new" problems to the old myths.

The Great Society did not exclude Native Americans from the protections it legislated, but these were explicitly targeted mostly at urban and rural Blacks. When the new Hollywood liberalism generalized this platform, it often inadvertently exposed the inadequacy of prevailing political solutions. For all the specious attitudinizing of *Cheyenne Autumn*—which uses the old Hollywood version of politics as personal expedient to suggest that most whites always knew how unjust the official policies were—the Cheyenne might as well be the Jews of *Exodus* (1960) or, for that matter, the Israelites of *The Ten Commandments* (1956), glorified nomads bent on the recovery of a homeland made great by the nobility of their commitment, and made safe by being relegated to the sphere of myth. That this sphere seems far less secure in *Cheyenne Autumn* than in any previous Ford western, for all the film's continuing efforts to shore it up, makes the movie a key turning point on the way to the death of the genre.

It could also be seen as a chapter in the death of the auteur, but that perception is complicated by the degree to which the auteur's death coincides in America almost precisely with the moment of his belated birth. American directors like Ford and Hawks, while their work slipped out of fashion in many quarters, were simultaneously being confronted, for the first time, by the idea that they were auteurs, a notion they were quick to reject with gruff modesty, if loath to refute, for the greater cultural prestige it could confer (Bogdanovich 102–07). At least one filmmaker of the old order, Alfred Hitchcock, was eager to embrace this new prestige, and *Marnie* is an especially significant example of how the auteurist debate made its way into Hollywood cinema.

Like so many films of the year, *Marnie* is a rich amalgam of old styles and new aspirations. It seems at least in outline like a vanquished reversion to older forms, redolent of forties melodrama and the woman's film, and beginning with credits unfolding over the pages of a gilt-edged book, a now-hoary device harking back to the oldest of the old Hollywood. The plot turns on a sensational pop Freudianism in its tale of a kleptomaniac (Tippi Hedren) who compulsively steals from her patrician employers until one of her victims, a millionaire businessman (Sean Connery) with psychoanalytic leanings, entraps her into marrying him. Though he claims his ambitions are curative, the film makes clear that his therapeutic aims are laced with fetishistic pathologies of his own. In a feverish climax where Marnie relives the childhood trauma that is the source of her neurosis, the movie's psychology of repression links to social marginality and exploitation, with both seen as effects of poverty in light of a raised awareness fully in keeping with the Great Society.

Initiating a final turn in Hitchcock's late phase, *Marnie* expresses a certain wistfully bereft quality due in part to the loss of the previous generation of "star" actors—now replaced by Hedren, Hitchcock's own prepackaged creation (though the role was originally intended for Grace Kelly). This feature is accompanied by a curious combination, not by any means unknown among Hollywood auteurs of the day, of assured mastery and waning authority. Privately, Hitchcock admitted the difficulty of finding new material, and as dissatisfied with the new crop of screenwriters as he was with the new generation of stars, he followed the French New Wave model of hiring novelists as screenwriters. At the end of the year, after the commercial and critical failure of *Marnie*, he wrote to Vladimir Nabokov, proposing ideas for "emotional, psychological" stories that would still "give me the opportunity to indulge in the customary Hitchcock suspense" (Bruccoli and Nabokov 363). In one sense, this was a bid for a greater cultural prestige that would also draw on the cult of the new as exhibited most pointedly, before *Dr. Strangelove*, in Kubrick's previous movie, the 1962 film version of Nabokov's best-selling novel *Lolita*, with a script credited to the author himself. In another, it reflected Hitchcock's sense that such prestige was already rightly his, even if it was obscured by his position in popular culture as "the master of suspense." Before and after the production of *Marnie*, Hitchcock was engaged in a series of interviews with François Truffaut that, among other things, highlighted the director's longstanding influence on the traditions of the art film.

In *Marnie*, Hitchcock returns to familiar territory with a heightened awareness of his auteurist profile, and this self-consciousness infuses the movie with a current of ardent neo-expressionism played out in devices such as stylized rear-projection—in equestrian interludes, for instance, where Marnie seems to be riding a stationary rocking-horse against a wash of cut-out sky—that seemed to some like corny throwbacks and to others like hollow imitations of new trends in cinema. The film is filled with geometrical compositions suggestive of Antonioni—as in the weirdly angular train platform of the opening shots, or the surreal exterior of an office with its cubist structure and zigzagging parking spaces—and it is fraught with a fervent irony that has clear affinities with the New Wave. On the eve of the film's release, Hitchcock sent copies of Truffaut's auteurist tributes about him to American critics who slighted him as an artist, hoping the evidence of these panegyrics would encourage them to mend their ways (Kapsis 92–93). The strategy backfired, and *Marnie* was viewed in most quarters as both pretentious and old-fashioned. Bosley Crowther in the *New York Times* found that the director was "taking himself too seriously—perhaps the result of listening to too many esoteric admirers" (quoted in Kapsis 94). In the pages of *Esquire,* Dwight Macdonald continued to declare Hitchcock senile, with direct snipes at *Marnie* (Macdonald 475). Simultaneously, in the same pages, Hitchcock was admitted to the club of the new—but it was a club of which he would probably not have wanted to be a member, that of the New Sentimentality, of which he was dubbed an icon, in testament to his "manipulation of the audience; the humor of horror; cynical control; tension as art" (Benton and Newman 31).

The auteurist status of another major figure of the old order, Billy Wilder, was less secure than Hitchcock's, as Andrew Sarris (to cite one example) ultimately consigned him to the "Less Than Meets the Eye" category in his rankings. Though Wilder probably wouldn't have wanted to be a member of that club either, his efforts to adjust to new currents express distinctive pains of their own. *Kiss Me, Stupid* is set in Climax, Nevada, a desert backwater on the road from Las Vegas to Los Angeles, midway between the seat of American vulgarity and greed and the country's self-professed Dream Factory. An acrid study in the pathology of celebrity culture, the film uses its setting as a stand-in for a middle America that no longer exists, because the prurient and rapacious values of the culture industry have seeped into every quarter of the nation's life. Wilder was clearly as struck as Hitchcock by the new possibilities suggested by *Lolita*: the name of the town in *Kiss Me, Stupid* alludes to both Nabokov's novel and Kubrick's film, where the title character is shipped off to Camp Climax, a rustic retreat meant to instill wholesomeness, that is really a hotbed of barely concealed debauchery. But Nabokov's buoyant vision of corruption is complete, while Wilder's more sour one is only partial, coated with the director's characteristic haplessly applied veneer of sweetness. Though *Kiss Me, Stupid* exploits the new freedoms of Hollywood in advance of the final suspension of the Production Code, it does so with an air of self-contempt that expresses a preference for a more "innocent" era of a recent past, now seen as lost.

The movie stages this theme as a clash between old-fashioned values and something like a consumerist, show-biz version of the new sensibility. The plot concerns a composer, Orville (Ray Walston), who gives piano lessons in his home and pairs with a gas station attendant to write songs they both hope will allow them to break into the big time. When a star comes through town, they conspire to detain him, arranging a tryst with a local waitress (Kim Novak) posing as Orville's wife to indulge the star's well-known taste for lechery, currying his favor to persuade him to adopt their songs in his repertoire. In a turn of oleaginous self-parody, Dean Martin appears as the star, and the thinness with which Martin's own persona is disguised—his character is named Dino—produces a low-level titillation that is one of the film's defining features. In Wilder's film, Dino is still a major celebrity, but his status is in question in a shifting cultural landscape where he represents the residual style of the crooner in a field swept with emerging fashions—Barbra Streisand, the Beatles, and rock 'n' roll, to list the examples the film cites. His Vegas show, portrayed in the movie's first sequence, punctuates pop songs from the heyday of Tin Pan Alley and big-band showmanship with leering asides and dirty jokes. Despite such compensatory jabs at updating an outmoded act, another character in the film still tells Dino outright that he's simply "old-fashioned," even by comparison with younger crooners of the rising order like Jack Jones or Bobby Darin. Though the song Orville proffers is as much a throwback to the old style as the other numbers in Dino's portfolio, he hawks it as a novel commodity to modernize the singer's act.

Wilder initially cast Peter Sellers as Orville in *Kiss Me, Stupid,* while assembling a hectic catalog of Philistine vulgarities to surround him, in a vision of America as a carnivalesque ribbon of roadside tourist stops and ramshackle gin joints, gaudy vaudeville showplaces and decrepit trailer parks, torn between flagrant obscenity and makeshift morality as *Playboy* and *Ladies' Home Journal* battle for the nation's conscience, emphasizing the thematic link to and influence of *Lolita*. As it happened, Sellers departed from the film after bitter conflicts with the director and a subsequent heart attack (Hopp 149). He was replaced in the role by Walston, who did little to legitimate the movie's ties to the new trends, trends toward which *Kiss Me, Stupid* still frantically continued to gesture.

Wilder's source was an Italian boulevard farce, a riff on Georges Feydeau with shades of *commedia dell'arte*. Transplanting this material to the American desert, the director brings out a strain of crudity as a populist counterpoint to the effete refinements of the material—a tendency visible in similar adaptations throughout Wilder's career. The sources for a number of his films exemplify a species of marginally cosmopolitan European bawdry—what's supposed to be funny is an old-world hedonism that cloaks itself in hypocritical respectability. In Wilder's Hollywood movies, by contrast, American Puritanism is both the object of his satire and the saving grace of his eleventh-hour moralism. His characters are not sophisticates

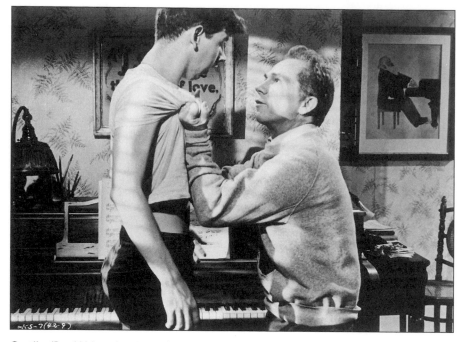

Orville (Ray Walston) accuses his pupil (Tommy Nolan) of being a "male Lolita" in *Kiss Me, Stupid* (Billy Wilder, Allied Artists). Personal collection of the author.

pretending to be genteel, but innocents who find themselves in compromising situations and degraded settings. In *Kiss Me, Stupid,* Orville imagines dissipation everywhere. Though married to a faithful woman, he is pathologically jealous, even suspecting one of his adolescent pupils of luring his wife into infidelity, and chasing him from the house while chastising him, in yet another reference to Nabokov/Kubrick, as a "male Lolita."

As an unapologetic proponent of the New Sentimentality, Wilder flirts with a faddish perversity to clear the way for traditional married love, and the comedy usually comes from how straight the characters really are under the surface. Despite its Nabokovian overtones, Wilder's film neatly reverses the dynamic of *Lolita*: in the novel, as to a lesser extent in Kubrick's film, America is portrayed as all pristine, glittery surface, with carnality roiling everywhere beneath, while in Wilder's movie, the wantonness is strictly superficial, overlying a reservoir of old-fashioned chastity. Despite Wilder's great success with a quite similar movie—*The Apartment* (1960)—only four years earlier, *Kiss Me, Stupid* was greeted with a critical scorn from which the director's career never really recovered. What made the difference was how directly in *Kiss Me, Stupid* Wilder expresses his own distaste for Hollywood's new directions, even as he tries to follow them.

■ New Hollywood and the Great Society

While auteurs of the old generation attempted to keep pace with the times by aiming for a modified form of a—if not *the*—new sensibility, filmmakers of the rising order, less concerned with achieving an artificial novelty, busied themselves producing work that amounted to a resurgence of the old Hollywood social problem film, addressing much the same catalog of social ills that Johnson identified in the Great Society speech. Samuel Fuller was one of a small handful of directors who managed at least briefly to bridge the divide between old and new. His work of the forties and fifties exemplified the kind of tough, hard, fast, unpretentious B-movies celebrated by Manny Farber as the most viable alternative to middlebrow Hollywood (Farber 21–22). For the same reasons, Fuller was also a favorite of the French auteurists, who continued to lionize him after they became auteurs in their own right. Like younger directors who often took to the new ideas and forms as their natural birthright—figures like Lumet, Frankenheimer, Arthur Penn, or Robert Mulligan—Fuller showed less anxiety in his work of the sixties about his ability to grasp the real issues confronting American society than other aging auteurs did.

The Naked Kiss mixes a rowdy tabloid spirit with a weirdly magnanimous streak of social criticism in an edgy meditation on the underpinnings of the Great Society. The plot concerns a prostitute named Kelly (Constance Towers) who, after a skirmish with her drunken pimp, flees a darkish metropolis for a small town where she starts a new life as a nurse in a ward tending to handicapped children. In an acrid synthesis of Norman Rockwell and film noir—abrogating Johnson's old city/country dualism—Fuller portrays the town as a bright landscape of public squares and tranquil lanes still shadowed with a sparse penumbra of gloom, harboring a core of resolute perversity under its veneer of agrarian values. This mixture is enabled, in *The Naked Kiss*, by a hovering sense of loss that generalizes the malaise earlier noirs located almost exclusively in the city; Fuller shows how the same woes infect the country despite the appearance of surface tranquility. Nearly every resident speaks of a personal trauma relating to the nation's recent wars, and just under their folksy hospitality lurks a dead-alive look and a melancholy that could turn to hostility any minute. Kelly seems to be welcomed by the townsfolk, but the Cinderella story she thinks she is reenacting is fundamentally conditioned by an unspoken awareness of her past as a circumstance she can never rise above.

For much of the film, the plot appears to address private philanthropy as a solution to social inequity, in line with conservative criticisms of the socialized "entitlements" of the New Deal and the Great Society. The ward where Kelly works is a private clinic supported by a wealthy donor (Michael Dante), and it benefits a cross-racial population of children whose diversity the film celebrates. Though with shadings of Barry Goldwater–like hucksterism, the millionaire is initially portrayed not as a Dickensian miser—as in virtually every other American movie along these lines—but as a benevolent steward, the counterpart for the commonwealth at large of the hard-boiled cop (Anthony Eisley) who uses his office as crime fighter to oversee the individual moral lives of the citizens. The millionaire's ownership of the town is seen as a positive force, freeing the people from needs of government intervention—and Kelly's impending wedding to him may be her ultimate redemption—until a wrenching turn sends the plot spinning into shrill Gothicism. In a scene of electric delirium, Kelly discovers that the millionaire is a pedophile who uses his charity to facilitate systematic abuse of children, and in its final stretch, the film moralizes against the violations of the private sphere as feverishly as it had earlier appeared to promote the liberties of individual enterprise. By implication, *The Naked Kiss* becomes, in the end, an unlikely call for just the kinds of reform the Great Society promised, invoking the same rationale of the social limitations of the private sector.

At the same time, a not-so-hidden agenda of *The Naked Kiss* is to position itself implicitly as an anti-abortion tract. The film begins and ends with Kelly gazing longingly at babies in strollers, yet throughout she has a troubled relation to the maternal role in which her job as nurse casts her. Her former prostitution obviously contributes to this problem, and it is strongly implied that she has ended a pregnancy, perhaps resulting from her sex work, in an operation that has left her unable to bear children. When one of her co-workers at the clinic becomes pregnant, Kelly gives her money to help her leave town, with the pointed instruction, "No abortion—understand?" Kelly's relationship to the mostly orphaned children in the ward is loving and nurturing, explicitly linked to motherhood in a song they all sing together—a sentimental pastiche with echoes of Doris Day singing "Que Sera Sera": "Mother dear, tell me please, is the world really round?" sing the children, to which Kelly answers in verse, "What you really seek is right here where you are."

This placid reassurance rings hollow considering the children's victimization by the millionaire pedophile, but it takes on added weight if understood as exalting their very births, as if to celebrate the simple fact of their not having being aborted—an interpretation that also helps to explain the unusually charged gaze of the camera at the children throughout the film, particularly in abstract montages of close-ups, their faces framed and lit to

Kelly (Constance Towers) remains entrapped in her past in *The Naked Kiss* (Samuel Fuller, Allied Artists). Personal collection of the author.

emphasize the pathos of their pluck, resignation, and beseeching vulnerability. Discovering the millionaire's pedophilia, Kelly kills him in a protective and self-defensive rage, but she cannot persuade an abused child to corroborate her testimony to this motive until she is instructed to speak to the girl "as a mother." Fuller's glorification of motherhood here is especially striking considering his characteristic assaults on "Momism" as a weakening or corrupting influence (Rogin 270–72). In *The Naked Kiss,* it appears to countermand the movie's provisional liberalism, as a corrective to feminist demands for reproductive freedom that many conservatives feared would be sneaked in through the back door under the banner of programs like the Great Society (Walker, *Cold War* 232–33).

The Naked Kiss was a production of Allied Artists, one of the minor studios to arise after World War II—a transformed version of the B-movie studio, Monogram—to compete with the remaining majors. Another of these, American International, averaged about twenty-five films a year by 1964, nearly twice as many as the number being produced by the major studios (Monaco 27). In large part this decline in studio production was due to the new arrangements of freelancing and outsourcing in Hollywood, effects that rendered a majority of American movies theoretically "independent," developed and financed outside studio coffers—though usually with co-operation of several entities including studios—before being distributed through studio channels (Wasko 111–15). A new "changes of elements" clause appeared in most contracts, however, dictating that no part of a production package could be altered after a first entity offered financing unless that entity was guaranteed a subsequent buyout, a factor that ensured continued studio control over production (Monaco 25–26). Companies like Allied Artists and American International marketed their products as being edgier than big studio fare—if not as outright exploitation films—but despite this institutionalization of the B-movie as quasi-independent, truly independent production remained rare.

Nothing But a Man is perhaps the most important such film of the year, shot on location in Alabama and dealing with what Benton and Newman called "The Problem"—that is, racial conflict—with a directness far beyond anything on offer in Hollywood, even after its turn to a self-styled liberalism. Hollywood movies about racism after World War II were typically products of a specifically white liberalism; often they were about light-skinned Blacks passing as white, a theme that enabled a putative critique of racism while also retaining white actors in the main roles. *Nothing But a Man* has a cast made up almost entirely of African American actors, a claim few Hollywood films of the sixties could make. Though the filmmakers, Michael Roemer and Robert M. Young, were white, this cast brought a level of authenticity to *Nothing But a Man* wholly unknown in the Hollywood race film.

Hollywood movies about racism tend to frame the issues as personal drama, in which white characters overcome their racism through a growing affection for a Black character. By contrast, *Nothing But a Man* never loses sight of the social dimensions or effects of racism. As if to illustrate systematically the ills the Civil Rights Act was intended to resolve, the film concerns discrimination in education, housing, and employment, and shows how the everyday lives of the characters are determined by social and economic disenfranchisement. The film tells the story of the relationship of Duff (Ivan Dixon), a section hand on a railway construction team, and Josie (Abbey Lincoln), a teacher, and though class differences between the two are noted in passing—"You've got some very primitive ideas, don't you?" Josie tells Duff teasingly—these are overridden by their shared experience of institutional racism as a fact of daily existence. Reacting with a mix of pained forbearance and forthright impatience, neither is surprised when they are harassed by hostile whites or denied housing opportunities when they move in together. Such moments are presented with a piercing casualness, not as the melodramatic spectacles of typical Hollywood treatments, with their hypocritically triumphal claims to expose hidden injustices, but as overt features of a society the inequity of which, it is implied, we should all recognize by now.

That the film takes the social context of civil rights for granted, instead of elaborating it in sociological terms, is evidence of the filmmakers' resolve to avoid the sort of ethnographic gaze visible even in such otherwise worthy essays in Black experience by white directors as Shirley Clarke's film about African American youth in Harlem, *The Cool World*. Unlike that movie, *Nothing But a Man* is anything but a study in the aesthetic of cool as a product of oppression, even though it also takes for granted that lives of great dignity take place in conditions of social abjection. The film's portrait of Black culture is resolutely incidental—snatches of gospel music or Motown hits as background, for instance—presented as part of the fabric of everyday life, not as signs of exotica to be showcased as novelty. The movie gestures toward debates between accommodationism and separatism, as when Josie's father, a preacher, states his view of the best way to talk to white people: "Make them think you're going along. . . ." It even skirts the notion that the trouble with racism is that it emasculates Black men, in a scene where a frustrated Duff hits Josie. Overall, though, it retreats from such psychosexual analysis, associated with contemporary figures such as James Baldwin or Eldridge Cleaver, in favor of a more starkly political one with explicit overtones of Martin Luther King Jr.

In his book *Why We Can't Wait*, King eloquently laments the sidetracking of Kennedy's massive civil rights campaigns into more localized objectives in voting rights, and his standpoint was surely a model of the "indignation" Johnson welcomed as a force for change. As King writes, "The Negro felt that he recognized the same old bone that had been tossed to him in the past—only now it was being handed to him on a platter, with courtesy" (King 7). But it is tempered with a measured anger that refuses to let white liberalism off the hook: "[Kennedy's] administration appeared to believe it was doing as much as was politically possible and had, by its positive deeds, earned enough credit to coast on civil rights" (8). *Nothing But a Man* may be a product of white liberalism, but it rejects the usual strategies of that ideology in movies—there is no spokesperson for it in the film itself—and in the detailed, subtly moving performances of its main actors, it amounts to a powerful plea for just the kind of direct action that King advocated.

If most films of the younger generation in the course of the year bid for a variant of the new sensibility by virtue of such social commitments, at least one, John Frankenheimer's *The Train*, combines a late Cold War social-problem earnestness with a concern for the politics of culture as such. Set in the final days of the German occupation of France during World War II, the film tells of the attempt by a Nazi colonel (Paul Scofield) to usurp a cache of French paintings by transporting them to Berlin aboard a French train, and of counter-efforts by French resisters to undermine this appropriation. A virtual catalog of the new sensibility in its high-culture mode, the art in question comprises work of the great modernists, from the Impressionism of Renoir and Monet to the Cubism of Picasso. The colonel's plundering of these works is motivated by his appreciation for them as art, and the film makes clear that he has, for the same reason, been covertly protecting the works from destruction throughout the occupation, at the risk of his own political standing.

In outline, the film clearly turns on the question of culture as a vehicle of political action, a concern that goes beyond the deracinated, Manichean politics of Cold War Hollywood in its earlier phases. On the one hand, the movie portrays modern art as a lofty refuge, a realm of pure aesthetics illegitimately co-opted by the world of politics through the colonel's scheme. On the other, it shows how the intrusion of culture into the political sphere complicates the affiliations of social actors. Especially in light of the wholesale Nazi condemnation of modernism as "degenerate art," the colonel's fealty to this art trumps his loyalty to Nazi doctrine, and his confiscation of the paintings contradicts in more immediate terms the national interest he is supposed to be defending. Though Nazi appropriation of art was common during the war, it was typically conducted as an extension of imperialism, often on a pretext of censorship, with avowed contempt for the art itself (Petropoulos 130). In *The Train*, by contrast, the colonel's proprietary love of modern art is portrayed as both a mark of his treachery and fanaticism, and a sign of cultural commitment, of his willingness to put aside political efficacy in favor of a "higher" cause, and of his participation in a cult of art that did indeed prompt some Nazis to pillage works of modernism despite their own involvement in the "degenerate art" movement (Petropoulos 85). The French resisters, meanwhile, are thoroughly indifferent to art, even as cultural value or national symbol. They initially submit to the colonel's plan to transport the paintings, only gradually uniting to sabotage the plot, not to retain the cache but to solidify an impending national victory in which the art figures only as expendable loot.

The Train is part of a more general turn away from standard Cold War concerns about communist infiltration in postwar Hollywood movies. With its interest in the implications and legacies of wartime fascism—a subject rarely treated seriously in American film—it revived a dormant strain that had long been eclipsed by fantasies of the atomic age and allegories of the

Red Menace. This development coincided, however, with an increasing tendency to treat those fantasies and allegories themselves, with a mounting cheekiness, as expressions of outright paranoia rather than articulations of justified fears—a tendency that culminated with *Dr. Strangelove*. The case of *The Train*, though, suggests that Frankenheimer had already been fully assimilated to the Hollywood model of filmmaking, as he was brought on to the film to replace Arthur Penn, on the assumption that Frankenheimer would turn in a more traditional action movie and deemphasize the cultural politics of the overall conceit (Buford 236–39). Although Frankenheimer moves beyond a conventional combat movie and embraces an international cast in a spirit of cosmopolitanism quite novel in Hollywood— with the burly French actor Michel Simon standing in for the Old Guard and the beautiful Jeanne Moreau representing the New Wave—that was largely what happened.

The Train is a clear illustration of the limits of the new sensibility in Hollywood. Even though what the film has to say about the Nazi occupation and the French resistance is filtered almost entirely through this cultural lens, its treatment of the material is constrained by a familiar kind of parochial equivocation. In recurrent low-angle shots of trains as hulking leviathans looming through ashen night and fog, the movie explicitly recalls the horror of the concentration camps, yet the camps themselves go largely unmentioned in the film. In its eagerness to treat modern art with due reverence, the movie adopts an obsequious reticence that encompasses both the resisters' earthy disregard of art and the colonel's worshipful adulation of it. When the leader of the resistance (Burt Lancaster) pointedly asks the curator of the art, "Do you think your paintings are worth these men's lives?"—the four-square conviction of his query makes the answer clear enough. Yet when the colonel proclaims that "beauty belongs to those who can appreciate it," his speech is granted a certain credence and even an odd pathos. The antidemocratic overtones of his screed only barely obscure underlying truths about the importance of art that the film obviously supports. Skeptical as it is of the Nazi cult of aestheticism, the movie is still eager to uphold the persisting aura of modern art and thus to secure its own half-hearted allegiance to the new sensibility.

Beyond the New Sensibility

Recalling Nevil Shute's prophecy, J. Hoberman wrote that "what was truly fresh in 1964 was the post-Kennedy euphoria. The apocalypse had happened and we remained. The fever broke. The crisis passed—

anything seemed possible" (92). Most Hollywood movies conveyed this sense only in their timid, cautious approaches to the idea of the new, but what emerged in retrospect as the most prescient film of the year—*Dr. Strangelove*—pointed forward to just this condition in its brash, misanthropic ebullience.

An impudent satire on the nuclear arms race, *Dr. Strangelove* wrote an end, at a stroke, to the anxious contemplations of the Cold War in American movies since World War II. Previous films like Hitchcock's *North by Northwest* (1959) or Frankenheimer's *The Manchurian Candidate* (1962) had already made sport of dominant concerns of the nuclear age, but the attitudes of Kubrick's movie gave the lie to pieties of the Great Society, expressing a new effrontery that bowed neither to liberal entreaties nor to conservative fears. Compared to contemporaneous efforts like *Fail-Safe* or *Seven Days in May,* both earnest cautionary tales, *Dr. Strangelove* brings to bear an unyielding, wicked sarcasm that, coupled with its blunt *Mad* magazine accessibility, makes it the ultimate in Medium Cool, and the closest any Hollywood movie of the year came to capturing the new sensibility.

So insinuating is the film's comedy, so integral to its vision, it is surprising to recall that Kubrick's initial conception was to produce a straight Cold War thriller, in the manner of the novel he adapted, Peter George's *Red Alert*—a work so much in the mode of *Fail-Safe* that George, whose book was published first, sued the authors of that novel for plagiarism. By Kubrick's own report, he began to feel in the course of the film that its materials were so extreme they could only work as comedy, and he proceeded—with his collaborators on the script, George and Terry Southern—to elaborate the extraordinary cocktail of sophisticated absurdism, corrosive satire, and outright slapstick that infuses the film. This range is evident in the styles of Peter Sellers's three roles. As a dimwit president of the United States, he plays with the restraint of satire; as a stiff-upper-lip British officer, with the pomp of parody; and in the title role, as a crazed scientist, with the exuberance of sheer caricature. Strangelove's comic battles with his own errant limb, an uncontrollable mechanical arm bent on strangling him, provide the most sustained slapstick, buffered by even broader scenes such as one involving a battle with a Coke machine that spritzes cola into a hapless soldier's face. In production, Kubrick went so far as to shoot a long scene showing a pie fight in the war room, but this was cut, perhaps because it went too far into the realm of slapstick and violated the eclecticism of the movie's comic palette (although the classic line, "You can't fight in here—this is the war room," remains).

In a sense, this production history underscores the film's roguish subtitle, "How I Learned to Stop Worrying and Love the Bomb." What the film demonstrates most keenly is a jauntily euphoric sense of anxiety overcome, surrendered to a vision of apocalypse both uncompromising and flippant. Even what remains in the film of its original serious premise takes on an air of blithe, antic prankishness: the haughty voice-of-God narration inflected with achingly arch overtones, the pseudo-documentary combat footage looking like a parody of itself, the use of musical standards like "When Johnny Comes Marching Home" given an excruciating edge through maniacal repetition. The prickly insouciance of the film's attitude—which led more than one outraged viewer to see it as an inhumanly Olympian contemplation of the world's end—gives the sense, despite the prevailing immoderation, that it could all turn deadly serious again in an instant, with the slightest shift in angle. The fact that it retains its anarchic comic spin to the bitter end is surely the clearest evidence of its invincible cool.

Though the new sensibility celebrated a breakdown of cultural hierarchies, such stratifications were by no means abolished, a fact suggested by Sontag's response to Kubrick's film. In her role as doyenne of the new sensibility, Sontag discussed *Dr. Strangelove* in tandem with Charles Chaplin's *The Great Dictator* (1940), which was being exhibited concurrently in re-release for the first time in twenty years. Where one might have expected Sontag to dismiss Chaplin's spoof on Hitler as a tasteless throwback while upholding Kubrick's film as forging the path of the new—as many critics did—instead she found the two films of a piece (Sontag, *Against* 148). If Sontag's reaction shows mostly how her streak of moral seriousness ultimately trumps her championing of the new sensibility, it also illustrates how that sensibility's entry into the commercial realm remained hampered by some of the same old polarities of highbrow and lowbrow. For Hoberman, writing nearly forty years later, "*Strangelove* was Pop Art" (92)—pure and simple. But if that sensibility were ever to take hold of American movies as a truly dominant force, it would not happen for years. Meanwhile, Hollywood was stuck with its poor cousin, the New Sentimentality, grasping simultaneously for high-mindedness and a species of hip equanimity, while yearning nostalgically for a time when it had been possible, without giving a thought to the shock of the new, both to "care and not give a damn" (Benton and Newman 27)—the age of Humphrey Bogart and *Casablanca* (1942). But Hollywood was so much older then; especially after this pivotal year, it was younger than that now.

NOTE

Thanks to Stefanie Altman, Dunbar Fellow at Claremont McKenna College, for her expert research assistance for this essay.

1965

Movies and the Color Line

DAVID DESSER

While the war in Vietnam was escalating to the point that there were almost 185,000 troops in country by year's end, one would be hard pressed to find any evidence of that in mainstream films. By the same token, another war—President Lyndon Johnson's much ballyhooed War on Poverty—also seems to have left little trace on celluloid images of the year. One learned from protest singer-songwriter Phil Ochs that 23,000 U.S. troops landed on the shores of Santo Domingo in the Dominican Republic, but the movies were silent on this score, too. Bubbling beneath the surface, however, even within the mainstream, one could easily detect the restlessness and disillusionment that would threaten to break apart the fabric of American society later in the decade and that certainly ended the ride of Hollywood's family-style, Production Code–restricted cinema.

Perhaps Hollywood remained moribund as it felt itself torn between producing middle-of-the-road fare that yielded the occasional big hit and continued, for the most part, to garner coveted Oscar statuettes, or delivering more offbeat fare to a growing audience of art film aficionados and disaffected teens whose numbers, thanks to the Baby Boom, were ever increasing. Traditional cinema with aging stars like James Stewart and Bob Hope barely returned a profit, while Golden Age directors like Howard Hawks and Henry Hathaway similarly found themselves increasingly out of step with younger audiences, try as they might to connect. In short, mainstream films left the mainstream audience largely apathetic and younger audiences unimpressed; to some, it seemed that the magic had slipped away from the silver screen.

Those hoping for a return to form for the movies might have seen a savior not in George Stevens's *The Greatest Story Ever Told,* a biblical epic whose paltry return of $7 million on a bloated $20 million budget was all too indicative of the industry's sad state of affairs, but in a film that would prove to be not simply a blockbuster smash but one of the most successful movies ever made—a film that would in real dollars amount to one of the biggest hits in Hollywood's history. While Hollywood in the next few years would try, with often disastrous results, to duplicate this feat of adapting popular musicals to the screen, *The Sound of Music* remains the most successful such venture. Hollywood feted the film and reveled in its box office winnings, but more astute cultural critics could hear far more complex sounds and stirrings in the social nexus of the year's truly momentous events.

One such issue that America would face is one that *The Sound of Music,* with its feel-good story and sentiments, avoids: race. The genocidal racism that helped the Nazis rise to power is repressed in the Oscar-winning film, but many in the United States thought the time was ripe to confront racism in its many and varied forms. Thus, when President Johnson forcefully and eloquently admitted to America's racial divide in a speech to Congress on 15 March (boycotted by the entire Mississippi and Virginia delegations, as well as other members from southern states), it appeared as if something significant was stirring, something whose time had arisen and, indeed, was threatening to boil over. Acclaiming the heroism of those who marched in Selma, Alabama, one week earlier and who had been met with brutality, violence, and death, Johnson launched into a speech that unhesitatingly castigated the nation for its failure to live up to its own promise: "We have already waited a hundred years and more and the time for waiting is gone." It was time already, he went on, for American Negroes to "secure for themselves the full blessings of American life. Their cause must be our cause, too. Because it is not just Negroes, but really it's all of us, who must overcome the crippling legacy of bigotry and injustice. And—we—shall—overcome" (Branch 113–14). Quoting the title of the iconic civil rights song was obviously no accident, and it must have seemed to the civil rights warriors of the time, especially Dr. Martin Luther King Jr., who led the march on Selma just the previous week, that Johnson would do what no one since Lincoln had done or could do. Just five months later, amid the smoke from a south central Los Angeles neighborhood, how different the world would look.

That questions of race and the escalating war in Vietnam would eventually become linked was perhaps the only factor not apparent this year, but otherwise race rose to the forefront of the national agenda while the war in Vietnam found its way onto the political and cultural radar in a major way. Early in the year, the war in Vietnam underwent significant escalation. It is arguable that the United States looked for any provocation in order to justify increasing military activity. So, for instance, in retaliation for attacks on the barracks at Plieku, U.S. forces conducted a series of air attacks against North Vietnam. On 5 March, the United States initiated the first sustained attacks against the North, in an action named "Rolling Thunder." On 7

March, the first two battalions of U.S. combat troops arrived to defend the air base at Danang. Some Americans were already leery of this adventurism and on 17 April a demonstration estimated at 15,000–25,000 people was held in Washington against the U.S. bombing of North Vietnam.

The demonstration hardly put a dent in the escalation of the conflict. Instead, on 8 June, President Johnson authorized American troops to engage in direct combat operations in Vietnam, removing the idea that they were there solely as advisors. The ever-increasing activity on the ground led to ever-greater anti–Vietnam War demonstrations. On 15 October there were forty U.S. cities hosting antiwar demonstrations. Still, the escalation of the war continued with a substantial increase in troop strength, including the conscription of nineteen-year-olds and the abolishing of draft deferments for married men, long a staple of the post-World War II military policy. However, deferments remained in place for all students in good standing in colleges and universities, the so-called II-S draft board classification: "Registrant deferred because of activity in study."

Antiwar sentiments at this point hardly characterized the opinion of the majority of Americans. Conversely, another war, this one actually and officially declared, did meet with some staunch opposition—the War on Poverty. In his first State of the Union address the previous year, President Johnson announced the launching of a comprehensive plan to wage war on poverty, but it was not until 24 August of this year that he signed the Economic Opportunity Act into law. This was part and parcel of the president's Great Society agenda, and though a controversial piece of legislation, perhaps another of Johnson's policies was even more so: the Voting Rights Act, signed on 6 August, prohibited states from using poll taxes or literacy tests to limit voter registration among minorities.

Both the War on Poverty and the Voting Rights Act were in response to ever-increasing divides between Black and white and a consequent rise in Black militancy. The assassination of Malcolm X, the controversial Black Muslim activist, shot and killed in a public auditorium in New York City on 21 February, was something of a first salvo detailing rifts in the Black community and the violent turn civil rights activism and Black discontent would soon take. Though it appeared that Malcolm was killed by a fellow Black Muslim, white violence directed against Blacks followed, as when on 5 March the integrated Freedom School in Indianola, Mississippi, was burned to the ground. Shortly thereafter, violence directed against demonstrators on a march from Selma to Birmingham to promote voting rights turned into "Bloody Sunday" when state troopers attacked the demonstrators. The unblinking eye of TV cameras caught this senseless and unprovoked attack against the peaceful marchers and led directly to President Johnson's impassioned and eloquent plea for an end to the racial divide.

How far America was from ending the racial divide became all too clear when, on 11 August in the Watts section of town, a Los Angeles police officer pulled over a Black motorist whom he suspected of driving drunk. The confrontation with the driver and his brother in the car escalated when their mother showed up and a scuffle ensued. Meanwhile, an increasingly angry crowd gathered and more officers were called to the scene. Soon the antsy officers lost their temper and hit the driver and his brother with their batons. Though the police hustled the boys away, the mood of the crowd could not be contained and a shocking six days of riots followed. More than thirty-four people died, over one thousand were injured, more than four thousand arrests were made, and there was an estimated $50–$100 million in property damage.

Amid the War on Poverty, the Voting Rights Act, and the escalation of the war in Vietnam, the Johnson administration also found time to create new governmental agencies with far-reaching implications for the health of American culture. The Federal Aid to the Arts Bill created the National Endowment for the Arts (NEA) and the National Endowment for the Humanities (NEH), organizations that were not particularly controversial at the time. Meanwhile, among significant cultural events was the appearance of Truman Capote's "non-fiction novel" *In Cold Blood*, serialized in the *New Yorker*. Based on the cases of convicted killers Richard Hickock and Perry Smith, who were executed during the year, Capote's celebrated work gave rise to a new form of literature: the true-crime novel.

In contrast to the blandness of this year's Hollywood films, television unveiled some interesting developments. "I Spy" (1965–1968) featured the first African American actor in a dramatic series in the person of Bill Cosby. At the same time, certain genre deconstructions may fairly be said to have been symptomatic of the stirrings of dissatisfaction in the culture at large. Programs like "Green Acres" (1965–1971), "Get Smart" (1965–1969), "F Troop" (1965–1967), and "Hogan's Heroes" (1965–1971)—all making their debuts this year—began to tweak the mythos of the mainstream. The intentional surrealism of "Green Acres" made the more cloying "Petticoat Junction," of which it was a spin-off, a bit easier to accept; James Bond, though well represented by the big-budget feature *Thunderball* this year, had some of the wind taken out of his sails by the bumbling Maxwell Smart; the less-than-heroic cavalry soldiers of "F Troop" put a different spin on frontier life than John Ford's cavalry films ever imagined; and the POWs housed in Stalag 13 made even the midshipmen of "McHale's Navy" (1962–1966) blush with envy at their antics.

In terms of popular culture, it was music that ruled the roost, particularly for America's youth. Bob Dylan's turn to the electric guitar may have alienated an older generation of folkies at the Newport Folk Festival, but his electrified recording of "Like a Rolling Stone" hit #34 on the *Billboard* Top 50 Singles of the Year, while The Byrds' famed guitar riff on their version of his "Mr. Tambourine Man" propelled that song to #21. Fully 40 percent of the songs on the *Billboard* chart were the product of British artists, with the Beatles and the Rolling Stones dominating. The Stones' "Satisfaction," one of the greatest rock 'n' roll songs of all time, topped the *Billboard* charts. Meanwhile, the rhythm and blues emanating out of Detroit's Motown Records indicated that crossing racial barriers was far less a problem if expressed musically, with groups like Diana Ross and the Supremes, the Four Tops, and the Temptations placing almost as many songs on the charts as the Beatles and Stones.

In comparison to the excitement in music and the strides taken by the small screen, Hollywood movies left much to be desired. If the health of a film industry must be judged not by the big-budget spectacular, the event picture, or the blockbuster but by the routine programmer, the kind of film released week after week, the kind of film nobody expects to garner prizes or take home awards, then Hollywood was in a bit of trouble. The old standbys were beginning to fail. Take Bob Hope, for instance. Never a box office or an Oscar perennial, Hope nevertheless turned out film after film beginning in the 1930s. *I'll Take Sweden,* Hope's entry this year, is something of an embarrassment, an obvious and obviously forced effort to merge Ol' Needle-nose with the young generation. Frankie Avalon, who went on a *Ski Party* and played *Beach Blanket Bingo* that year, co-stars with Hope and Tuesday Weld in this would-be risqué comedy that is sadly light on both laughs and sex. Jerry Lewis, too, seemed to be losing if not his touch, then his hold on the audience that had made him one of the most successful comic actors of the postwar era, both as one half of the comedy team of Martin and Lewis and as a popular writer-director-star. *The Family Jewels* didn't shine at the box office, while *Boeing (707) Boeing (707)* saw Tony Curtis brought in to try and recapture some of that Martin and Lewis magic. Things got so bad that even Vincent Price found himself on the wrong side of the comedy bandwagon in the beach-party-meets-the-horror-spoof *Dr. Goldfoot and the Bikini Machine.*

All was not lost, to be sure. The frothy musicals of Elvis Presley continued to be reasonably reliable. *Girl Happy* was certainly a decent hit in the spring and *Tickle Me* a virtual smash that summer, but *Harum Scarum,* the fall Presley entry, didn't, as *Variety* might say, scare up much coin. Blake Edwards's *The Great Race,* with an all-star cast including Tony Curtis, Jack

Lemmon, Natalie Wood, and Peter Falk, returned most of its extra-large budget, while another Jack Lemmon film, the more modestly budgeted *How to Murder Your Wife*—a comedy very much in the Italian style replete with sex kitten Virna Lisi—did the sort of respectable business that kept such comedies a staple for the next few years.

Something of a European flavor spiced up two of the year's more challenging films. The outrageous and scandalous *The Loved One,* from the novel by satirist Evelyn Waugh, was British director Tony Richardson's backhanded tribute to Southern California's crazy trendiness and an affront to good taste with its caustic look at the funeral business, including a prescient look at pet cemeteries. Arthur Penn's *Mickey One* was perhaps less a comedy than a film about a comic, but whatever it was, its Kafkaesque nightmare vision and ultra-New Wave stylistics left audiences cold.

Teach Me Gold

If race and the escalating war in Vietnam were truly the issues most on people's minds or percolating just below the surface of consciousness, it is no surprise to find that the most challenging films of the year dealt rather directly with these concerns. War or its aftermath was the prime subject of a handful of significant films, while race made its presence felt in a number of movies—large and small—across a variety of genres. And a focus on race and racism should not imply a focus on discrimination solely against African Americans. Antisemitism, especially in its most virulent form as expressed during the Holocaust, became the subject—implied or overt—of no fewer than three important films of the year.

The first such film was *Ship of Fools,* directed by Stanley Kramer, best known for his social consciousness expressed through films like *The Defiant Ones* (1958), about racism, *Inherit the Wind* (1960), about the famous Scopes monkey trial, and *Judgment at Nuremberg* (1961), about the war-crimes trials of the Nazi perpetrators of the Holocaust. Reteaming with screenwriter Abby Mann, with whom he had worked on *Judgment at Nuremberg,* Kramer's adaptation of Katherine Anne Porter's highly regarded 1962 novel provides a direct confrontation with racism, antisemitism, and other forms of discrimination. Set aboard a passenger ship sailing from Cuba to Germany in the all-too-symbolic year of 1933, *Ship of Fools* relies on a veteran cast to interweave a number of stories that rather portentously speak to the coming conflagration. In addition, the high-gloss cinematography of Ernest Laszlo (who earlier in the year was the director of photography on *Baby the Rain Must Fall*) lends the film a deceptively soap-opera quality, as if the film were a frothier classic Hollywood all-star extravaganza. Kramer lets the photography and high-profile cast carry the ever-more serious and probing examination of a society in moral decay. Siegfried Rieber (José Ferrer), an openly antisemitic German publisher, spouts his vicious drivel to German Jewish salesman Julius Lowenthal (Heinz Ruhmann). Lowenthal's rueful remarks that surely "all will get better in Germany" and that "there's almost a million Jews there; what are they going to do, kill all of us?" couldn't be more ironic. But Kramer links issues of antisemitism to other forms of racism, such as that directed against Blacks. Lee Marvin's washed-up baseball player remarks to fading beauty Mary Treadwell (Vivien Leigh) that he never knew what a Jew was until he was fifteen; her arch reply, "You were too busy lynching Blacks," suggests that antisemitism and racism go hand in hand. By the same token, antisemitism is linked to the discrimination meted out to Carl Glocken (Michael Dunn), a dwarf deemed unfit to sit at the captain's table and who is instead segregated off to a side where he is joined by Lowenthal. For that matter, Simone Signoret as a drug-addicted political prisoner, banished from Mexico for helping exploited workers stage an uprising, is similarly ostracized. George Segal, as a would-be activist painter, is something of an audience stand-in. Though Michael Dunn's dwarf provides ironic and pointed commentary from his position as the outsider, Segal's David is our surrogate who learns about social injustice and the true stakes of racism.

The passenger ship at sea as a microcosm of society worked well for *Ship of Fools* to explore in miniature the kind of beliefs that launched Hitler to power in Germany in 1933 and the failure of the rest of the world to stop him. Another film of this year used the same idea of a floating microcosm, this time with a war-time setting along with numerous elements of a Hitchcockian thriller. Released in August, just a month after *Ship of Fools, Morituri,* although a far different film, had just enough similarities to the former to make it sink at the box office despite respectful reviews and a cast headed by Marlon Brando and Yul Brynner. (The title probably didn't help either; even the original title, *The Saboteur, Code Name: Morituri* was little better. In fact, the title is derived from the Latin phrase immortalized by Roman gladiators: "Morituri te Salutant" [We who are about to die salute you].) Here the floating microcosm contains a patriotic but anti-Nazi German ship's captain (Brynner) charged with ensuring delivery of a much-needed load of rubber to the German war machine in Europe; an antiwar demolitions expert (Brando) hiding from the German authorities; a staunch pro-Nazi first mate; and various and sundry soldiers, sailors, and prisoners of war, including a young woman who survived the horrors of a concentration camp. A reasonably effective suspense thriller, shot in appropriately noirish black-and-white by cinematographer Conrad Hall, the film is also interested in exploring issues of conscience: how can the ship's captain support a war machine to which he is opposed while at the same time maintaining some sort of self-respect by doing the job to which he has been assigned? Can heroism overcome cynicism and is violence the only means to prevent further violence? The ambiguous answer to these questions—the refusal to see things in black and white—lends a great deal of complexity to the film. In addition, the conscience of humanity is once again called into question via Janet Margolin's fetching vulnerability as a Holocaust victim.

Both *Ship of Fools,* with its foregrounding of antisemitism, and *Morituri,* with its inclusion of a Jewish survivor of a concentration camp and the overt rejection of Nazi antisemitism evinced by the film's major characters, bring the Holocaust to bear, even if it remains something of an undertone. Not so with Sidney Lumet's searing film version of Edward Lewis Wallant's controversial novel *The Pawnbroker.* Although both novel and film are controversial for their characterization of the Jewish Holocaust survivor, both are unflinching in their portrayal of a man shattered by his experiences in the Nazi death camps.

Also potentially controversial were two scenes of female nudity. Hollywood, of course, still labored under the restrictive Production Code of 1934, and although foreign films had fairly consistently featured exposed female flesh (as did the ever-more popular "sexploitation film"—this year saw Russ Meyer produce one of his "classics" of the genre, *Faster, Pussycat! Kill! Kill!*), the mainstream, even independent productions like *The Pawnbroker,* shied away in fear of audience rejection, being associated with exploitation or litigation. Leonard Leff, in an exhaustive rehearsal of the film's laborious production and post-production history, notes that distributors were wary of releasing the film due in part to the delicate subject of the Holocaust, but mostly because of the nudity. Leff notes, "Hoping to establish the bona fides of the picture and soften the censors' anticipated resistance to it, [the producers] arranged to open *The Pawnbroker* abroad." In particular, it was felt that the Berlin Film Festival was a place where a film could acquire an international reputation which "could not only trump the Production Code Administration (PCA) office but help a 'serious' film set box office records. In early summer 1964 a motion picture trade association panel sponsored by the United States Information Agency chose *The Pawnbroker* as the American entry for Berlin" (Leff 367). Despite good notices at Berlin, the film could find no distribution in the United States until April, following a protracted battle with the PCA (Leff 267–371).

The Pawnbroker tells the grim story of Sol Nazerman (Rod Steiger), a former professor of philosophy in Germany who lost his entire family to the Nazi death machine. Now a mere shell of a man living in New York, he is alienated from both his rather typical, bland, suburban middle-class in-laws and the people he works and deals with at his pawnshop in Spanish Harlem. He is cold and unfeeling toward the pathetic souls who come to pawn the shattered remnants of their sad lives or who come in just for some human contact. Nazerman can provide none. He is similarly unfeeling in his relationship and even his lovemaking to another survivor, the wife of his best friend whom he saw killed in a concentration camp screaming out her name. And, most tragically, he is out of touch with the wants and needs of his young, vibrant assistant, symbolically named Jesus (Jaime Sanchez). After Nazerman's final rejection of him, Jesus engineers a robbery of the pawnshop that results in his own death while saving Nazerman from a gunshot. Though Nazerman had learned that his pawnshop was being used as a money-laundering front for the various unsavory activities of big-time gangster Rodriguez (Brock Peters), and was horrified and outraged by his newfound knowledge (a knowledge Rodriguez rightly understands that Nazerman was merely repressing), it is only with Jesus's death that he returns to some sort of human consciousness and feeling.

One of the most striking features of *The Pawnbroker* is the way in which it attempts to visualize the intrusion of traumatic memory into the present. In this respect the film very much borrows the flash editing and jump cuts popularized by the French New Wave. In particular, *The Pawnbroker* has much in common with Alain Resnais's classic documentary short of the Holocaust, *Night and Fog* (1955), and his feature-film debut about the atomic bombing of Japan and the German occupation of France, *Hiroshima, mon amour* (1959), borrowing from them a structure that mixes the present and the past and sifts them through a haunting poetry that refuses an easy separation between temporal realms. *The Pawnbroker* uses its flash cuts to signal these intrusions in perhaps a clearer way than Resnais's more formally challenging film is able to do (the difference between the French New Wave and an emerging style of post-classical cinema in Hollywood), but the effect is the same: to signal through graphic edits that Nazerman is haunted by his past as events of eerie similarity occur in the present. For instance, a series of eight flash cuts (less than one second) intrude upon Nazerman as he walks by a schoolyard fence behind which a young man is being beaten. This is graphically linked to a shot of a man in a concentration camp also desperately trying to climb a fence to safety. Another scene finds a depressed Nazerman riding the New York subway. Flash cuts and graphic

Sol Nazerman (Rod Steiger, right) behind a psychological prison of his traumatic memories in *The Pawnbroker* (Sidney Lumet, The Landau Company). Digital frame enlargement.

matches soon transport him to a cattle car carrying his family to their deaths. The longest death-camp sequence occurs when a prostitute offers herself to him in the back of his pawnshop, and in the sight of her bare breasts he is confronted with the memory of his wife's forced servitude in a concentration camp brothel. Interestingly, for all the film's willingness to confront the horrors of the death camps directly, less than four minutes of running time are in fact devoted to the past. It is the present with which the film is most concerned.

With Nazerman's horrific memories coming to him unbidden, *The Pawnbroker* is ultimately a film about vision: the refusal to see versus being forced to see. Nazerman engages in a kind of deliberate "not seeing" and in this not seeing we detect a pattern of "Nazi-ing." Nazerman does not see the humanity of his customers. He calls them "creatures, scum, rejects." In rejecting their humanity, Nazerman becomes a "Nazi man," taking away the humanity of his customers just as the Nazis had dehumanized the Jews as part of their overall strategy of eliminating them, first from the body politic of Germany and then from the face of the earth. Instead of this "not seeing," Nazerman is forced to see. And being forced to see means to acknowledge: Nazerman must acknowledge the racism that goes on around him, must acknowledge his kinship with the lost souls who enter the pawnshop, must acknowledge his failure to acknowledge Jesus and accept responsibility for his death, just as we all must accept responsibility for the things we see and refuse to acknowledge. As Lester Friedman expresses it: "[Nazerman] can no longer close his eyes to his own part in the oppressive exploitation of other human beings" (Friedman, *Hollywood's Image* 185). Nazerman learns, albeit too late to save Jesus, to live not by the rule of gold but by the Golden Rule. A simple message, perhaps, even a cliché, but no less true for all that, especially during this year of racial strife.

Tolerance: A Better Word than Friendship

To live by the Golden Rule is no less the message of *A Patch of Blue*, a film that confronts racism head on, albeit with the vision of class as a kind of distorting view. While Shelley Winters made horrific mother figures something of a specialization in her repertoire, she has never been more frightening than here in the role of Rose-Ann for the casual way in which she mistreats her blind daughter—memorably played by Elizabeth Hartman in her Oscar-nominated film debut. In a drunken fight with her husband after a night of adulterous debauchery, Rose-Ann blinded their daughter Selina. The husband understandably abandoned her, but tragically also the little girl, whom she has abused and mistreated ever since. Keeping Selina a veritable prisoner in a tenement apartment, Rose-Ann makes her daughter do all the cooking and cleaning and forces her to string beads for cheap necklaces sold to a kindly neighbor. Although Winters never makes Rose-Ann sympathetic—she is also a virulent racist—we are still able to see something of the life forces that have beaten her down. A woman of little education and with no social or economic prospects, she understands that as she ages her life will not improve. And maybe there is more than a hint of jealousy in her voice when she insists that Selina is ugly and will never amount to anything. With little to look forward to, she lashes out with violence both physical and emotional. Such a forceful presentation of the psychology of social class was itself rare in the American cinema. Unfortunately, in its presentation of racism and clear antiracist message, the film makes a move typical of the Hollywood cinema, ascribing racism among whites only to the working class. By the same token, in highlighting the interracial relationship between Gordon Ralfe (Sidney Poitier) and Selina, the film must insist on the class superiority of the Black man to the white woman, as if a relationship among class equals would be impossible to envision.

Gordon (Sidney Poitier) rescues the poor white girl Selina (Elizabeth Hartman) from her racist mother Rose-Ann (Shelley Winters) in *A Patch of Blue* (Guy Green, MGM). Digital frame enlargement.

In the film's most tense moment, Gordon and Selina exchange something more than a chaste kiss. Gordon quickly backs away and Selina misinterprets his hesitation. He, of course, cannot imagine making love to a white woman, which is to say that he very much can imagine making love to a white woman, but must not—by virtue of both social and cinematic norms of the times, of course. But she thinks it is because she's tainted, somehow dirty because she had been raped. When Selina finds out Gordon is Black it bothers her not one bit, and the film was rather daring for showing such an erotically charged interracial kiss. Indeed, in showing the obvious adultery that led to Selina's blinding, her rape when she was a teenager at the hands of an older man, and in less overtly but still clearly implying that Rose-Ann and her friend Sadie intend to start a brothel (and perhaps pimping for Selina in the process), *A Patch of Blue*, no less than *The Pawnbroker*, contributed to the ever-weakening hold of the Production Code on American cinema. It is surely no surprise that two of the year's most powerful and satisfying films so willingly break major commandments of the old Hays Code run by the restrictive Breen Office.

Still, one cannot imagine any actor being able to pull off this daring feat other than Sidney Poitier. The only major Black star of this era, Poitier was nevertheless (or as a consequence) confined to relatively sexless roles and certainly roles without hints of interracial romance or sex. As the more militant Black Power era of the sixties arose, Poitier became notoriously (and wholly unfairly) disrespected for the kinds of sexless, often demasculinized roles he played. Yet that is precisely what is necessary to pull off the otherwise racially charged kiss in this film. Left unspoken in *A*

Patch of Blue, however, is not what Selina "sees" in Gordon, but rather what Gordon might see in the ignorant, unsophisticated, girlish Selina. Her character is only eighteen and while we don't know Gordon's age, we do know he is the older brother of a medical intern; what we also know is that star Sidney Poitier was thirty-eight at the time of the film's release (Elizabeth Hartman was twenty-two). We can only conclude that, just as the class discrepancies "permit" the crossing of the racial divide, so, too, the age discrepancy allows Selina to value Poitier in a way that an older, more sophisticated white woman could not be allowed, and that the value that Gordon sees in Selina is simply that she is white.

None of this should take anything away from the film. Director Guy Green, a cinematographer of note in his native England before moving to Hollywood to direct in 1961, utilizes Cinemascope framing to go with Robert Burks's glowing black-and-white photography. Though not unheard of, it was rare for a film shot in the widescreen format to be accompanied by black-and-white cinematography. Otherwise an intimate drama, *A Patch of Blue* utilizes its 'Scope framing as a nice index for the idea that Selina's world need not be so closed off and confined. Similarly, the film's editing, though not as flashy or experimental as that on view in *The Pawnbroker*, shows something of the European influence, too. Wonderful scenic transitions are made across seeming continuity edits, for instance, as seen in a shot of Selina setting the table in her squalid apartment. As she reaches to put a plate on the table, it is across a cut such that the table is now in Gordon's apartment. Such creativity shows an expansion of the American cinema stylistically as much as the film's look at interracial romance pushes the boundaries of Hollywood's thematic maturation.

Viva Dundee

The crossing of the racial divide, or what critic Matt Wanat calls "border crossings" (98), is very much apparent in *Major Dundee*, Sam Peckinpah's truncated cavalry epic. Race is often at the heart of the Hollywood western, though far too often in the genre's history it has been repressed as the simple triumph of the Euro-American man over the hostile wilderness. White/Native relations have certainly formed the backdrop to many well-intentioned films, to be sure, but few westerns have truly explored what was at stake in the genocidal confrontation that gave rise to America and the American character. The postwar western also occasionally tackled or at least tried to acknowledge the long-lasting problem of the twentieth century, the problem of the color line, as W.E.B. Du Bois famously intuited. While not at the heart of Peckinpah's mangled *Major Dundee*, race is never far from the surface. What turns out to be surprising in this film first screened in March is how predictive it is about the American character and how these qualities of character led to the particularities of the conduct of the Vietnam War. Although a big-budget effort and a film of enormous interest, *Major Dundee*, even in its restored form, does not rank among either Peckinpah's major efforts or the genre's true masterpieces; but as a prescient product of its time, Peckinpah's probe across the color line and into Third World adventurism have much to say about how the western genre seems always to capture the dark heart of the American character. But before turning in earnest to Peckinpah's flawed demythological epic, it is important to consider other westerns of the year to see how the genre was being pushed—sometimes gently, sometimes forcefully—to tackle issues bubbling underneath the ever-more troubled surface of American mainstream culture.

The Great Sioux Massacre, directed by Sidney Salkow, was part of a pattern begun in the postwar era of films attempting to redress the image of the Native American and which also see American "heroes" as at least flawed, if not quite the raving racists or total psychopaths that later westerns, under the impetus of the ever-more unpopular war in Vietnam, would promulgate. In this film, Custer's Last Stand at the Battle of the Little Bighorn is owed to a combination of ever-encroaching white settlement on Indian lands and Custer's political ambitions at the expense of the Sioux nation. Another lower-budget western also reworked the Custer story, this time more overtly fictionalizing it and making its Custer-like protagonist into more of a xenophobic gloryhound. And if *The Glory Guys* also more overtly recalls the more famous and ambitious *Major Dundee,* released just a couple of months earlier, it is no coincidence: with a script by Sam Peckinpah himself, and featuring co-stars Michael Anderson Jr., Slim Pickens, and Senta Berger, *The Glory Guys* is very much in keeping with the demythological trend of so many westerns made that year, including Peckinpah's would-be epic. Peckinpah was not particularly fond of the film, though it reunited him with the creative team with whom he had worked on TV's "The Rifleman" (1958–1963). Peckinpah's claim that the film shifted the focus from his intended white-Indian conflict into a love-triangle amid the backdrop of a U.S. cavalry defeat at the hands of the Apache seems another example of the Peckinpah versus Hollywood myth (Simmons 76). Now largely forgotten, *The Glory Guys* was part and parcel of the reshaping of the western at the time, an attempt to both keep it alive and make it more relevant to an increasingly younger, more alienated audience.

The big-budget *The Sons of Katie Elder,* directed by Henry Hathaway, provided mainstream audiences with a more typical western, although Hathaway is not immune to recognizing John Wayne's aging body and recent lung surgery. Reteaming the Duke with Dean Martin (they had worked together in the Hawks classic *Rio Bravo,* 1959) and featuring the seemingly ubiquitous Michael Anderson Jr. (he also appeared in *The Greatest Story Ever Told*), the film is a bit of a shaggy dog story—a violent revenge saga interspersed with some Hawksian horseplay that doesn't amount to very much. But for Wayne's fans—he still ruled the box office roost while others his age had long since faded or passed away—and fans of the traditional western— itself in danger of fading away in this demythological era—it was more than satisfactory. The comic byplay rampant in *The Sons of Katie Elder* prevents one from taking the film particularly seriously. There was no danger of that happening, either, in the even more overtly comic parody *Cat Ballou.* In a dual role, each of which spoofed a traditional western icon—the menacing gunfighter outfitted all in black and the ex-gunfighter brought low by alcohol who seeks redemption—Marvin hams up the screen while an earnest Jane Fonda plays it relatively straight as a farmer's daughter out for revenge against the rapacious railroad men who killed her father. Parodies of westerns have been part of the genre almost from its inception, and thus it would be too strong to say that in so easily demolishing the western's iconography on the part of this film it is possible to see something of the death of the genre foreshadowed. Still, amid all the deconstruction going on, with even John Wayne putting his tongue a bit in his cheek, the western was certainly hobbled.

For Sam Peckinpah, however, as evidenced by *Major Dundee,* the western still had much to offer, even if it was to speak about how the genre and history were sometimes at odds and the image of the western hero always contained more fiction than fact. In one of his finest dramatic roles, Charlton Heston appears as the monomaniacal titular hero Amos Dundee, banished to the southwest from the mainstream of the Union Army during the Civil War to run a POW camp. When a renegade band of Apaches under the ruthless command of Sierra Charriba raids a ranch, kidnaps a group of white children, and slaughters a cavalry patrol, Major Dundee determines to reclaim the children and capture or kill Charriba. Lacking the manpower to accomplish this mission alone, however, he offers the Confederate prisoners on his watch an opportunity for freedom if they will accompany him. The African American guards at the camp also seek to accompany him and Dundee manages, too, to enlist a group of assorted misfits. Most important among Dundee's cobbled-together command are the Confederate officer

Benjamin Tyreen (Richard Harris), ordnance officer Lieutenant Graham (Jim Hutton), and one-armed Army scout Samuel Potts (James Coburn). Brock Peters, Senta Berger, and Peckinpah regulars Ben Johnson, Warren Oates, L. Q. Jones, and R. G. Armstrong are also along for the wild ride as Dundee, without authorization or seemingly much good sense, chases Charriba into Mexico, even pursuing him after he has recaptured the children.

Major Dundee is both a classic and deconstructionist western. On the one hand, with its story of a renegade band of Indians whose cruelty is matched by their cunning, *Major Dundee* seems little different than countless westerns that portray the Native as savage and senseless. The Apache here are given little nobility beyond their fighting prowess and, indeed, the defeat of Charriba, upon which so much of the film seems dependent for its plot, turns out to be rather anti-climactic and does not, in fact, mark the film's climax. Instead, that distinction belongs to Dundee's battle with French troops, of all things—though again, the presence of the French in this "Third World" territory should not be overlooked. On the other hand, race relations are much foregrounded by Peckinpah in more progressive ways. The film attempts a kind of integration of a number of races and ethnicities: African Americans, Mexican Americans, Native Americans, and Southerners (Wanat 98). African Americans, in particular, are highlighted in the manner in which Dundee allows them to join his fighting forces. Peckinpah endows these men with a great deal of dignity, especially Brock Peters's Sergeant Aesop, and in one particular scene confronts white racism directed against Blacks quite directly. Yet here, too, we may see something of the sociocultural context slipping through in the inability of Aesop to fight his own battle against racism. Confronted by the racist epithets of Confederate soldier Benteen (John Davis Chandler), Aesop is initially loath to stand up for himself. And when it appears he might just do that, instead Reverend Dahlstrom (R. G. Armstrong) fights his battle for him, giving the southerner a sound beating to the accompaniment of biblical epithets. It is as if no Black man at this time could be allowed to stand up for himself, could be permitted to engage racism directly with violence, and instead a more paternalistic white figure (a representative of organized religion no less) would fight that battle for him and thus displace white racism onto only a select few—the poor white southerner.

It is in its vision of Third World adventurism that the film achieves transcendence beyond its successes (and failures) as even a demythological western. And here the specter of Vietnam is everywhere apparent. To begin with: in pursuing Charriba into Mexico, Dundee is confronted with a type of guerrilla warfare far different than his West Point training or even the

Charlton Heston as the would-be savior of Mexico in *Major Dundee* (Sam Peckinpah, Columbia 1965). Digital frame enlargement.

conduct of the (rather savage) Civil War might have prepared him. It is only when Dundee learns from his enemy, can apply the enemy's tactics, that he is able to defeat Charriba. In this respect, Charriba's band of fighters represents the dreaded Vietcong, guerrilla fighters at home in that hostile terrain. When the old Apache delivers the kidnapped children to Dundee, he explains that although he was tired of fighting, he joined Charriba because it is, after all, their land. So, too, the Vietcong used any means necessary to fight the better-armed American soldiers who were, truth be told, trespassing on their land.

This is a rather small point in the film's Vietnam allegory (intentional or not), but more pointed is the attitude of Amos Dundee, whose single-minded vision of himself first as a would-be hero who rescues children from savage Indians and then as a liberator of Mexican villages is eerily on target to the single-minded tunnel vision characteristic of America's military commanders in Vietnam. Convinced it was their duty to liberate the peasants of Vietnam from communist oppression, American military commanders all too clearly recall Major Dundee and his sudden sense of himself as a hero of the people who will win their hearts and minds. That Dundee liberates the Mexican village from French troops, and that the climactic battle features Dundee's rag-tag bunch against the better-equipped but actually less skilled imperial French troops is also eerily connected to Vietnam, where the United States followed the (defeated) French into Indo-China but were themselves defeated by less traditionally trained and equipped fighters. In seeing American interventionism as much the product of megalomania as liberation, Peckinpah presents us with a film that captures the irony, and tragedy, of Vietnam.

Kings of Cool

Following the difficult production that was *Major Dundee*, Peckinpah signed on to direct *The Cincinnati Kid*. Film history is certainly the worse for the temporary delay in the successful pairing of director Peckinpah with star Steve McQueen. McQueen, like Peckinpah, a veteran of television westerns, was a rising film star, and the story of big-time card players, adapted from a popular novel by Richard Jessup, was a perfect vehicle for the brash McQueen to team with the genre-bending Peckinpah. Unfortunately, disagreements between producer Martin Ransohoff and the soon-to-be notoriously difficult Peckinpah forced the director's withdrawal after only four days of shooting (Simmons 73–74). Norman Jewison, another TV veteran and director of only innocuous, albeit successful comedies previously, took over the reins and turned in a more than competent film and one that very much captured the tenor of the times.

In fact, however, the less star-studded *Bus Riley's Back in Town*, featuring the film debut of Michael Parks, seems today the more prescient of the two films. Though screenwriter William Inge took his name off the screenplay (in favor of the pseudonymous Walter Gage), it everywhere shows Inge's particular characteristics, especially generational conflict expressed through barely contained sex and sexuality and the stifling effects of small-town life. As Bus Riley (Parks) comes back to town after a stint in the navy in order to find himself, he sees that his small town is much changed, but in particular that his ex-girlfriend has married a much older, well-to-do man. Though often the stuff of film noir, this particular configuration is more the set-up for a coming-of-age drama in the style of the earlier films of James Dean and the contemporary work of Steve McQueen. Unfortunately, Parks's striking resemblance to James Dean probably worked against him here. Moreover, Ann-Margret's barely contained sexuality also works against Parks's extremely low-key performance, but at the time Ann-Margret was the more dominant star, despite Parks's inhabiting the title role.

Yet it was a film released earlier in the year than either *The Cincinnati Kid* or *Bus Riley* that best captured the increasing alienation of the leading edge of the Baby Boom. In *Baby the Rain Must Fall*, Steve McQueen's Henry Thomas, like Bus Riley later in the year, returns to his small town, except here after a stint in prison. Yet he is no less alienated and out of sorts with his new life, desperately trying to make it (as it is clear he never will) as a singer. The importance of music was never in doubt for any motion picture throughout film history. But popular music, particularly rock 'n' roll, was increasingly a factor in a film's overall syncretic strategy. *Baby the Rain Must*

Fall doubly impacts the use of music, not only by its story of a struggling, alienated singer, but by its use of Glenn Yarbrough's singing of the title song. Indeed, this memorable tune went as high as #12 on the *Billboard* pop chart. Like *Bus Riley*, too, this film is the work of a playwright, Horton Foote. Foote understands even more than Inge that much of film acting takes place in the small moments, in the close-ups, and so he writes a character study where it is the journey, not the destination, the characters, not the action, that is important. And if neither of the McQueen vehicles or Parks's debut impressed the folks who hand out the Oscars (or overwhelmed the box office, for that matter), it was only a matter of time before the sorts of characters they played would resurrect the Hollywood cinema.

▄▄▄▄▄▄▄ A Thousand Clowns to the Rescue

If a caustic comedy like *The Loved One* or an existential look at a comedian like *Mickey One* couldn't quite grab both critics and audiences, a good compromise between them was *A Thousand Clowns*. Like all of the Oscar nominees for Best Picture this year, save for the British film *Darling* (directed by John Schlesinger), *A Thousand Clowns* is an adaptation, here from Herb Gardner's Tony-nominated 1962 play. Gardner adapted his own work for the screen, and much of the original cast, including Jason Robards Jr., Barry Gordon, Gene Saks, and William Daniels, appear in the film in the roles they originated on Broadway. Though it uses the world of children's television as the basis of much of its humor and satire, *A Thousand Clowns* has slightly bigger fish to fry. At once a tract against conformity and a mature recognition that life is filled with compromises, the film seems rather prophetic about how much an emerging counterculture would be willing to sacrifice in an effort to accommodate the slings and arrows of modern life.

Murray Burns (Robards) is a burnt-out writer of an asinine children's television show. He has come to believe that life should be lived, not worked, that a thousand clowns should always be in evidence. Happily unemployed and a free spirit as much as possible, his only responsibility, besides berating his neighbors from his New York City fire escape each morning, is to try and bring up his nephew (Gordon) with the same anarchic attitude. To that end, he has allowed the boy to try on various names until in a kind of bar mitzvah at age thirteen (the primary protagonists of the play are Jewish, but nothing of the issues impacted in the dramas discussed above are present) he must choose a permanent one. The intellectual life of uncle and nephew may be gauged by the sorts of names the boy toys with—Raphael Sabatini, Dr. Morris Fishbein, Lefty—and by the kind of humor they exchange, such as a comedy bit with voice imitations of Alexander Hamilton and Thomas Jefferson. When a pair of social workers comes to investigate how Murray is raising his nephew, currently calling himself Nick, a crisis ensues. Murray must seek employment or risk losing custody. He returns to the very TV show that he despises, but in a kind of compensation, he wins the heart of social worker Sandra Markowitz (Barbara Harris).

It is interesting that the film utilizes the world of television as stand-in for corporate conformity. The first generation brought up on television was beginning to enter their troubled teenage years in the 1960s. Was TV to blame for the social ills and alienation beginning to appear; or had the medium turned from an exciting Golden Age of socially committed dramas to a bland "vast wasteland"? Murray certainly thinks the latter; for him television represents the essence of selling out, and he makes no bones about that to his neighbors each morning from his steel podium. Even when he is told that he must get back to reality, he comments, "I'll only go as a tourist!" Yet on that very first morning back to work, ready to announce his thoughts for the day, he finds that "I'm sorry. I can't think of anything to say." Thus the film recognizes that with conformity comes a loss in spontaneity and creativity, but it enables Murray to keep custody of his nephew. Yet when Murray agrees to return to his job, Nick throws a temper tantrum in what is the film's most moving and interesting scene. Suddenly, Nick is a petulant child, no more the miniature version of Murray, no longer the little wise guy who speaks his mind with a wit and cynicism beyond his years. Murray is both puzzled and shocked by his nephew's uncharacteristic behavior. The comic tone is suddenly dropped here, a moment of pause, of hesitation, a reality check, so to speak. We realize that in this fit of pique, this childlike lashing out, it is as if Nick recognizes the loss of Murray's innocence and something of his own, and the culture's, carefree childhood. Torn between rebellion and acquiescence—like the culture at large—*A Thousand Clowns* opts for conformity and compromise. The culture itself was poised for a different strategy.

1966

Movies and Camp

HARRY M. BENSHOFF

By most accounts, this was not a strong year for American cinema. Commentators observed that Hollywood seemed to be out of touch with the era's countercultural sensibilities. Audiences were turning away from Hollywood films in favor of underground and exploitation films, as well as more idiosyncratic auteur films from Europe such as Ingmar Bergman's *Persona,* Roman Polanski's *Cul-de-sac,* Claude Lelouch's *A Man and a Woman,* and Jean-Luc Godard's *Masculine-Feminine*. If and when counter-cultural audiences attended mainstream Hollywood films, they often viewed them through an ironic lens, a distanced and distanciating reception practice known as camp.

At its most basic level, camp is a form of comic negation—a refusal to take seriously the serious forms and artifacts of dominant culture. Camp is a sort of "queer discursive architecture" that in the act of reception allows one to "pervert" "all 'originary' intention, deviating it toward unpredicted—and often undesired—ends" (Cleto 11). Most cultural historians agree that the origins of camp can be traced back to Western male homosexual sub-cultures of the last few centuries. The word is believed to have evolved from the French term *se camper,* which means "to flaunt," and as such, camp is something a spectator can *do*: one can "camp up" a film, a room, or even a persona. However, camp is also a means of textual production. A film may be called deliberately campy if its makers have purposefully encouraged outlandish plotting, baroque visual design, corny dialogue, and wooden acting. As Susan Sontag's seminal essay "Notes on 'Camp'" (first published in 1964 and anthologized in 1966) describes the phenomenon, by the mid-1960s camp was a sensibility that was shared not just by homosexuals, but by increasingly larger numbers of straight Americans turning away from the dominant ideological structures of Western culture. Furthermore, by this year, audiences were not only decoding mainstream texts as camp (what Sontag called "naïve camp" or the camp of failed seriousness), but Holly-wood itself was beginning to produce texts of deliberate camp (Sontag).

Camp's ironic way of seeing things, of turning the terrible into something grotesquely amusing, was understandable in a year when there was no shortage of troubling issues plaguing the country. Racial unrest, the war in Vietnam, the sexual revolution, and the burgeoning youth movement all posed significant challenges to the nation's sense of itself. Although the year saw the election of the first African American senator since the Reconstruction era (Edward Brooke from Massachusetts), race riots plagued Chicago and Cleveland throughout the summer. Violence against civil rights leaders continued to escalate: Martin Luther King Jr. was hit with a rock during a protest in Chicago, and James Meredith was shot and wounded by a sniper. Partially in response to such attacks, the militant Black Panther Party was founded in Oakland, California. More random, less ideologically motivated acts of violence were also occurring with alarming frequency. Serial killer Richard Speck killed eight women in Chicago, and Charles Whitman killed fifteen and wounded thirty-one more at the University of Texas at Austin. Truman Capote's *In Cold Blood,* famously chronicling another senseless murder spree, was one of the year's best sellers. Such violence at home was mirrored by the violence in Southeast Asia, as the Vietnam War continued to escalate. In October alone, over 46,000 men were called up to serve. In response to the war, demonstrators mounted a series of massive protests in the capital and around the nation, and even the Senate Foreign Relations Committee conducted televised hearings questioning U.S. involvement in Vietnam.

Antiwar and civil rights groups were but two segments of the year's growing countercultural movement. Young people in general were turning away from the nation's proscribed course, proclaiming a new platform of sex, drugs, and rock 'n' roll. Masters and Johnson's *Human Sexual Response* added fuel to the sexual revolution, as did the founding of the era's best-known feminist group, the National Organization for Women. LSD guru Timothy Leary launched his League for Spiritual Discovery even as the previously legal drug was criminalized by the courts. The Beatles were riding the crest of their popularity, allowing John Lennon to observe that they were now more popular than Jesus. Nonetheless, their infamous "Butcher Block" album cover was censored by Capitol Records: the original image, featuring dead baby dolls and raw meat, was considered too overtly political and (metaphorically) antiwar, and replaced by an innocuous image of the Beatles around a steamer trunk with a plain white background. Other musical artists including Bob Dylan, the Byrds, the Beach Boys, the Mamas and the Papas, and the Rolling Stones released albums that gave voice to the era's new sensibilities. In January, the Grateful Dead performed the first of their many subsequent light-and-music concert "happenings," events designed to simulate a new world order based on peace, love, and harmony. By the end of the year the countercultural newspaper the *San Francisco Oracle* had begun publication, chronicling the news most important to this new youth-oriented movement.

Perhaps unsurprisingly, Hollywood was a bit befuddled by these social changes and had a difficult time connecting with its changing audience. In truth, Hollywood itself was changing rapidly. Jack Valenti became president of the Motion Picture Association of America and began the process of replacing the Production Code with a ratings system. Lew Wasserman at Universal/MCA reached an agreement with NBC to start making movies for television. Paramount was absorbed by Gulf+Western, and Columbia narrowly escaped being taken over by European investors. In fact, the industry was becoming increasingly globalized, often via complicated production deals between Hollywood studios, foreign filmmakers, and foreign investors. For example, Twentieth Century Fox released a series of British horror films (including *Dracula: Prince of Darkness, The Reptile*, and *Plague of the Zombies*) that did well at the box office. Other internationally made but Hollywood-released films of the year include *Alfie, Georgy Girl, Fahrenheit 451,* and *Blowup,* all attempting to appeal to some extent to countercultural sensibilities.

Many commentators felt that Hollywood was outmoded or even dying. *New York Times* critic Bosley Crowther included only three American-made films on his "Ten Best" list for the year. Figures representative of classical Hollywood filmmaking and traditional social mores (the most iconic being Walt Disney) passed away. Films directed by older Hollywood veterans—such as Alfred Hitchcock's *Torn Curtain,* John Ford's *Seven Women,* and Billy Wilder's *The Fortune Cookie*—were deemed by many to be tepid rehashes of their previous successes. When Hollywood tried to attract a youthful, hipper audience with films like *The Swinger, Not with My Wife, You Don't! How to Steal a Million, Spinout,* and *Kaleidoscope,* they too were met with only lukewarm response. The faltering box office for both traditional films and the newer, more mod ones was the result of Hollywood's increasingly fragmented audience. Star of the year Julie Andrews (as selected by the *Motion Picture Herald*) was emblematic of this split. Not only did the British-born star signal the industry's trend toward globalization, but Andrew's very persona embodied many of the year's social contradictions. Both she and her 1965 film *The Sound of Music* (which was still playing widely throughout this year) were the epitome of traditional wholesome values to many Americans, but simultaneously they were also the object of derision to many others.

This rift between traditional Hollywood filmmaking and the era's newer countercultural sensibilities opened up a space for camp reception practices. Camp was now evident to a wide variety of spectators in outlandish spy melodramas, Hollywood biblical epics, Japanese science fiction films, and Italian peplum films. And as Hollywood continued to release "serious" film melodramas, many were received as naive camp. For example, the science fiction film *Fantastic Voyage*, about a microscopically shrunken ship and crew that travels through a human body, may have been created as a straight-forward fantasy film, but overwrought performances by Stephen Boyd and Raquel Welch—most memorably as she is attacked by giant antibodies that cling to her skin-tight costume—push the film toward camp (a fact observed by its *Mad* magazine parody). Similarly, *The Oscar* and *Madame X* may have been attempts to make old-fashioned Hollywood melodramas, but they were often laughed off movie screens because of their outrageous dialogue and wooden acting. The year's best-selling novel, *Valley of the Dolls*, was met with a similar response when Hollywood filmed it the following year.

More-or-less deliberate camp was also prevalent in many of the year's most popular and memorable television shows: "The Munsters" (1964–66), "The Addams Family" (1964–66), "The Man from U.N.C.L.E." (1964–68), "The Green Hornet" (1966–67), "Lost in Space" (1965–68), "The Monkees" (1966–68), "Dark Shadows" (1966–71), and "Star Trek" (1966–69). Hollywood contributed to the trend with films like *Ghost in the Invisible Bikini*, an amalgamation of American International Pictures' beach party and horror films meant to "camp up" both genres (which were arguably pretty campy to begin with). Similarly, AIP's reigning master of menace, Vincent Price, deliberately camped his way through *Dr. Goldfoot and the Girl Bombs*, itself a hybrid international sequel to *Dr. Goldfoot and the Bikini Machine* (1965). Joseph Losey's *Modesty Blaise* was yet another deliberately campy super-spy thriller, as were *Our Man Flint*, *The Silencers*, *The Last of the Secret Agents?*, and *What's Up, Tiger Lily?* And although most of these texts were resolutely heterosexual on the narrative level, their campy styles (and the occasional casting of gay or gay-coded actors like Aron Kincaid, Tommy Kirk, and Dirk Bogarde) still queered "normality" to some degree.

Although camp was everywhere, there was little consensus among critics, commentators, and consumers about its precise meaning(s). Camp did then and does now "bleed into" other popular textual forms such as parody, satire, black comedy, pop, mod, and kitsch. However, unlike (most of) those terms, because of its origins in gay male subcultures, camp also carried homosexual connotations. (Some dictionaries still list "homosexual" as one possible definition of camp.) As such, those commentators who acknowledged camp's ties to homosexuality often considered it to be either apolitical non-sense (thus dismissing the challenges being posed by the era's nascent gay liberationist discourse), or else part of a subversive plot by members of a dangerous "pink mafia" to corrupt American values (thus perhaps over-estimating the power of those same challenges). Yet only rarely were those positions stated forthrightly: the most common approach to acknowledging camp's homosexual origins was via a sort of sly, winking suggestion, since homosexuality itself was still mostly a taboo subject. Homosexuals had only been officially permitted to appear in Hollywood films as characters since 1961, following a special amendment to the Production Code.

Each of the films discussed below embodies different political implica-tions in relation to camp, (homo)sexuality, and dominant ideology. How-ever, they all share a coolly ironic, distanciated, or blank style that draws attention to issues of performance and theatricality, so central to the camp aesthetic. In so doing, the films tend to make unstable commonly held notions of authenticity, identity, reality, and even cinema itself. Their highly theatricalized visions and their insistence on blurring boundaries (between art and exploitation, the serious and the comic) confounded those critics and filmgoers who demanded generic purity, moral seriousness, and absolute meaning. The controversies these five films engendered were also expressed via censorship struggles: several either battled fiercely with the crumbling Production Code Administration or met with legal attempts to block their screening. Still, regardless of the myriad ways that camp infil-trated the year's films—whether in G-rated mainstream fare or in under-ground and/or exploitation cinema—camp did create a space that was more-or-less critical of dominant American institutions, a "discursive archi-tecture" within which countercultural ideals could be and were expressed.

Holy Bat-Camp!

The most widespread camp phenomenon of the year was undoubtedly *Batman,* as both an ABC television series (1966–68) and a fea-ture-length Twentieth Century Fox motion picture rushed into production to capitalize on the TV show's success. *Batman* (both movie and TV show) might best be classified as deliberate pop camp: its producers intentionally set out to write corny dialogue and encourage their actors to be either wooden and/or (in the case of the villains) excessively melodramatic, while simultaneously trying to mute the property's more overtly homosexual connotations. Critics of the era repeatedly used the term camp when they described *Batman,* yet they rarely explained what they meant by the term, and only occasionally alluded to its homosexual connotations. They sometimes made puns out of the term, referring to *Batman* fans as "well-encamped followers" (Archerd 1966), or entitling a publicity piece about the film "Summer 'Camp' Note." Only the most daring journalists hinted at camp's homosexual contexts. For example, one review suggested that "if you are interested in High Camp we refer you to *Seduction of the Innocent* by Dr. Fredric Wertham" ("Bat Man"). *Seduction of the Innocent* had been published over a decade earlier as part of a larger federal attack on the comic book industry. While much of the outcry over comic books had resulted from the gore and violence of titles like *Tales from the Crypt, Seduction of the Innocent* alleged that Batman and Robin were role-modeling male homosexuality to impressionable children. In response, the comic book's writers developed more female characters, including Aunt Harriet, Batgirl, and various female super villains. The producers of the *Batman* movie and TV show would follow a similar path, doing what they could to keep *Batman* "straight," even as the subtext and deliberately campy style of the property continually raised the specter of male homosexuality. So did the many queer or queerly coded actors who guest-starred on the TV show and/or the film, including Cesar Romero, Vincent Price, Roddy McDowall, Victor Buono, George Sanders, Van Johnson, Anne Baxter, David Wayne, Tallulah Bankhead, and Liberace.

In the *Batman* film, unlike the TV show, Batman/Bruce Wayne gets a heterosexual love interest named Miss Kitka (Lee Meriwether), who is quite obviously the arch villainess Catwoman in disguise. She is joined in her machinations by the Joker (Cesar Romero), the Penguin (Burgess Meredith), and the Riddler (Frank Gorshin), and together as the United Underworld they hatch a plan to kidnap the world's leaders via a diabolical dehydration device. Batman (Adam West) and Robin (Burt Ward) eventually save the day with the help of their noble allies and a host of new Bat-technology devices, including the Bat-Copter, the Bat-Boat, and even a can of Shark Repellent Bat-Spray that saves Batman from one of the more (deliberately) phony sharks ever put on screen. "Men Die! Women Sigh! Beneath that Batcape—He's all man!" screamed the film's ad copy, simultaneously raising and then repudiating the specter of homosexuality via its assertion that Batman was indeed a "genuine" man.

Such spin control—keeping *Batman* straight enough for mainstream viewers—was evident throughout the run of the TV show and in the film. Although Batman and Robin wore rather fruity tights, care was allegedly taken to minimize the prominent bulge in Burt Ward's briefs. In the press, producer William Dozier took repeated pains to distance himself from

The pop camp villains (left to right): the Penguin (Burgess Meredith), the Riddler (Frank Gorshin), Catwoman (Lee Meriwether), and the Joker (Cesar Romero) hatch a plan for world domination in *Batman* (Leslie H. Martinson, Twentieth Century Fox). Personal collection of the author.

camp's queerer aspects: "I hate the word camp," he told the *New York Times*. "It sounds so faggy and funsies" (quoted in Schuster). Dozier instead explained *Batman*'s style as "exaggerated seriousness and exaggerated use of the cliché. That becomes what a number of people choose to call camp— funny when it's done properly and squarely and without any attempt to be funny. Lots of people say it's so bad it's good. This is so about *Batman*, but it's no accident. You can't be that bad unless you work very hard at it" (quoted in Scheuer). Star Adam West also distanced himself from the word camp, preferring to think of *Batman* as "Pop Art . . . farce . . . [or] lampoon," although West also went on record stating that if homosexuals were enjoying the property it was all right with him—as any and all viewers counted in the media popularity game (West 98).

Actually, Bat-camp predated the arrival of the film by several years, if not decades. Created as a comic strip by Bob Kane in 1939, Batman first reached the screen in two Columbia serials, *The Batman* (1943) and *Batman and Robin* (1949). In 1965 and continuing throughout 1966, enterprising theater owners in college towns and urban areas programmed the *Batman* serials as midnight movie events, generally attended by countercultural audiences eager to laugh at the serials' naive dialogue and cheesy costumes. *An Evening with Batman and Robin*, as these screenings were entitled, became four-hour-plus audience-participation happenings, as audiences hooted and talked back to the screen. When *An Evening with Batman and Robin* made it to London, the covertly gay cinema journal *Films and Filming* reported that "the audience convulsed itself with knowing laughter every time Batman so much as smiled at his little friend" (Durgnat). *Time* ran a story on the phenomenon, and the *Los Angeles Times* even referenced Susan Sontag's "Notes on 'Camp'" when it tried to explain the appeal of the show ("He Flies Again"). A later review of the show in the *Los Angeles Times* linked *An Evening with Batman and Robin* directly to the more overtly queer underground cinema when it suggested that only "those who have managed to sit through six hours of *Sleep* [1963], by that other noted camper, Andy Warhol, are likely to find it less than a marathon" (Thomas, "Batman").

The blur between high and low, good and bad, naive and knowing—so integral to the camp project—was evident in all aspects of the *Batman* phenomenon. Avant-garde film critic Gene Youngblood called *An Evening with Batman and Robin*—previously a Hollywood B-movie serial—a "4 1/2 hour Pop Art orgy" (Youngblood, "Batman" 1). Film scholar Raymond Durgnat compared the serial's re-release to the high art films of Robert Bresson, Alain Resnais, and Alain Robbe-Grillet (Durgnat). And when the TV show was given a gala premiere in New York City, it was attended by "Andy Warhol, Roy Lichtenstein, Roddy McDowall, and five hundred of the Manhattan elite" (West 87). Clearly the worlds of the gay male underground, the urban intelligentsia, and the mainstream entertainment industry were mixing and mingling, even if the producers of *Batman* sought to suppress those ties. And although they never mentioned it in the press, it seems inconceivable that they were not aware of the naive camp following that the old *Batman* serials had created. Thus, by suppressing the property's gay innuendo and employing a colorful comic book visual style, the *Batman* movie transformed a naive (and more overtly queer) camp phenomenon into a deliberate pop one suitable for all ages.

Arguably, it was the film's colorful villains that appealed to queer and countercultural audiences, while children and "squares" could still root for Batman and Robin. Producer Dozier, perhaps ingenuously, repeated over and over in the press that *Batman* was really about teaching moral lessons and respect for law and order, chastising those who would overanalyze it

(Scheuer). Yet clearly camp—even in this mainstream pop manifestation—still functioned as a moral solvent, allowing the text to celebrate and ridicule simultaneously the forces of law and order. As if acknowledging that, the *Batman* film begins with an elaborate crawl across the screen assuring viewers that the producers "wish to express gratitude to the enemies of crime and crusaders against crime throughout the world for their inspirational example." Yet as the crawl continues, it itself becomes rather campy: "To them, and to lovers of adventure, lovers of pure escapism, lovers of unadulterated entertainment, lovers of the ridiculous and the bizarre—to funlovers everywhere—this picture is respectfully dedicated." At this moment a spotlight reveals a man and woman kissing in a dark alleyway, before the crawl returns for its punch line: "If we have overlooked any sizable groups of lovers, we apologize." The "overlooked" lovers in the shadowy netherworld are here presented as explicitly heterosexual, but the implication is also made that the overlooked group of lovers might also be queer. As with most pop camp artifacts, even as queerness is allegedly purged from the text, it nonetheless continues to linger.[1]

Black Comedy, Satire, Camp

Camp, queer, and countercultural sensibilities also linger throughout *Lord Love a Duck*, George Axelrod's bleak satire of American mores. Based on a novel by Al Hines, the film centers on a high school senior, Alan "Mollymauk" Musgrave (Roddy McDowall), and his Svengali-like control over a teenage nymphet, Barbara Ann Greene (Tuesday Weld). Mollymauk, a manipulative genius, is given to squawking like a duck as he makes all of Barbara Ann's dreams come true. This loose narrative structure allows the filmmakers to satirize the crassness and vacuity of the modern American dream. Axelrod himself described the project as a cross between Andy Hardy and Dr. Strangelove, and the film was advertised as being "against teenagers . . . their parents . . . beach movies . . . cars . . . schools . . . and several hundred other things. It's about a guy living in this insane world who suddenly goes stark raving sane and commits a mass murder. It's a comedy." Even before its release, the film's subject matter created controversy. Based upon the proposed script, the Production Code Administration warned that it would not be able to approve a sequence "in which the members of the high school class . . . draw straws to see who shall go out and fornicate for votes for head cheer-leader" (Shurlock). Other concerns over the picture's morality were reported in *Variety*, but the film was eventually awarded a Seal of Approval (Archerd 1965).

Lord Love a Duck tries very hard to be hip. It opens with a montage of still and moving images from the rest of the film (including shots of the film-makers themselves), cut to an upbeat title song performed by The Wild Ones. In style and tone the film recalls *A Hard Day's Night* (1964), although *Lord Love a Duck* is considerably darker. Various patriarchal authority fig-ures—policemen, school principals, psychiatrists, filmmakers, and parents—are mocked throughout the film, as is the vapidity of the younger generation. School principal Emmett (Harvey Korman) is easily manipulated by Barbara Ann, who seduces him by blowing suggestively on his prized microphone. In fact, sex, and the hypocrisy it creates when it is repressed, is a key subject of the film. Principal Emmett has an oral fixation, meant to suggest his repressed desire for his students. In one amusing scene, he chas-tises the botany teacher for discussing pistils and stamens, facts of nature Emmett can only conceive of as "smut" and "filth." Similarly, a psychiatrist is appalled when Mollymauk refuses to see "dirty" things in her ink blots. One of the film's more audacious sequences occurs when Barbara Ann guilt-trips her divorced father into buying her twelve cashmere sweaters (so she can join a clique of wealthy popular girls). The scene begins as a dis-placed orgy of consumer consumption that recalls the famous food-seduction scene from *Tom Jones* (1963), as Barbara Ann and her father lasciviously devour hot dogs and onion rings. She then proceeds to try on an array of tight-fitting sweaters with names like "grape yum-yum," "papaya surprise," "lemon meringue," and "periwinkle pussycat." Framed in wide, canted angles, the father's almost orgasmic response to his daughter's display is made into a grotesque comment on his repressed incestuous desire.

It is within the Mollymauk/Barbara Ann relationship that the film seems most queer, with Mollymauk coming off mostly as campy gay man, a fact underlined by thirty-seven-year-old perennial bachelor Roddy McDowall playing the high school senior. While the film's press book refers to him as a "fey young high school senior," a review in *Playboy* raised (and then dismissed) another reading of the character, calling Mollymauk a "resourceful fairy godfather (Grimm rather than gay)" ("*Lord*"). And although Mollymauk's confession at the end of the film would have us believe that he did what he did out of "love" for Barbara Ann, it is made quite clear throughout the film that they are not sexually involved with one another. Speaking of himself in the third person, Mollymauk tells Barbara Ann early on that "Mollymauk doesn't park . . . Mollymauk doesn't fool around." Instead, he prefers to invade the local Lovers Lane specifically to disrupt the heterosexual couples who *are* parking. When Barbara Ann, thinking Mollymauk might be interested in her sexually, tells him that "I

In *Lord Love a Duck* (George Axelrod, United Artists), perennial Hollywood bachelor Roddy McDowall brings his fey persona to the queer trickster role of Alan "Mollymauk" Musgrave. Personal collection of the author.

don't do bad things with boys," Mollymauk responds, "You don't have to do anything." Finally, when Barbara Ann asks Mollymauk what he does get out of their relationship, he cryptically replies, "I think of things." By the end of the film, as Mollymauk is attempting to murder Barbara Ann's newly-wed husband (because she has grown tired of him and he is impeding her desire to become a Hollywood starlet), Mollymauk is flitting about the house, spouting French phrases, and making cocktails and dinners laced with poison. He is the "fag" to Barbara's "hag," a queer trickster figure glee-fully attacking a seedy, hypocritical, and bankrupt culture.

The film's advertising copy also traded on campy queer insider knowl-edge about other Hollywood movies: a series of ads were prepared that referred to other then-popular films. Thus, in a nod to Alfred Hitchcock's famous tagline *"The Birds* [1963] is coming," one ad for the film announced that *"Lord Love a Duck* are Coming!" Another ad, recalling one of the most notoriously homosexual films ever to be awarded the Production Code's Seal of Approval, proclaimed that *"Suddenly, Last Summer* [1959] Roddy

McDowall, Tuesday Weld, Lola Albright, Martin West and Ruth Gordon discovered that they were being used for something evil. . . ." Another queer in-joke within the film itself centers on an isometric facial exercise called the "silent scream," a suggestive-of-fellatio opened-mouth stretch that Barbara Ann's mother (who is a cocktail waitress/prostitute) insists is practiced religiously by Cary Grant, an actor about whom homosexual rumors had been circulating for decades. Although *Lord Love a Duck* was received by most American critics as a scattershot black comedy satirizing contemporary American culture, its knowing use of camp also allowed it to speak to queer moviegoers and sound a queer critique of heteronormativity.

▄▄▄▄▄▄▄▄ "What a Dump!": Camp and the Serious Drama

Who's Afraid of Virginia Woolf? is a film perhaps best remembered as a serious adult drama from a major Hollywood studio. Yet the film, like the award-winning Edward Albee play on which it was based, has many interesting links to the year's developing debates over the forms and meanings of camp. In addition to the film's full-throttle performances by Elizabeth Taylor, Richard Burton, Sandy Dennis, and George Segal as two battling and embittered married couples employed at a New England college, *Who's Afraid of Virginia Woolf?* foregrounds the performative nature of identity, continually theatricalizing the quotidian. Its unrelenting bitchy wit and its insistence that the borders between "truth and illusion" are always blurred sound a strident critique of bourgeois heterosexuality, making it one of the year's queerest camp artifacts.

Although most contemporary critics did not label *Who's Afraid of Virginia Woolf?* as camp per se, there was certainly an air of camp about the film's official tag line: "You are cordially invited to George and Martha's for an evening of fun and games." Skipping over camp directly to the label homosexual, some reviewers understood the film (as they did the play) as really being about two homosexual couples and not two heterosexual ones. For example, *Newsweek* opined that "Albee is using his harrowing heterosexual couples as surrogates for homosexual partners having a vicious, narcissistic, delightedly self-indulgent spat. He has not really written about men and women, with a potential for love and sex, however withered the potential may be. He has written about saber-toothed humans who cannot reproduce, and who need to draw buckets of blood before they can feel compassion for each other" ("Who's Afraid"). Continuing in this vein, the review suggested that "deep down inside [the film and the play], in a tiny envelope from a Cracker Jack box, is a tiny plastic statue of a playwright thumbing his nose at the world." While this particular view of the work has rightfully been critiqued as homophobic (i.e., homosexuals are essentially "vicious" and "narcissistic" and incapable of creating heterosexual characters) and self-serving (actual heterosexuals could never be so monstrous), it does correctly suggest that the dynamic power of the work is connected to a queer writer's critique of dominant culture.

From its opening moments, *Who's Afraid of Virginia Woolf?* references the history of camp role playing, as Martha (Taylor), performing as Bette Davis in *Beyond the Forest* (1949), arrives home and intones the infamous line "What a dump!" Sounding as much like a drag queen performing Bette Davis as Bette Davis herself, the slovenly Martha further distances herself from Davis's alleged Hollywood glamour by gnawing on a chicken bone and telling George (Burton), "You make me puke!" The multiple intersections of reality and fantasy in this one scene—Martha is role playing but clearly referring to her own home and marital situation—become even more reflexive as Martha notes that the line was from some "Goddamned Warner Bros. epic," a line that might also aptly describe *Who's Afraid of Virginia Woolf?* (Such Pirandellian excess would have been taken to further sublime heights had Bette Davis herself actually been cast as Martha, as had been briefly considered.) Throughout the film, George and Martha continually enact various personas that suggest the ultimate unknowability of their "true" identities: Martha lisps "I'm thirsty" in a little girl voice when she wants another drink; when George brings Martha flowers he pretends to be a tongue-tied schoolboy. Ultimately, the various stories they tell Nick (Segal) and Honey (Dennis)—about a young man who may have killed his parents, about the existence of their son, or the quality of their own "happiness"—are neither true nor false, but something else altogether. Similarly, Nick and Honey's marital issues (Was her pregnancy hysterical or aborted? Was her preacher father a man of God or a con man who bilked his flock?) are never resolved. It is the playing of the game, the verbal exercise of cruel and campy wit as a defense against bitter realities, that ultimately matters the most to George and Martha, just as it did for generations of gay men and women in pre-liberation eras.

The acting of all four leads (but especially by Taylor and Burton) is itself firmly grounded in camp, in part because of the film's theatrical flavor, which first-time film director Mike Nichols took pains to preserve. The actors bite into Albee's bitchy dialogue with relish, milking each line for its fullest release of irony and sarcasm. "I don't bra-a-a-ay!" Taylor-as-Martha brays. Martha, delighting in humiliating George in front of Nick and Honey, christens him "a bog, a fen, a G.D. swamp!" before bellowing "Hey Swampy!" at

"Movie star vaudeville team" Elizabeth Taylor and Richard Burton give full-throttle camp performances in *Who's Afraid of Virginia Woolf?* (Mike Nichols, Warner Bros.). Personal collection of the author.

him from across the room. George responds with bitchy *bon mots*, as when he refers to Martha's sleazy lounge outfit as her "Sunday chapel dress." In a moment of nonverbal irony, when Martha attempts to seduce Nick at the roadhouse, George programs the jukebox to play "The Anvil Chorus," the music suggesting that a blacksmith hammering on an anvil is like having sexual intercourse with Martha. While Burton and Taylor's tour-de-force verbal sparring (perhaps mirroring their real-life romantic complications) earned them high praise, it would be only two years later that at least one critic would refer to them as a "movie star vaudeville team [that] has become one of the greatest camps of our time" (Kauffmann). And while George Segal as Nick mostly plays it safe as the straight man of the group, Sandy Dennis as Honey gives an excessive performance filled with nervous tics, twitches, and quivering lips, screaming one moment and vomiting the next. Yet, true to camp's usage within queer subcultures, there are also moments of great tenderness and understanding in the film. Martha's desolate search for companionship after her tryst with Nick (shot in a single high-angle long shot) suggests pity more than contempt, as does her climactic confession that she is indeed afraid of Virginia Woolf, or rather the mental illness and suicide to which she succumbed. As George puts it, although no one may know the difference between "truth and illusion" anymore, we all must carry on as if we did.

As with many of the other films discussed herein, *Who's Afraid of Virginia Woolf?* created controversy during its production as well as after its release. The film's battles with the Production Code Administration began in 1963 when Jack Warner optioned the play and sent the Code Administration a copy of the script for comment. For over two years the film's producers tried in various ways to rewrite the script, but eventually it was filmed with most of its raunchy and/or blasphemous dialogue intact (Leff and Simmons 241–66). When the National Catholic Office for Motion Pictures rated the film A-IV (for adults, with reservations), the Production Code Administration felt obligated to concur, and *Who's Afraid of Virginia Woolf?* was released with a Seal of Approval but also with a strict "adults only" policy. Warner Bros. even hired Pinkerton guards to enforce the policy at the Pantages Theater in Los Angeles ("Pinkertons"). But not everyone was happy with that situation. In other parts of the nation, attempts were made to stop the film from being shown altogether. In Nashville, Police Sergeant Fred Cobb (who was also a Baptist church deacon and Sunday school teacher) shut down a screening of the film and arrested the theater manager ("Woolf Too Hot"). There was also an attempt to file criminal charges against a local exhibitor in Des Moines ("Dubuque"). Eventually the furor waned and *Who's Afraid of Virginia Woolf?* became an American film classic. Although it uses aspects of queer camp to critique American culture—George and Martha being pointedly named after George and Martha Washington—those aspects of the film are perhaps subtle enough for the film to continue to pass as serious cinematic art (as opposed to being dismissed as "merely" camp or queer).

█████████ **Camp and Exploitation**

The year's exploitation films almost always held a camp appeal, whether they were Herschell Gordon Lewis gore-fests, Russ Meyer "roughies," or soft-core sexploitation films. As a type of cinema that promised to reveal more sex and/or violence than Hollywood could, exploitation films were inherently ripe with campy excess. Concomitantly, their low budgets, disingenuous aspirations, and self-conscious acting all worked together to create a naive camp effect. On the other hand, some exploitation filmmakers, realizing their films' limitations, chose to fashion them as more obvious deliberate camp. Thus, while some of the year's drug/sexploitation films like *Hallucination Generation* are campy due to their overwrought and badly fashioned melodrama, others like *Movie Star, American Style; or LSD, I Hate You* deliberately established a winking camp tone. Similarly, more mainstream exploitation hybrids like *Billy the Kid versus Dracula* and *Jesse James Meets Frankenstein's Daughter* are hard to appreciate as anything other than camp. Their mixture of western settings and gothic motifs, cheap sets and goofy dialogue, combined with William "One Shot" Beaudine's hurried direction, make them minor camp classics. *Jesse James . . .* even features elements seemingly aimed directly at queer audiences, such as a female mad scientist and a bare-chested hunk of a monster.

Amidst this milieu, Roger Corman fashioned his box office hit *The Wild Angels* as part exploitation roughie and part art film. A loose, meandering narrative about a gang of outlaw motorcyclists, Corman's film careens from the atrocious to the poetic, confusing many critics even as it contributed to its camp effect (Heard). While not deliberately campy in most senses of the term, Corman's dispassionate style—refusing neither to condemn nor condone the violent biker gang—does allow for a camp response. So too does much of the awkward and purple dialogue performed by stars Peter Fonda and Nancy Sinatra. In his climactic speech that addresses the gang's principles, Fonda's character, Heavenly Blues, spouts the immortal lines, "We wanna be free! We wanna be free to do what we want to do . . . to ride our machines without being hassled by the man! And we want to get loaded! And we want to have a good time!" Aside from the incongruity of such children of Hollywood royalty playing low-life bikers (and even performing alongside actual Hell's Angels members hired for "authenticity"), the film's hyperbolic publicity campaign also encouraged a campy response: "Their credo is violence . . . their God is hate . . . THE MOST TERRIFYING FILM OF OUR TIME!" Another scene, in which Sinatra, as the sleazy biker Mama "Mike," pretends to be a straight "good girl" by donning a white dress and gloves (in order to help rescue a captured biker), also verges on the precipice of camp theatricality. And surely the planned (but never realized) creation of a musical rock group to be called the Wild Angels and marketed in the mode of the Monkees would have tipped the property into the realm of deliberate pop camp.[2]

Although the queerer contexts of the postwar biker phenomenon were downplayed by Corman throughout much of the film, they were the central topic of the still-popular underground film *Scorpio Rising* (1964), which itself had riffed on the earlier Hollywood biker film *The Wild One* (1953). In a later interview, Corman did admit that his research for the film uncovered gay bikers, although he decided not to linger on them in his film. (Actually, during the final funeral/orgy in the church, one biker can be seen in another biker's arms, and one rather gay-sounding biker exclaims, "Good Heavens Lucifer! Don't tell us about evil being good and good being evil— that—well—it's absurd! It's ridiculous!") The fact that Corman had muted the potential homosexuality of the bikers deeply disturbed *Saturday Review*'s film critic Hollis Alpert, who argued that Corman, "presumably having seen *Scorpio Rising*," had made an irresponsible film "bereft of social purpose, satire, or meaning." In Alpert's formulation, had Corman shown more homosexual bikers, such "pathology" would have adequately served to discredit them, and thus restored conventional morality to the film.

Despite its seemingly neutral ideological stance, *The Wild Angels* does contain an indirect critique of dominant American institutions and the ways in which they limit personal freedoms. The film opens with a young boy on a tricycle being dragged back to his squalid yard by his mother, a scene that suggests perhaps the immaturity of the biker gang, but also their genuine yearning to be free of a smothering lower-class domesticity. As embodiments of American masculinity, the bikers "get loaded," snort drugs, beat up Mexicans, and rape women, but they are unable to sustain any kind of intimate human relationship beyond a bland homosocial loyalty to their buddies. They long to be free, but they don't really know what to do with that freedom once they've achieved it. In a small metaphorical scene early in the film, Loser (Bruce Dern) unties a horse specifically to set it free, but it merely stands there, suggesting that perhaps humans as well as horses are incapable of actually being free—that both enjoy or are at least inured to the structures that limit them. And when the "normal" townies at the end of the film degenerate into violent thugs as bad as the bikers themselves, Corman's point is clear: it is not just the bikers who are violent and limited, but American society as a whole. Heavenly Blues, burying his buddy Loser (who had been shot by police earlier in the film), speaks the final line of the film: "There's nowhere to go." Even the open road cannot provide escape from the social structures that define and limit America's promise of freedom. Resigned to that fact, Heavenly Blues continues to bury Loser and waits for the imminent approach of the cops.

Perhaps unsurprisingly, *The Wild Angels* was quite controversial, even as it became American International Pictures' biggest grosser to date. When it played at the opening night of the Venice Film Festival, many American critics were outraged by its blank, amoral tone, and they were mortified to think that the rest of the world was seeing such a seamy image of American culture. The bikers' prominently onscreen Nazi paraphernalia (even the film's title card is adorned with a swastika) also angered many viewers; the film was banned outright in Denmark, and its exhibition in England was delayed (*"Wild Angels* Banned"). Five days after the film was released in the United States, Peter Fonda was arrested for possession of marijuana, blurring the line between actor and social miscreant and generating much free publicity. Then, in December, the Hell's Angels attempted to sue Corman for defamation of character. The case ultimately went nowhere, although Corman did receive a few death threats from the angry bikers. The success of *The Wild Angels* is often credited with creating the biker genre that followed it.

Underground Camp

The era's queerest cinematic camp was undoubtedly located within the underground film scene, a movement of urban avant-garde film-making that often employed camp aesthetics and overtly (homo)sexual themes. By this year, Andy Warhol was arguably the best-known underground filmmaker in America; his works frequently showcased camp style and forthright depictions of homosexual behavior. However, the audience for underground films was rather limited, as the films were screened at urban cine-clubs, late night dives, and countercultural happenings rather than regular theaters. Thus, when Warhol's *Chelsea Girls,* a three-hour-plus film of side-by-side double-projected images, was released to more conventional art house theaters, it was hailed by *Newsweek* as "the *Iliad* of the underground" (Kroll). In both its form and content, *Chelsea Girls* embodies a deliberately queer campiness that constantly questions its own veracity. The film also offers a critique of violence: the violence of the Vietnam War as well as more subtle forms of violence inherent in dominant, heteronormative institutions such as the church and the nuclear family.

Chelsea Girls is shot in Warhol's signature blank style: the movie is composed of only twelve long-take shots, each one lasting the length of a reel, or a little over thirty minutes. (Since the reels are double-projected, the film lasts a little over three hours and not six.)[3] Warhol had employed this long-take style in his earlier silent and singly projected films, as well as in the *Screen Tests*, a series of cinematic portraits he was experimenting with at the same time. As in those films, Warhol's use of long takes in *Chelsea Girls* was meant to challenge the norms of Hollywood storytelling and continuity editing, as did the nature of his "actors"—frequently the junkies, transvestites, hustlers, and socialites who hung around his studio, The Factory. In a campy parody of the Hollywood star system, many of them proclaimed themselves to be Superstars and went about New York City aping the glamour and exclusivity associated with Hollywood celebrities.

Unlike most of Warhol's earlier films, *Chelsea Girls* was shot with sound, (partial) color, and a scenario—of a sort—provided by playwright Ronald Tavel. Yet in most cases, the film's "scenario" was really more of a situation than a fully realized script, one that allowed Warhol's Superstars to do what they did best: improvise as the camera rolled. This format produced a very unstable cinematic space in which campy queers like Ed Hood or Bob "Ondine" Olivio "acted" out roles and situations for the camera that may or may not have been "real." For example, we are led to believe that the performers really are shooting drugs or doing LSD, but the lines they speak appear to be improvisations based as much upon their own "real life" personas as any situation suggested by Tavel. Furthermore, offscreen voices can sometimes be heard directing the action and giving cues to the "actors," again confounding the expectations of Hollywood form. This unusual cinematic construction caused confusion and consternation among many critics. "It is a hoax," wrote *Variety*. "They are not actors, but just some uninteresting people who sit in front of a camera and talk. There is no suggestion of performance" (Hirsch).

In fact, quite the opposite is true—*everything* in the film is a self-conscious performance. Nowhere is this more apparent than in the two reels featuring Ondine, who seems to "enact" a range of characters between himself (as when he injects himself with speed) and that of his "Pope Ondine" persona, the Pope of "homosexuals . . . perverts of any kind . . . thieves . . . criminals of any sort . . . the rejected by society." Even the dialogue plays with this self-reflexive style on occasion: when the young woman whom Pope Ondine is "counseling" asks him, "What are you doing as a priest?" he quickly blurts out "Posing!" Such an exclamation underlines Ondine's performance but also suggests that all priests are themselves merely playing a role—one dependent upon the unequal power relationship of the confessional. When Ondine slaps Rona Page in the penultimate reel and becomes visibly shaken by his violence, it appears to be real; however, that violence was instigated by the assertion that he—or his act—is (note the oxymoron) a "real phony." After asking camera operator Paul Morrissey to stop filming (to no avail), Ondine resumes playing with his necklace, rinsing out his syringe with Coke, and nonchalantly telling everyone, "By the way, the *Bride of Frankenstein* [1935] is the greatest movie ever made—it's just fabulous!" It is difficult to know whether in these final moments one is watching Pope Ondine, Bob Olivio, or someone else altogether—the only thing one can say for sure is that one is experiencing the antics of a campy queer cinephile.

Other portions of the film are equally unstable in terms of their veracity, as various other actors "perform" sketches that link together several of the era's chief concerns: sex, drugs, violence, and power. For example, the "Hanoi Hannah" sequence (one of the two in the film usually credited to Ronald Tavel) features Mary Woronov as a lesbian dominatrix. Playing a sort of Oriental Dragon Lady/Tokyo Rose figure, Woronov brutalizes several young women, one of whom briefly enacts being a captured GI talking about "his" girl back home. The voluntary aspects of sadomasochistic role playing are also stressed, and by extension the scene suggests that all violence—including that of the Vietnam War—is merely a rather tired act that one might choose to put on or just as easily discard. The veracity of the scene is also placed in quotes via its positioning in the film's overall flow. An entire reel featuring many of the same performers runs on the left while Hanoi Hannah cavorts on the right, creating a meta-cinematic effect in which the performers appear to be watching themselves. (This also happens with reels nine and ten, in which Eric Emerson appears to be watching himself trip on acid.) Mary Woronov shows up again in reel eight, a "domestic scene" between a mother (played by experimental filmmaker Marie Menken) and her son (Gerard Malanga). Menken wields a whip and tells Malanga she wishes she had had an abortion, all the time questioning him on Woronov's silent, surly presence in the room. Much of this scene is juxtaposed with reel seven, in which Ed Hood as a pudgy homosexual john constantly fondles and berates his pretty-boy hustler, implicitly asking the audience to compare the violence and hierarchy in the mother/son and daddy/rent-boy relationships being depicted. Discussing politics directly, Hood refers to the "Johnson menstruation" (as opposed to the Johnson administration), bitchily noting that both are "pretty bloody, wouldn't you say?" The film ends as it began, with a reel of the terminally blank Nico staring into space.

Most mainstream critics were not amused by Warhol's campy, excessive, and overtly queer opus. Critic John Mahoney named Warhol "the greatest showman of dubious footage since Kroger Babb," the pioneering exploitation film exhibitor. Others damned it because it dared to represent forthright homosexuals, sadomasochists, and drug users. *The Hollywood Reporter* suggested (rather bitchily itself) that the film was "effected without taste, responsibility or art, but is nonetheless fascinating in the same way as paintings by parrots and chimpanzees" (Mahoney). That same review called Warhol's blank style "dangerously cynical and completely without compassion or humanity," while *Cue* suggested Warhol's style made "even perversion dull"—which was precisely one of the film's points (Wolf). Local censorship boards also were outraged by the film. A theater owner in Boston was found guilty on four obscenity counts for exhibiting it, and a print of the film was confiscated in Chicago while the FBI was called in to investigate ("Hub's Judge," "Chicago Cops"). The few reviewers that did praise the film nonetheless did so in moralistic terms. Gene Youngblood, an active chronicler of the era's experimental film scene, called it a "vision of hell," and compared it to the work of serious dramatists Jean Genet, Edward Albee, and Henry Miller. Jack Kroll in *Newsweek* also compared *Chelsea Girls* to the work of Edward Albee, precisely for the ways in which its campiness calls attention to the layers of performance that make up the "lives" of the "characters" and, by extension, that of America itself.

Conclusion

If camp was the cinematic flavor of the year, it manifested itself in a variety of ways. It appeared as deliberate pop camp in films like *Batman,* blurred into black comedy in films like *Lord Love a Duck,* and lurked around the edges of exploitation films such as *The Wild Angels.* In other, more overtly queer formations, camp sounded a forceful critique of dominant American institutions in films like *Who's Afraid of Virginia Woolf?* and *Chelsea Girls.* In the latter, camp was even used to destabilize and question the nature of cinema and reality itself, one of camp's more radical functions kept more or less muted in most other films of the year. Such varying usages of camp's deconstructive capacities also correlated to the films' broader appeals. The "safe" pop camp of *Batman* (i.e., camp that was not too critical and not too gay) allowed the film to reach mainstream as well as countercultural audiences, while the deliberately queer and deconstructive camp of *Chelsea Girls* prevented it from escaping the confines of urban art house theaters. In other instances, the campy queer critique of heteronormativity inherent in films like *Who's Afraid of Virginia Woolf?* were subsumed under the banner of "serious adult drama," laughed off in *Lord Love a Duck,* and/or dismissed as the irresponsible ravings of an exploitation film-maker, as with *The Wild Angels.* Nonetheless, regardless of its form, visibility, and/or critical potential, the many uses of camp left a strong imprint on this year's films.

NOTES

1. The homosexual implications of camp in relation to *Batman* have lasted across the decades and even affected the course of Hollywood's more recent *Batman* blockbusters: many heterosexual fans of the series disdain *Batman Forever* (1995) and *Batman and Robin* (1997)—two films made by queer director Joel Schumacher that play up the property's campy appeal—compared to their embrace of the more grimly serious and resolutely heterosexual *Batman Begins* (2005).

2. "Based on the success of the film and follow-up albums, American International Pictures is in the process of formulating a contemporary musical group to be called 'The Wild Angels.' They will be given a 'big promo buildup' similar to Screen Gems' campaign for The Monkees." A TV pilot was also in the works, presumably to feature the biker-band ("AIP 'Angels').

3. The twelve reels of *The Chelsea Girls* can theoretically be run in any order. My analysis is based on a version of the film prepared by Paul Morrissey for British television in the 1990s, available for study at the Andy Warhol Museum in Pittsburgh. The twelve reels—in brief—run as follows:

1) Nico cuts her hair in a kitchen (B&W, right screen)
2) Ondine does premarital "counseling" (B&W, left screen)
3) Brigid Berlin does drugs and discusses her life (color, right screen)
4) Ed Hood and Gerard Malanga taunt a hustler (B&W, left screen)
5) "Hanoi Hanna," lesbian S&M with Mary Woronov (B&W, right screen)
6) Continuation of (5), lesbian S&M (B&W, left screen)
7) Continuation of (4), men and women with hustler (B&W, right screen)
8) Marie Menken and Gerard Malanga play Mother and Son (color, left screen)
9) Eric Emerson grooves on himself (color, right screen)
10) People in a gallery, including Eric Emerson, watch a light show (color, left screen)
11) Pope Ondine shoots up and freaks out (B&W, right screen)
12) Nico under light show (color, left screen)

1967

Movies and the Specter of Rebellion

MURRAY POMERANCE

If history, as Todd Gitlin once reflected, "could be picked up by the scruff of the neck and made to dance" (224), this was surely a choreographic year. The Super Bowl, the Monterey Pop Festival, and the American Film Institute began; Sir Francis Chichester soloed his yacht around the world; Mickey Mantle hit his 500th homer; New York's Stork Club vanished; Che Guevara was butchered by Bolivian troops on 9 October; Dr. Christiaan Barnard performed the first heart transplant in Capetown on 3 December; Israel won a six-day war, capturing the Golan Heights from Syria, the Sinai from Egypt, and the West Bank and portions of Arab Jerusalem from Jordan; and Charles de Gaulle, visiting Montreal for Expo 67, outraged English Canadians by shouting, "Vive le Québec libre!" Readers plunged into William Styron's *The Confessions of Nat Turner,* Sue Kaufman's *The Diary of a Mad Housewife,* and Ira Levin's *Rosemary's Baby.* Theatergoers marveled at Joe Orton's *A Day in the Death of Joe Egg,* Tom Stoppard's *Rosencrantz and Guildenstern Are Dead,* and Brendan Behan's *Borstal Boy.* The musically attuned bounced to "Up, Up and Away," crooned "Ode to Billy Joe," or, as of 1 June, dreamed along with the Beatles' *Sgt. Pepper's Lonely Hearts Club Band,* arguably one of the landmark popular albums in history.

On many fronts routine was smashed as generational conflicts, antiwar protests, and race riots burgeoned. Early on Wednesday, 26 July, National Guardsmen heard shots from the vicinity of Detroit's Algiers Motel; investigating, they found ten Black males and two young white females; shortly thereafter, three of the men were brutally beaten and murdered, by forces never to be formally identified. This seemed a perfectly typical event in a summer when America's long-lived trauma of race was on everyone's mind, riots enflaming not only Detroit but 126 other cities, including Newark, Atlanta, Boston, Buffalo, Cincinnati, Tampa, Birmingham, Chicago, New York, Milwaukee, Minneapolis, New Britain, Conn., Plainfield, N.J., and Rochester, N.Y.; when it was over, seventy-seven people had died, and more than four thousand were injured. The Blacks and whites of Detroit, John Hersey wrote within the year, had long been "encroaching and elbowing and giving way to each other" (15). The Student Nonviolent Coordinating Committee's Stokely Carmichael urged Blacks to arm for "total revolution" on 17 August, two days after the Rev. Martin Luther King Jr. called for a national campaign of "massive disobedience."

Not only in racial matters were revolt, rebellion, and civil disobedience in the air. The Vietnam War had reached the point where American citizens were gathering openly to protest it, a hundred and fifty thousand persons taking to the streets of New York and San Francisco on 15 April and the same number protesting again on 21 October at the Pentagon (while Joan Baez was being arrested at the Oakland Draft Induction Center for standing up to say "No"). Lewis B. Hershey, director of the Selective Service, made it known that any antiwar demonstrator who had been arrested would lose his draft deferment. Dr. Benjamin Spock and Allen Ginsberg were arrested protesting the war in New York. "Hell no, we won't go!" young men chanted across the nation. Meanwhile, Jann Wenner premiered *Rolling Stone,* a publication that would soon become the voice of a generation, setting itself against the stuffy formalities and governmentally sanctioned tastes of the *New York Times.* Off-Broadway, *Hair* opened 29 October, celebrating youth, eroticism, drugs, and the ceremonial burning of draft cards, with a young cast stripping onstage at the end of the first act. At the finale, "Answer for Timothy Leary, dearie!" they sing deliriously, mocking middle-class America and pushing it away, it seemed, forever.

Hollywood was thriving, if traumatized: a number of early screen icons were lost—composer Franz Waxman; heart-throb Nelson Eddy; character actor Claude Rains; blonde pin-up Jayne Mansfield; Vivien Leigh, who had made Scarlett O'Hara and Blanche Dubois come alive; gaunt and menacing Basil Rathbone; bouncy and pretty Ann Sheridan; and the haunting Paul Muni. More structurally, the Production Code was in severe decline, threatened by the demands of an audience that—catered to by American filmmakers influenced in turn by European auteurs—wanted to see reality onscreen and could very easily retreat to the pervasive glow of television. As production costs of films continued to skyrocket, with some directors taking million-dollar-per-picture salaries, conglomerate financing took hold: Transamerica Corporation bought out United Artists on 11 April, and just about three months later Seven Arts took over Warner Bros. In September, Universal Newsreel ceased production, ending the pattern of newsreel projection in theaters. But through all this, almost eighteen million viewers were watching movies every week—eager for Julie Andrews,

Lee Marvin, Paul Newman, Dean Martin, Sean Connery, Elizabeth Taylor, Sidney Poitier, John Wayne, Richard Burton, and Steve McQueen—and the box office brought in just under a billion dollars. Even when a fire burned sets at Universal on 15 May, the fever of production did not abate.

Many films of the year seemed to rebel stylistically and gain dramatic effect through innovative excesses of cinematographic, directorial, writing, or performance style, while at the same time being as smoothly polished as freshly opened M&Ms. Comedy is a particularly rich genre, a powerful attraction at a time when real life is beset by racial, generational, and political strife. Audiences could choose, among many other films, Stanley Donen's *Two for the Road,* with Audrey Hepburn and Albert Finney migrating back and forth in time; Theodore J. Flicker's *The President's Analyst,* with gangly, grinning James Coburn traumatized by the constant need of his principal client for on-the-spot therapy; Val Guest and Ken Hughes's *Casino Royale,* with Peter Sellers, David Niven, *and* Woody Allen as James Bond; David Swift's *How to Succeed in Business Without Really Trying,* from the Broadway show, with toothy, boyish Robert Morse showing more vertical ambition than a mountain goat; or Jerry Lewis's *The Big Mouth,* a film whose title would be an exercise in obviousness if it did not contain *two* Jerries with twice the wackiness and twice the mouth. There were also Roman Polanski's *The Fearless Vampire Killers,* Gene Saks's *Barefoot in the Park,* and Richard Quine's film of Arthur Kopit's *Oh Dad, Poor Dad, Mama's Hung You in the Closet and I'm Feeling So Sad* (one of the longest film titles of this and many other years).

For viewers who wanted adventure or more serious fare, there were Robert Aldrich's *The Dirty Dozen,* in which Lee Marvin trains Ernest Borgnine, Charles Bronson, John Cassavetes, Robert Ryan, and eight other luminaries to work in harmony as a World War II assassination team; Lewis Gilbert's sexy James Bond classic, *You Only Live Twice,* where 007 (Sean Connery) joins up with a Tokyo ninja force to stop the weaselly Ernst Stavro Blofeld (Donald Pleasence); Richard Brooks's *In Cold Blood,* from the pioneering nonfiction novel by Truman Capote, following Perry Smith (Robert Blake) and Richard Hickock (Scott Wilson) from their failed attempt in 1959 to rob the Clutter family in rural Kansas, through their trial and imprisonment, and finally their drop through the gallows; and Terence Young's *Wait Until Dark,* which puts a blind Audrey Hepburn in the sights of thieves (the oily Alan Arkin, the creepily suave Richard Crenna) who invade her tiny apartment.

Curious new visions, or strange hallucinations, came to the screen in Jim McBride's *David Holzman's Diary,* the first "mockumentary," with audiences pondering where the reality was as a man onscreen made a movie of his own life; D. A. Pennebaker's *Dont Look Back,* a definitive look at the 1965 English tour of iconoclastic musical poet Bob Dylan; Frederick Wiseman's stunning and blatant *Titicut Follies,* a scathing portrait of the abysms of life inside a Massachusetts asylum; Richard Fleischer's fantasy musical *Doctor Doolittle,* with Rex Harrison "talking to the animals" and negotiating with a two-headed llama, the Push-Me-Pull-You; John Huston's *Reflections in a Golden Eye,* a symphony of perversity, vituperation, retaliation, nude horseback riding at night through the woods, effeminacy, adultery, nipple-slashing, and more. Mark Robson's *Valley of the Dolls,* from Jacqueline Susann's wildly popular 500-page novel, has Barbara Parkins, Sharon Tate, and Patty Duke tumbling into the subworld of pharmacological addiction, but no Judy Garland—the ultimate Hollywood rebel—who was cast but soon thrown off the set.

However, it was rebellion that the most perduringly interesting films of the year all promised to directly address. Stuart Rosenberg's *Cool Hand Luke* followed a recalcitrant antihero as he bucks the rural southern prison system. Arthur Penn's *Bonnie and Clyde* recounted the origin, development, and bloody resolution of the short but glamorous career of two charming miscreants whose regard for the social order is hilarious and disgusting at the same time. Norman Jewison's *In the Heat of the Night* explored racism and masculine bonding as North meets South in a murder investigation. Stanley Kramer's *Guess Who's Coming to Dinner* purported to editorialize on American race relations by testing the authenticity of middle-class liberal sentiment. Roger Corman, King of the B's, released *The Trip,* about a man who tries LSD in order to establish contact with his true self. And Mike Nichols's *The Graduate* worked to pose youth in rebellious confrontation with their parents through an intergenerational love affair gone strictly sour, seen against a cutting portrait of smug suburban life.

The Rebel Runs

Stuart Rosenberg worked almost exclusively in television before making *Cool Hand Luke* for Warner Bros., so it's hardly surprising to see him using the cinematic frame principally for containing and isolating a space in which dramatic performance can be played out. The compositions are static but engaging, and the weight of the film rests on meticulous casting and startling performance. Cinematographer Conrad Hall has a preference, here and elsewhere, for light over movement, so the scene is always magnificent in its shabby, dusty, cruelly soft color. In a sense, we are trapped in a prison camp in the 1930s just like Lucas Jackson (Paul Newman), who committed the infraction—labeled as a VIOLATION by a glowing full-screen sign that is the first shot of the film—of sawing off parking meter heads in a public lot in his town. Now for two years he is subject to the perverse discipline of the Captain (Strother Martin), a fey and lisping, not to say dandified, planter manqué—who can be a "nice guy" or a "real mean s'uva'bitch!"—and his crew of stiff-backed, taciturn goons who patrol the camp with rifles and grim-jawed stares. Among the other prisoners is the garrulous, dominating "good ole boy," Dragline (George Kennedy), with whom Luke plays out a typical Hollywood boy-meets-boy scenario that moves from alienation through hesitant testing through a demonstration of strength and ultimate bonding. The two end up as soulmates, Dragline seeing in Luke an "almost existential defiance" (Lax 118), an indomitable spirit and humor, a purist rebel attitude that coolly dismisses the camp, the Captain, the social order to which this punishment is dedicated, and the folly of human desire. When Luke tries twice to escape and is subjected to debasing punishment by the guards, we feel that it is Dragline's unwavering fixation upon him and unremitting sense of loyalty that pull Luke through. For the chaste love of Luke, indeed, Dragline overcomes his fear of the Captain and jumps to join Luke in a third escape attempt, which ends with the two men cornered and Luke shot.

The prison bunkhouse is managed by a chubby, cigar-chomping capo, Carr (Clifton James), whose introductory invocation of the house rules beautifully encapsulates the sense of debilitating and invasive social anxiety about order that this film reflects. This camp is the last bastion of a world obsessed with putting everything in its place, controlling every impulse, correcting every deviation, profiting upon every exertion and every drop of sweat. Carr is pacing up and down between the bunk beds, looking at nothing, intoning by rote:

> Them clothes got laundry numbers on 'em you remember your number and always wear the ones that has your number any man forgets his number spends a night in the box. These here spoons you keep with ya [spoons clatter to floor], any man loses his spoon spends a night in the box. There's no playin' grab-ass or fightin' 'n the buildin,' you gotta grudge against another man you fight 'im Saturday afternoon, any man playin' grab-ass or fightin' 'n the buildin' spends a night in the box. First bell is at five minutes of eight, you get into a bunk, last bell is at eight. Any man not in his bunk at eight spends a night in the box. There's no smokin' in the prone position in bed, to smoke you must have both legs over the side o' yo' bunk any man caught smokin' in the prone position in bed spends a night in the box. . . . No one will sit in the bunks with dirty pants on, any man with dirty pants on sittin'

on a bunk spends a night in the box. Any man don't bring back his empty pop bottle spends a night in the box. Any man loud-talkin' spends a night in the box. . . .

By now, most of the inmates have yielded to the absolute oppressiveness expressed by Carr's unyielding rhythm. Dragline, principal among them, hates it, but he has swallowed it, given up his soul. What is charming about Luke is that his soul is still, apparently, his own.

Cool Hand Luke thus functions as a textbook illustration of the systematic repression of healthy animal instinct and vivacity (in what is clearly just an overgrown boy) by a ressentient system committed to brutalization, planning, and control. This system was the banking, government, big business, and the military-industrial complex of LBJ's America, that young people and antiwar and antiracist protesters were trying to confront with derision, withdrawal, mockery, abandon, delirium, and denial. Luke therefore represented onscreen a vision of the oppositional personality in full blossom: smiling in his agony, always moving himself forward to (even momentary) freedom, he epitomized in a pure and nondenominational form the sacred creed to which so many people were pledging themselves. But did Cool Hand Luke, as Dragline affectionately tags him, actually personify a rebel spirit at the story's conclusion?

In two ways the film seemed, even as it screened, to sell out. First, symbolically. Luke bets that he can eat fifty eggs within an hour, and soon Dragline has organized the bookmaking and taken money from everyone. Methodically he starts popping hard-cooked eggs into Luke's mouth, and in a montage sequence this proceeds for several minutes from one camera angle to another as Luke's belly starts to swell and he becomes nauseated. With two seconds to go, and Luke supine on a table, the final egg is slipped between his lips. Then Rosenberg and his editor Sam O'Steen cut to a shot looking down from above on the satiated and bloated, half-nude, glistening body, the arms hanging out and the ankles beatifically crossed. "Newman really looks like he's on the crucifix, even his ankles are crossed," O'Steen wrote. "But Rosenberg was into that kind of stuff" (52). Luke's sustained show of personal strength and courage, then, wraps up as an homage to codified, state-sanctioned religious iconography, the furthest thing from rebellion. By contrast, toward the end of the film, and just before he is shot, Luke is alone in a chapel talking to God. "Old man," he calls him, in a casual, sweet, unaffected tone completely at odds with the conventionalized and rather formal image of him as a Christ.

But the actual finale of the film is even more compromising. Originally Rosenberg had Luke being driven off with the Captain to the prison hospital

Because director Stuart Rosenberg was unsatisfied with the original ending of *Cool Hand Luke* (Warner Bros.), he tacked on an upbeat ending that would reprise the protagonist's (and Paul Newman's) trademark smile. Digital frame enlargement.

an hour away, a wan smile on his face, blood streaming from the bullet wound in his neck. Clearly, he wouldn't make it. He'd been slaughtered, sacrificed by a system that never tolerated his passion for liberty (a system, in effect, that had surrendered its own idea of America). "We gotta have a happy ending," said Rosenberg, telling O'Steen to cull all the moments when Newman smiled (53). He shot a new scene, with Dragline telling the cons how he fondly remembers that "Luke smile," to which we now cut, smile after smile after smile, as though everything is somehow all right. After a film that exploits an eccentric man's search for liberty against insuperable odds, delving in the most painful close-ups into fractions of his moments of struggle, we are left with only a sugary resolution. Luke is less what Bosley Crowther called him, "a fugitive not only from the chain gang, but also from society, and, indeed, from life" ("Forceful"), than a mask Paul Newman wore over that trademark marquee smile that keeps shining after everything else has faded.

A very different experience of the rebel criminal awaits in *Bonnie and Clyde*, a film Roger Ebert called "a milestone in the history of American movies, a work of truth and brilliance . . . pitilessly cruel, filled with sympathy, nauseating, funny, heartbreaking, and astonishingly beautiful" ("Bonnie"). We emerge spattered with metaphorical blood and riddled with wounds that were not only narrational (spurred, in part, by editor Dede Allen's half-dissolves matched to slash cuts) but also emotional. After all, "the film stood," as Lester D. Friedman reminds us, "at a profoundly significant cultural crossroads: a point where American values veered from a comfortable fifties' mentality to a more complicated reconfiguration of the world; where the old Hollywood system cracked under the impact of new ideas and technologies; . . . where film became as intellectually legitimate as literature and painting" (3).

The real Clyde Barrow and Bonnie Parker died in a hail of bullets about fifty miles east of Shreveport, Louisiana, on 23 May 1934. They were twenty-four years old and had spent some three years rampaging the Texas countryside in the commission of small, but violent, bank robberies. The film versions (Warren Beatty, Faye Dunaway) seem a little older, Bonnie composed and vixenish even in her expression of desire, sexual and other- wise, and Clyde a man whose ambition shows no timidity or rawness for all his emotional immaturity. Within minutes of meeting Clyde, Bonnie dares him to commit an armed robbery, which he does. Off they scoot in his jalopy, to the happy, bouncy backwoods plunking of Flatt and Scruggs, their rebel career, and their love affair, off and running. A swank lothario by all accounts, Clyde turns out to be "not much of a lover boy," which is to say, for all intents and purposes impotent, to Bonnie's abject dismay. But he per- suades her that she is the best girl in Texas, and his respect and genuine devotion win her over. Soon enough they have formed a gang of five with C. W. Moss (Michael J. Pollard), a loyal but dimwitted gas station attendant, Clyde's vociferous brother, Buck (Gene Hackman, who steals the film), and Buck's squealing, sanctimonious wife, Blanche (Estelle Parsons, in a per- formance that is magnificently developed and turned). Running from the law, these outcasts—each of them a study in white trash—land in motel after motel, their safe havens continually busted up by police. Buck is killed, Blanche captured, C.W. sold out by his father (Dub Taylor) to the Texas Rangers for setting up Bonnie and Clyde's execution. "At the time," writes Beatty's biographer Suzanne Munshower, "the graphic depiction of Blanche Barrow receiving a bullet in her eye, Buck getting the top of his head blown off, and Parker and Barrow writhing in slow-motion balletic grace as they are riddled with bullets was enough to shock all but the most jaded audiences" (63). The story, by David Newman, Robert Benton, and Robert Towne, moves gently and inexorably to its gruesome conclusion, with Burnett Guffey's appropriately dusty Technicolor cinematography, Dean Tavoularis's carefully designed 1930s Texas (all dry desperation and poverty), and Theadora Van Runkle's costumes seizing the eye throughout. (Women across the country rushed to imitate Bonnie's beret just as Bonnie, tickled by watching *Gold Diggers of 1933* with Clyde and C.W., ran home to jangle a golden coin-studded necklace around her neck.)

In a number of ways *Bonnie and Clyde* sets up, then contradicts, an argu- ment for rebellion against the system. For example, Bonnie Parker is played by Dunaway ("to the majority of filmgoers . . . an unknown commodity unhampered by associations with past performances" [Hunter 43])—as one of the first, perhaps *the* first, blatantly sexually hungry females in American film. The film opens on her lustful mouth, and we quickly see her naked in bed, twisting and turning with burning frustration, then, naked in a window, calling down to Clyde in an inverted vision of Juliet and Romeo. Within a minute she is bouncing into his company, and soon afterward he has to push her off to save himself from her touches. Far from a possessive, domineering, and devouring maternal, or a sensitive, cultured, and restrained princess, this hungry heroine stands on the wrong side of not only the law but also conventional proprieties of femaleness. When she meets the prurient Blanche, she is revolted by the woman's faux-bourgeois sentimentalities and self-absorption. In wanting to have everything, and to have it now, she is a harbinger of the liberated, desirous female, someone who wanted the body that Clyde Barrow's (and Warren Beatty's) appearance continually promised to give. But Bonnie doesn't actually get much in *Bonnie and Clyde*. "When we started out," she says when things have turned sour, "I thought we was really goin' *somewhere*, but this is it. We're just goin,' huh." Her passion involuted, her drive made dissolute, her energy and hope for an adventurous future are eaten away by a series of tawdry small robberies and desperate flights—"what you get," the film might be taken to say, "for makin' whoopee."

Several times Clyde tries unsuccessfully, with mounting desperation, to make love to Bonnie, finally succeeding "perfectly." But this resolution of his sexual blockage and Bonnie's hunger tends to posit a sexual, rather than a moral, motive for the crime spree. Instead of being a rebel, he was only a horny young man whom Bonnie joined only out of lust. A contrasting motive is suggested much earlier, as, having spent a night in an abandoned house, Bonnie and Clyde awake to find a family of farmers who have stopped on their migration across the country. The husband informs Clyde that this was his place, but the bank foreclosed on him and threw him out. In the style of the Depression-era photography of Dorothea Lange, the abject, proud family is made heroic by their dignified posture and silence in the face of disaster. Clyde, who is holding a pistol because he has been teaching Bonnie marksmanship, takes a few shots at the sign the bank has nailed in front of the house, informing the farmer that he robs banks. He hands the gun over so the man, and then his hired hand, can get satisfaction, too. Here it seems evident that Clyde has made a willful decision to stand outside the system sanctified and represented by the bank, to become the avenger who can set things straight for America or at least strive to uphold values beyond the shabby inconsiderateness banks exemplify and work to spread. If, by the time he dies at the end, Clyde has become only a pent-up kid who has finally achieved release, then what was it all for, really? Pollard mused, "In [the original script] Bonnie was a nymphomaniac, Clyde was a homosexual transvestite. . . . I [playing C.W.] was supposed to have been picked up to keep 'em both happy. Warner Brothers decided to clean it up. . . . Maybe Warner's were right, but with the original script it's for certain none of us would have come out as heroes" (Hunter 54), and it seems clear that none of them do. The heroism in rebellion is in gaining distance from the system, not in capitulating to it by demonstrating that one can have normal sex.

Clyde's flight from abnormality and deficiency thus taints what could have been a greater, more responsible, motive. Even as, in a deliriously simple moment, they steal their first car, these two are stepping up in the world, gaining the status their crime spree will pretend to decry: it's a *better*, more expensive, car. Clyde takes possession boldly. "That's not our car," says Bonnie in surprise. "It is now," says he. As they disappear down the road, we have time to reflect that the nobility of taking what is there for the taking and leaving what one doesn't need behind is not what this theft is about. Bonnie and Clyde are social climbers, plain and simple.

The Rebel Yells

The "hot night" of *In the Heat of the Night* is many nights at once: one sweltering spate of time, in which a young white woman in a racist southern town takes pleasure in walking around her house naked, seduces a local young man, and gets pregnant; all the nights during which the story takes place, as police search for a murderer under pressure of time; and the long, dark, seemingly hopeless nightmare of American racism, an infernal and utterly unilluminated zone of hatred and fear from which it seems white consciousness will never emerge. The story of the film is fairly simple. Virgil Tibbs (Sidney Poitier) is visiting the town of Sparta and is taken in as a murder suspect; when Police Chief Gillespie (Rod Steiger) finds out that he is a homicide investigator from Philadelphia, Virgil is asked to assist in the case. Working beside Gillespie begins as a defensive standoff, since if Gillespie has no time for Blacks, and no patience with this superior from the North who knows more than southern sheriffs do about cadavers, murder techniques, evidence, and, it seems, hatred, Tibbs has no tolerance for intolerance. But slowly the two men eat away at one another's brittle exteriors and develop a *modus vivendi*. Tibbs manages to show Gillespie how the murder was done and, ultimately, who did it, but not before substantial grief, upheaval, and bloodshed mar the town. Photographed by Haskell Wexler in rich color, especially in the night sequences, *Heat* positions racial antagonism at the crux of every scene, always tipping us toward an explosive point and suspending us just before the explosion comes.

The film posits Virgil as a rebel in the racial standoff in America. He is above petty injustice and loathing, he is educated, he is a professional with dignity and stature (no actor in America had more physical poise or more dignity on camera than Poitier). But its well-meaning confrontations with racism do not amount to a remedy for a complex problem, and in the end Virgil is a mythic, not a real, rebel, no more capable of redeeming or transcending his social world than Luke Jackson or Bonnie and Clyde are. The racial tension that was boiling over in America this year was not about man-to-man confrontations, not a matter of Gillespies barking insidiously at Tibbses and hearing them bark right back. One key scene idealizes racial rebellion magnificently, but also reveals the film's limits in giving Virgil space for rebellion. The leading citizen of the town is Eric Endicott (Larry Gates), owner of a cotton plantation and a man with an orchid fetish. Tibbs and Gillespie visit him and he has his Black servant fetch a pitcher of lemonade. Paternalistically he walks Tibbs around the hothouse, where white, pink, and golden orchids are crammed together in the cloying sunlight. He admires Tibbs's choice of a favorite orchid that, he says arrogantly, "like the Negro," needs much care and attention and must develop "slowly." But when Gates realizes that the men have driven up to question him about the murder, he is outraged by what he takes to be Tibbs's impertinence and slaps him soundly on the face. Instantly, Tibbs slaps back. "This was," Norman Jewison later asserted, "the first time in an American movie that a Black man had slapped a white man back, and that fact added to the shock of the scene" (Jewison 143). As Endicott informs Tibbs that in times past he could have had him shot on sight, Tibbs gives off a stare that could kill and stomps out, with the servant shaking his head sympathetically as though to apologize for this "boy" who doesn't understand his real place in life. Tibbs's reaction here—his slow, silent gaze as he drinks in Endicott's decadence, his measured politeness, his unthinking reflex reaction to the slap—seem to add up to a sermon on equality: don't be superior, be the same. But finally, even such an elegant moment is dissolved by the story: Endicott is innocent, and Tibbs has to admit to personal animosity. The plantation mentality Endicott has kept alive is utterly gone from Tibbs's world.

Yet not from Gillespie's. As they take a morning drive through the cotton fields to Endicott's house (Ray Charles singing "In the Heat of the

Virgil Tibbs (Sidney Poitier) is not pleased to be reminded that cotton picking is beneath his station in *In the Heat of the Night* (Norman Jewison, Mirisch—United Artists). Digital frame enlargement.

Night" on the sound track), we see the world that Tibbs's birth and education have permitted him to eclipse: hands grasping cotton, African Americans laboring in the vast fields, Black children jumping up and down merrily on the cotton truck. Clearly, Tibbs is fully conscious of having grown beyond the ugly history this place represents. Yet, emphatically, Gillespie taunts him: "None a' that fer you, uh, Virgil!" Tibbs's slapping Endicott on the face was a way for the Hollywood Left to symbolically show allegiance to the concerns of Black America while at the same time holding back from depicting real confrontation: Poitier, in his natty gray suit and striped tie, is hardly getting into a real tangle with the plantation owner, nor is he addressing the laws and policies that make Endicott's entrenched racism so stable. Tibbs, indeed, has no real confrontations in this film: threatened by virulent crackers, he is saved by Gillespie or his own quick wit. The film manages to screen the look of rebellion and confrontation without engaging its protagonist in the real thing.

Gillespie—described by Steiger as "a most difficult character who was reticent to the point of hiding out in himself" (Hutchinson 127)—finally softens enough to have Tibbs over to his sanctum, something of a first: "You know, Virgil, you are among the chosen few. You are the first human being that's ever been in here." Thus, what began as the cold, impenetrable façade of racist division is transmuted—by Virgil's persistence and professionalism? by his gracefulness? by his authenticity?—to at least the beginning of a beautiful friendship. Gillespie takes him to the train, even carrying his bag, and the two part with smiles of acceptance on their faces.

While *In the Heat of the Night* puts southern white racism squarely in our sights, it permits us to swiftly escape it: into the energy of a police investigation, into the lascivious mystery of sexuality, into the formula of male bonding, and finally, in a helicopter shot, away from the South and the train that is evacuating Tibbs. Bosley Crowther's gushing rave, "It is most appropriate and gratifying to see Mr. Poitier coming out at this moment of crisis in racial affairs in a film which impressively presents him as a splendid exponent of his race" (qtd. in Goudsouzian 271), was no description of the real "crisis" in the South. In one scene, Tibbs is refused service in a diner and thus doesn't get a luscious-looking piece of lemon meringue pie—the worst that happens to him in this film.

Four months later, Poitier galvanized audiences again. In the "delightfully acted and gracefully entertaining" *Guess Who's Coming to Dinner* (Crowther "'Guess'"), he plays Dr. John Wade Prentice, an epitome of the human condition: a graduate maxima cum laude Johns Hopkins, he has been on the teaching faculty at Yale and the London School of Tropical Medicine and assistant director of the World Health Organization, has written two textbooks, and is heading a phenomenal new experiment in which, with a caravan of well-equipped trucks and a thousand adopted medical assistants, he has a plan to save millions of lives. He has fallen madly in love with Joanna Drayton (Katharine Houghton), who "happens not to be a colored girl." She is, indeed, a princess of the San Francisco bourgeoisie. The two have flown home to seek her parents' consent and plan after dinner to head off to marriage. Joanna is all no-nonsense purposiveness, determination, and bubbling enthusiasm, precisely as one would expect from the daughter of a woman played by Katharine Hepburn. Her father (Spencer Tracy, in his final role: he would die three weeks after shooting wrapped) owns a liberal newspaper and has for decades been the quintessence of white liberal conscience in the Bay area. Since the film begins with the revelation of the love these two young people have for one another, and promises their marriage, the dramatic suspense derives wholly from our doubts as to whether the wedding will in fact take place, entrapped as the characters are, and as were audiences at the time, in a culture of racist resentment and divisiveness. Can such a love as this really triumph?

The film presents no entrancing visions and vistas but is satisfied to concentrate on the electric performance of Poitier and on the rebirth of the Hepburn-Tracy marital struggle as exploited by George Cukor in *Woman of the Year* (1942) and *Adam's Rib* (1949). It is both saddening and strangely encouraging to watch these two icons of the American screen still working intensively, she with her Parkinsonian tremors beginning to show and he clearly in agony from emphysema, his eyes often glazed but his spirit ferocious. Christina and Matt have been set up for us by their daughter's advance publicity as paragons of liberal thought and attitude, so our initial trepidation comes at the realization that John's parents, a retired postal worker and his loyal wife (Roy E. Glenn, Beah Richards), with conventional attitudes toward race, do not yet know that their future daughter-in-law is white. There is, however, a virtual gauntlet of institutional barriers set in place by Stanley Kramer and screenwriter William Rose, and for all their devotion John and Joanna give us every fear that the affections of two isolated individuals will hardly serve as support while they run it.

First, Christina, whose initial reaction is shock but whom Joanna's ebullience and certitude win over, is a dutiful, not a rebellious, wife. Seeing that her husband is far from eager for this marriage to take place, indeed, that he intends to refuse his assent (and thus doom the couple, because John has promised Matt secretly that the wedding is off if he does not unreservedly give a blessing), she holds back from contradicting him in public. As an institution, the Drayton marriage is male-dominated, and Tracy's intelligent bluster, even in obvious physical decline, is precisely the cue that reveals this. Joey thus has a romantic but ultimately powerless mother and a father whose public positions and private sentiments are in conflict. Further, Christina operates in a social circle typified by Hilary (Virginia Christie), her wealthy gallery assistant and a harridan openly scathed by John and Joey's romance and outraged at the prospect they might wed. Christina must now fire her, and this she does in a punchy little speech outside the Drayton house; yet, we may wonder, who will operate the gallery now, and how easy will it be for Christina to find in this cloistered community another colleague whose attitudes toward race are less offensive? Loathsome as she is, Hilary hardly represents only herself. She is one of the "hundreds of millions of people," as Matt explains to John, who will resent and reject this match. John's mother is devoted to him and to his happiness, and, like Christina, wants to see the marriage succeed, although her initial reaction is shocked mortification. The father is enraged because his son does not realize what duty he has to the past, until John explodes at him, "You and your whole lousy generation believe the way it was for you is the way it's *got* to be, and not until your whole generation has lain down and died will the dead weight of you be off our backs! . . . You see yourself as a *black man*. I see myself as a man." The maid, Tilly (Isabel Sanford), resents John's uppityness and privately castigates him for having ideas above his station (recalling the attitude of Endicott's sympathetic manservant in *Heat of the*

Night). The very close family friend, Monsignor Mike Ryan (Cecil Kell-away), is all leprechaunish effervescence and sanctimonious charm, seeing in John and Joanna a vision of spiritual triumph over a dark evil that has too long held America in thrall; but his is a false position, a sweetened personal reaction rather than a projection of his institutional role. This institutional role and its impotence are clearer in the film's conclusion, when Matt seems on the point of destroying the lovers and Mike can only sit mutely in private despair. On racism, the church has officially nothing to say; much as the wives, mutely praying for a happy ending, have no formal voice against their husbands in public.

To be sure, the movie has its happy ending—which is to say, the ending the audience has been waiting for since the opening shot—but it is a resolution that does not address the racial riots in the streets outside the theater, or the long history of repression represented by those vast cotton fields through which Gillespie and Tibbs so serenely drive. Matt changes his mind! How, or why, we never learn. Kramer said in a Toronto press conference a few years afterward that he had designed the architecture of the film so that the obstacle to the marriage could be nothing other than race. What else could have been the problem? That John was irresponsible, immature, poorly bred, inarticulate, not committed to public service, not heroic, not a model of good looks, not passionate about Joanna, not brilliant and well educated, not a man of means in his own right? Only that he was Black. Kramer was gambling on his audience: that seeing Joanna and John together they could instantly wish for the happy resolution of this interracial love, rather than reacting against it as Hilary and Tilly do. He was right. On a four-million dollar investment, the film made seventy million dollars worldwide. Yet, from the start, *Guess* had never been intended to be serious politics. Meeting Poitier at the Russian Tea Room to sign him, Kramer had been frank that he had no actual revolution in mind: "The picture would be something less than honest social drama, instead presenting a light plea for tolerance" (Goudsouzian 278). It is not only John's father who must be lifted off his back, it is the entire complex institution of racial prejudice in America. How, precisely, that is supposed to "die" and disappear the film cannot bring itself to suggest.

The Rebel Withdraws

"A. A violent order is a disorder," Wallace Stevens wrote in 1942, and "B. A great disorder is an order" ("Connoisseur of Chaos"). If the first side of this equation neatly describes the social world portrayed in *Cool*

Hand Luke and *In the Heat of the Night*, and the second describes what we see in *Bonnie and Clyde* and *Guess Who's Coming to Dinner*, then in *The Trip* the relationship between order and disorder is entirely less clear, the nuances of rebellion harder to make out against a constantly fragmented world of waking dreams and nightmares. Roger Corman's motive for this film was to use a script by Jack Nicholson to dramatize the experience of taking lysergic acid diethylamide in a way as personal, subjective, optically enhanced, and "realistic" as was possible onscreen. "Corman was never slow to jump on a trend," writes Scott von Doviak, "so it's no surprise that he was first out of the gate when the LSD craze hit." It is fairly safe to assume that most of the eight million people who went to see this colorful bit of nonsense were humming "Lucy in the Sky with Diamonds" before, during, or after the experience. Smooth and silky Paul (Peter Fonda), a director of tacky television commercials on the brink of a divorce from the haunting Sally (Susan Strasberg), goes with his cheery, bearded friend John (Bruce Dern) to slimy Max's (Dennis Hopper) hippie drug den high in the Los Angeles hills and pops some acid. A copy of Allen Ginsberg's *Howl* is prominent on a bookshelf. We follow him as he rides the Roller Coaster of the Self, into a sexual liaison with Glenn (Salli Sachse) (Bob Beck and Allen Daviau's psychedelic slide show superimposed on their naked writhing bodies), an orgasmically mind-blowing meditation upon an orange as the center of life in the universe, a paranoiac freak-out in the swimming pool (with John yanking Paul out naked and gasping), a series of dream flights from two hooded horsemen, an off-beat encounter with a woman in a laundromat, and finally an escape from the Los Angeles Police Department that, he is convinced, is out to get him. This finale is cut as a mosaic of quick vérité shots interlarded with symbols, colored flashes, photographs, and graphics, as though the world has come apart into its constituent elements, which jam his consciousness. Paul wakes in the morning safe with Glenn, stares off into the sky, and the trip is over.

The dialogue is written to be evocative, not suggestive. There is no "point," no "meaning" to this film, but one gets a fairly accurate sense of the kinds of thought patterns and linkages made by trippers, at least at the time. One of the dominant popular aesthetic forces was the commercial graphic design of Peter Max, who used bold shapes and primary colors that would be stimulating to those on drugs but innocuous for straights who would choose his posters to decorate offices and waiting rooms. The influence of Max is visible in Leon Ericksen's design for the film—the aerie where Paul starts his trip is decorated with translucent banners over the windows and gaudy furniture around the interior/exterior turquoise pool. It is entirely indeterminate whether for most, or even many, who took LSD under the influence of Timothy Leary's philosophy at this time the experience really did maximize color sensibility in quite so concrete a way as Max's art and Ericksen's design continually suggest. Shapes did not necessarily twist and melt, colors did not always bleed into the environment; but the film does give a chilling sense of the way realistic everyday perception merged with fantasy. There are moments for Paul when it is difficult to tell whether he is fantasizing or not, the strongest of these being effected in conversations with John where John cannot quite make out how to resolve the ambiguities in what Paul is saying in his "realizations." "It's really like that!" Paul shrieks happily, looking at the most mundane objects, and John has, of course, no inkling of what he is seeing or thinking.

There is only one scene where the real quality of rebellion associated with drug-taking in the 1960s is fully realized. Being involved with a drug experience, we must remember, was a way of setting oneself—temporarily, and within the boundaries of one's social group at the time—apart from the society at large, migrating, as it were, into a purely conceptual space that left the cultural constraints of society far, and dimly, behind. Paul is wandering the neighborhood and walks into a house nearby. He turns on the television (which is broadcasting a delicious lime green static). Soon enough, a little girl (Caren Bernsen) walks down the stairs. "Who are you?" He raises his finger to his lips. "I'm just a man." She approaches, "What do you want?" With earnestness: "I'm resting . . . OK?" She asks for a glass of milk and with gentleness and civility he gives her his hand and lets her lead him to the kitchen. In a shockingly sensitive moment, where Fonda shows a great honesty in performance, Paul quickly smells the milk before pouring it for the kid—not to add to the sensuality of his tripping experience but to guard her health. "Where's my daddy?" she asks, and Paul says forthrightly, looking into her eyes, "He's upstairs asleep. Shall we go sit down?" When they are back in front of the television, the father comes down hastily and barks, "What are you doin' here!" Paul runs out. In this scene we see the clearest, and most challenging, separation between Paul's state of being and the bourgeois interior through which he moves as though it were an entirely foreign environment: the copper double-boiler on the stove, the plush furniture around the television, the food in the fridge, all entirely alien to him. He becomes a model rebel at this point, detached, peaceful, showing a different way of living life but respecting those with whom he comes in contact, the person for whom conventional life has become, at least temporarily and magically, strange.

Sniffing in *The Trip:* the tripper (Peter Fonda) pauses for assurance that the milk is fresh (Roger Corman, American International Pictures). Digital frame enlargement.

However, the film never really intends to support the tension produced in this scene. Over the final shot—Paul staring into the sky—a montage of broken glass is superimposed, as though to say, "Now he is fractured, wounded, damaged forever. Warning to all." Even at the beginning, right after the MGM trademark, a disclaimer appeared (and was read in voice-over)—a convention in exploitation films, although this could hardly be seen to be one. It predicted exactly such a problematic conclusion:

> You are about to be involved in a most unusual motion picture experience.
>
> It deals fictionally with the hallucinogenic drug, LSD.
>
> Today, the extensive use in black market production of this and other such "mind-bending" chemicals is of great concern to medical and civil authorities.
>
> The illegal manufacture and distribution of these drugs is dangerous and can have fatal consequences. Many have been hospitalized as a result.
>
> This picture represents a shocking commentary on a prevalent trend of our time and one that must be of great concern to all.

Yet is Paul fractured forever? And is his use of LSD "of great concern" to authorities? What we see in him is a discovery of the self, a realization of the importance of his actions by the man committing them, and a strong devotion to weaving oneself into a social scene that is inherently alienating to all of us. *The Trip* denies the rebellion that it offers.

The Graduate put its protagonist on a different kind of trip, promising a less temporary and more complex rebellion but failing to deliver it all the same. For a number of reasons—a stunningly acerbic script by Buck Henry, often shocking or hilarious editing by Sam O'Steen, explosive performances—*The Graduate* stunned audiences when it was released 21 December and has continued to stun them for years. This was not the first screen performance by Dustin Hoffman, but it was certainly his first moment of recognition—he was received as a stellar talent who had arrived overnight. Anne Bancroft had already established herself as a character player of supreme talent and polish, but her Mrs. Robinson, a seething cauldron of bitchy sophistication and pathetic loneliness, remains iconic. Hoffman plays Benjamin Braddock, just now graduated from college and ready for the "real world" into which his parents (William Daniels and Elizabeth Wilson), fussing neurotically over their fledgling, cannot wait to thrust him so that his successes may redound to their credit. At the graduation party, Ben has been explaining to his father that he is worried about his future, that he wants it to be "different." Now, mauled by his parents' friends: touched and retouched, having lipstick planted on his cheek, questioned, turned into the butt of expectations, he is victim to a tall and very serious man who comes upon him from behind:

> *McGuire:* Ben!
>
> *Ben:* Mr. McGuire!
>
> *McGuire:* Ben!
>
> *Ben:* Mr. McGuire.
>
> *McGuire:* Come with me for a minute. I want to talk to you. . . .
>
> *McGuire* (outside on the patio, with his hand on Ben's shoulder): I just want to say one word to you. . . . Just . . . one word.
>
> *Ben* (nodding): Yes, sir?
>
> *McGuire* (with gravity): Are you listening?
>
> *Ben:* Yes, I am.
>
> *McGuire:* Plastics.

There is a great future for Ben in plastics, if not just in getting girls, or zipping around in his new Alfa Romeo, but he is looking for an altogether new kind of future, one that will take him beyond the orbit that has been established by his father. His rebellion is thus self-creation, the making of a man no one imagines or anticipates—especially his parents, who have attempted to prepare him for everything, and to prepare themselves for his every move. In a later scene, the Braddocks insist that Ben show off his new scuba equipment to some intimate friends. As he steps out to the pool area, harpoon in hand, we cut to a position from his mental as well as physical perspective, as it were, seeing through the oval of his mask and hearing bubbling sounds from his breathing apparatus. In mime, we see the parents and their friends, all grins, urging him into the water. When he finally goes under there is no prize at all, just space, so he tries to emerge. But mom and dad reach down toward the lens and push him back—away from their world, or his own. Working with a number of professionals so early in his career made Hoffman something of a Braddock himself—pressured, confined, bottled up. "During the first three weeks of filming, Dustin was unsettled and self-conscious," writes Jeff Lenburg. "One problem was the fact that for the first time he was playing a character close to his own: a very shy, intelligent, not very articulate boy trying to be polite, trying to be honorable, trying not to lie" (23).

From his horrifying, self-contained cyst, he is ultimately rescued by the sordid sexual persistence of the lascivious and "very neurotic" Mrs. Robinson (whose husband [Murray Hamilton] is his father's business partner). If an early attempt to seduce him in her daughter's bedroom was doomed to failure—"Oh, my Christ!" cries he, drowning again—she finally has him cornered, clumsy as an untrained puppy, trying to kiss her when her mouth is full of cigarette smoke, unable to dislodge a hotel room hanger for her leopard-skin coat. He fears he'll never manage the sex: "For God's sake, can you imagine my parents?" Mrs. Robinson realizes he's a virgin, mouthing a single word, "inadequate," that seems sufficient to overcome his legion inhibitions. Afterward, as in their "Sounds of Silence" Simon and Garfunkel remind us that "the words of the prophets are written on the subway walls and tenement halls," we watch him in his pool, floating, relaxed, ascendant. And then, over "April, Come She Will," we see the two settling into a boring pattern, even taking their liaisons as humdrum, the lyric "A love once young has now grown old" summarizing this condition. "I don't think we have much to say to each other," she says, by way of diagnosis.

Mrs. Robinson having initiated Ben into the mystery of sex, he is ready for a girlfriend: her daughter, Elaine (Katharine Ross), although his teacher has nothing if not an entirely negative view: "Benjamin, don't you ever . . . take that girl out." The bond is broken, and Ben starts dating Elaine. But Mrs. Robinson warns him that to keep Elaine away from him she is "prepared to tell her everything." He runs to confront Elaine, to somehow confess himself. She is mortified and throws him out. As summer changes to fall, she goes back to Berkeley and he despairs (in a montage over "Parsley, Sage, Rosemary, and Thyme"), then decides he will find her in Berkeley and marry her, although "to be perfectly honest, she doesn't like me." He haunts the campus, surveilling her from a distance. When she confronts him and accuses him of raping her mother, he tells her what really happened. She warms to his sweetness and finally agrees that she might marry him. Whistling "Mrs. Robinson," he excitedly buys a ring. But in his rented room, Mr. Robinson waits in anger, calling him "filthy" and a "degenerate"; he is never to see Elaine again. He tries to find her at home in Los Angeles; her mother mentions a wedding. Racing back to Berkeley, he is told she is to be married to a medical student in Santa Barbara. Panting, desperate, he barges in to interrupt the ceremony. His run up to the church is a now-classical shot made in extreme telephoto, with the frantic Benjamin seeming to be covering no ground at all as he dashes toward the camera. Finally, having disrupted the ceremony, and with Elaine by his side, he uses a crucifix to fight off the Robinsons and the groom and retreats with his love to a city bus, where they ride off to their happily-ever-after future.

Ben's is to be, after all is said and done, a conventional, even a bourgeois, future. Rebelling against his parents and against the Robinsons as archetypes of bourgeois society, he has become, in the end, only one of them. After all, he is the flustered male with the girl in the bride's gown: they're as married as his parents, or perhaps as married as hers. What *The Graduate* promises is a break from convention, "elegant self-mockery" in its "plethora of sight gags" (Friedenberg); a gear shift away from the everyday. This it delivers in terms of production values but not in its plot, which finally, like so many other plots, spells a heteronormative love triumphing over every obstacle to achieve blissful harmony and nothing more. Was it really this and only this, we must wonder, that Ben's important education was preparing him for?

For all the glamorous promise of newness and unconventionality that illuminates their screen presence, neither hungry Benjamin Braddock nor tripping Paul Grove; neither the shining Dr. John Wade Prentice nor the snippy but brilliant Virgil Tibbs; neither Cool Hand Luke, with his unwavering smile, nor the insouciant and unruly Bonnie and Clyde really demonstrate success in detaching themselves from their social worlds. They do not, we may lament, transcend or change America in ways that people were pointing to, and calling for, this year, do not quite manage to "[fire] a subversive shot across the prow of mainstream American society" (Friedman, *Arthur Penn's* 3–4). The films in which we meet these rebel heroes are daunting in their directness and polish, unforgettable as visions, but ultimately only specters of rebellion.

1968

▪▫▪▪▪▪▪▪▪▪▪

Movies and the Failure
of Nostalgia

LESLIE H. ABRAMSON

During 1968, the actual assumed the status of the harrowing imaginary as history became an unmitigated American nightmare. This traumatic year proceeded with a series of horrific shocks and tumultuous confrontations as establishment and anti-establishment forces clashed on political, cultural, and geographic fields of engagement. Domestic icons, institutions, and policies were attacked, activism climaxed and was suppressed by extremist measures, Vietnam casualties peaked, and the legacy of Camelot was revived and silenced. In the turbulent wake of the assassinations of Martin Luther King Jr. and Robert Kennedy, wartime mortifications, a bitterly fractious presidential election punctuated by the chaos of the Democratic National Convention in Chicago and other eruptions of police brutality, campus takeovers, a spate of hijackings, protest marches, urban riots, strikes, and stalled Vietnam peace talks, figures and forces of arbitration no longer seemed to exist. In their absence, American cinema remained an institution of mediation, one that acknowledged with a new forthrightness the social turmoil and tendencies of the present, yet at the same time grappled with its own contemporaneity, thematizing memory and returning nostalgically to classical generic forms and traditional strategies of self-regulation to contain, commodify, and reinvigorate itself aesthetically, culturally, and economically.

Ubiquitously, the bearer of shock, upheaval, and horror was the documentary image. The mainstream visual culture of intensely visceral newspaper daily wire photographs, magazine spreads, primetime documentaries, and nightly network newscasts serializing the first "television war" in juxtaposition with scenes of domestic clashes together transmitted graphic depictions of Vietnam and the United States as physical and rhetorical battlegrounds. Among the year's inaugural images were those of the astonishing savageries of the Tet Offensive in January, a massive, deadly surprise attack against South Vietnam, which generated with new immediacy explicit footage of carnage in progress and a drastic shift in Americans' understanding of the status of the war. In the throes of Tet and its wake, two of the decade's most haunting photographs captured assassinations: South Vietnamese police chief Lieutenant Colonel Loan coldly executing a distraught Vietcong suspect on the streets of Saigon by thrusting a gun against his head (broadcast as video footage as well) and mortally wounded presidential candidate Robert Kennedy lying in a pool of light on the floor of Los Angeles's Ambassador Hotel. Resonant as these scenes were with regard to the brutality of U.S. foreign policy and the demise of American nostalgic idealism, ultimately the image itself became an object of culpability. The camera shot came under attack as a dangerous apparatus of domestic assault as government commissions, civic agencies, sociologists, and social commentators, casting about for the causes of what was newly perceived as the nation's pathology of violence, implicated its mechanisms of representation. In particular, cinema's proliferating war reportage–inspired aesthetic was indicted as, in the words of one *Newsweek* writer, "the sado-violence that is the new pornography on television and in movies" ("Understanding Violence"). Such intensifying criticism of the industry prompted *Variety* editor Abel Green to observe, "Bobby Kennedy's most vivid monument could be a change in the American scheme of entertainment" (Green, "Guns" 60).

Concurrently, the film industry was besieged by censorship challenges. As cinema's new aesthetics of sensation (see Monaco) were enunciated in the display of not only a profusion of violence but growing sexual explicitness, reflecting the surging sexual revolution and the graphic eroticism of the increasing influx of European films, the forces of conservatism that would sweep Richard Nixon into office in November's election mobilized in a series of nationwide civic and legal efforts to restrict exhibition that reached as high as the Supreme Court. Determined to preserve the industry's independence as it battled a near decade-low average weekly attendance of nineteen million by endeavoring to appeal to differentiated adult markets, Motion Picture Association of America president Jack Valenti returned to traditional strategies of protectionism by self-regulation, replacing the Production Code with a rating system on 1 November. Under the new system, studios and distributors of foreign films voluntarily submitted their films for classification in one of four categories: G (general), M (mature), R (restricted to those sixteen and over unless accompanied by a parent or guardian), and X (restricted to those sixteen and over). Meant to appease critics and bolster Hollywood's image, the ratings system simultaneously enabled the industry to safeguard both its aesthetic autonomy and efforts at commercial expansionism.

Amidst the year's profusion of shocks, cultural discourse became suffused with the lexicon of horror. Hours after Robert Kennedy was shot, historian Arthur Schlesinger Jr. declared in a commencement address at City University of New York, "[Americans] are the most frightening people on the planet." Schlesinger decried "the ghastly things we do to our own people [and] . . . to other people," cautioning that "we can no longer regard hatred and violence as accidents and aberrations, as nightmares which will pass away when we awake" (Schlesinger, "America" 19, 20). In cinema as well, manifesting not only social trauma and upheaval but the public's new commitment to confronting its own demons, the year's releases reflected upon domestic culture as one of appalling violence, violation, and struggle. An index of the increasing pervasiveness of psychic and graphic mortification, as well as the urge for its containment, both the independent and studio sectors nostalgically encoded contemporary anxiety in the horror film, reinvigorating the classical genre with *Night of the Living Dead* and *Rosemary's Baby*. Both films envision the nightmarish emergence of the ghastly from within and among patriarchy, a preoccupation of the year's multiple releases representing the murderer as lone assassin: *The Boston Strangler, Targets, No Way to Treat a Lady, Ice Station Zebra,* and *Where Eagles Dare*. More specifically evoking the Kennedy tragedies, *Wild in the Streets* contains an attempted political assassination of a rock-star president; *5 Card Stud* centers on a murder conspiracy plot involving a man who becomes a preacher upon his brother's death; and President Garfield and his assassin surface in *No More Excuses*. Other films, such as policiers and westerns *Bullitt, Madigan, The Detective, Coogan's Bluff,* and *Hang 'Em High*, cynically depict the dialectic between widespread social pathology and ineffectual or corrupt institutions of law and order, positing the archetypal lone anti-establishment figure of justice roaming urban and rural frontiers as the only individual capable of restoring a small measure of order to a nonetheless irredeemable culture.

Registering the central source of domestic and international hostility more explicitly than any other year during the 1960s, American cinema not only exhibited more images of the Vietnam War this year, but produced the decade's only mainstream commercial film on the conflict. These works inscribed the dynamic among the immediacy of the horrific, the nostalgic urge, and the problematic of memory construction in images both of the war and the figure of the troubled veteran, which surfaced repeatedly. Reenacting the climaxing struggle between pro- and antiwar forces, John Wayne's uber-patriotic Hollywood feature, *The Green Berets*, was challenged by a surge in independent antiwar documentaries, including *In the Year of the Pig, A Face of War,* and *Inside North Viet Nam*. Psychological baggage-carrying Vietnam and World War II veterans surfaced in *Targets, Angels from Hell, The*

Subject Was Roses, and *Tiger by the Tail,* constituting flashpoints of domestic turbulence. Draft dodgers emerged in *Windflowers* and even Russ Meyer's soft-porn *Vixen!* Comedies, too, were haunted by the war: *No More Excuses* and *Head* feature documentary footage of Vietnam; the family film *Yours, Mine and Ours,* which contains two generations of military men—a widowed navy officer (who marries a military widow) and his oldest son, who eventually leaves for basic training—displaces the anxieties of war onto the antics of the generation gap.

Other war films both reference and repress Vietnam by evincing nostalgia for earlier conflicts, principally by situating their plots during World War II or fantasizing war as a struggle between foreign powers and the British. *Where Eagles Dare, Ice Station Zebra, The Devil's Brigade,* and *The Secret War of Harry Frigg* are politically and geographically escapist films, locating the conflicts on landscapes diametrically dissimilar to Southeastern Asia. *The Devil's Brigade* begins with the U.S. Army voicing its "strong opposition" to a joint Canadian and American operation in Norway, in the figure of an American colonel who protests, with ironic resonance, to Britain's Lord Mountbatten, "But the most important thing is, once you get them there, how are you going to get them out? There's been no provision made for that!"

At the same time, the counterculture was represented in a group of films that captured the duality of the historical moment for anti-establishment movements that, at the height of activism not only in the United States but in Prague, Mexico, and elsewhere, were violently repressed. Evincing both exuberance and a jaded recognition of the ultimate inefficacy of rebellion, *Wild in the Streets* (which fantasizes the rock star as president, echoing both Robert Kennedy's celebrity status and the new political activism of performers), *Psych-Out,* and *I Love You, Alice B. Toklas!* represent an escapist urge to elude or expunge the ills of the establishment by seeking or constructing alternative cultures. Yet these films are bereft of happy endings. Appropriating patriarchal power structures for the purposes of social revolution, *Wild*'s initially iconoclastic rock singer becomes an instrument and victim of the urge for cultural hegemony, as radicalism becomes its own form of fascism in his edict to intern the older generation in detention camps. Such dramas as *Rachel, Rachel* and *The Heart Is a Lonely Hunter* depict establishment culture as a form of imprisonment so repressive that the main characters become marginalized, constituting their own counterculture. These films recognize that an alternate lifestyle can provide only momentary liberation, exhibiting a distinct collapse of idealism. The thematics of world weariness extended to the science fiction subgenre of space travel. Inspired by the highly anticipated Apollo moon missions launched at the end of the year, *2001: A Space Odyssey* and *Planet of the Apes* enact escapist fantasies of an intergalactic and temporal order, which similarly constitute no liberation from social struggles. These films, together with other productions, allude to the failure of nostalgia, coupling the urge to look back or retreat to familiar genres with a recognition that the past is no solace.

The Horror

George Romero's *Night of the Living Dead* constitutes the Vietnamization of the horror film, a self-conscious, politically and socially charged work allegorizing a country battling its own demons. This low-budget independent production, which shocked its original neighborhood theater youth audiences and eventually achieved cult status, portrays an America haunted by legions of the recently deceased, transmogrifying the landscape into a national war zone and a site of multiple anxieties. The troubling specter of the newly dead, battlefront news reports, military apparatus, and images of bloody flesh—displayed in a new graphic explicitness influenced by the stylistics of war coverage—manifestly reference the Asian conflict. Yet the film is haunted by the cataclysmic domestic past as well. The crisis originates in a cemetery; the inaugural trauma centers around a fallen figure resonantly named "Johnny," a young man whose demise leaves its witness in a state of shock and longing. The horror is compounded by the emergence of multitudes of largely middle-aged murderers from the graveyards, morbid carriers of radiation who bear the ghastly legacy of the atomic age into contemporary culture.

Employing classic signifying practices of the horror genre, this black-and-white film begins with a long shot of a solitary car winding its way through a bleak and deserted rural landscape. Suturing traditional codes to the contemporary horrific, *Night* announces its referentiality to the Vietnam War as a violent mass producer of the deceased when the car passes a sign, "Cemetery Entrance," riddled with bullet holes, soon followed by shots of American flags waving above the headstones, introducing what Robin Wood identifies as Romero's "metaphor of America-as-graveyard" (Wood, *Hollywood* 115). Two siblings have traveled to the gravesite of their long-dead father, an excursion to the site of memorialization to which the stridently unnostalgic brother, Johnny (Russell Streiner), cynically objects. As he both signals and satirizes the horror genre by hauntingly intoning, "They're coming to get you, Barbra," a grey-haired zombie in a black suit lurches through the cemetery and attacks his sister (Judith O'Dea). Johnny attempts to fend him off but is overcome. Barbra escapes to a nearby deserted farmhouse, and soon thereafter is joined by Ben (Duane Jones), who boards up windows, locates a radio, shotgun, and bullets, and fends off zombies. A turn of the radio dial reveals that the eastern United States is in "crisis," coalescing the lexicon of Vietnam War reportage with images of horror: "There is an epidemic of mass murder being committed by a virtual army of unidentified assassins. The murders are taking place in villages, cities . . . with no apparent pattern or reason for the slayings. It seems to be a sudden, general explosion of mass homicide."

The decisive and resourceful Ben, the only African American in the film, takes charge of the spectrum of Caucasians converging in the farmhouse: the catatonic Barbra; Harry Cooper (Karl Hardman), a cowardly and anxiety-ridden middle-aged man; his disdaining wife, Helen (Marilyn Eastman); their daughter, Karen (Kyra Schon), who, bitten by a zombie, lies infected in the cellar; and a level-headed teenage couple, Judy and Tom (Judith Ridley, Keith Wayne). They all watch television in alarm as the mass media becomes the apparatus of graphic shock and terror, detailing the gruesome progress of the flesh-eating zombies and transmitting interviews with those forces mobilized into battle. These images are juxtaposed with news clips exhibiting the disturbing dissimulations of a secretive and ineffectual government and the candid but equally futile theoretical discourse of scientists who posit that high levels of radiation emitted by a satellite destroyed by NASA upon returning from Venus may have caused the mutations.

In increasingly horrific developments, Tom and Judy are incinerated during a courageous attempt at rescue and their flesh graphically cannibalized; Ben shoots Harry; and Karen turns into a zombie, stabbing her mother to death and feasting upon her dead father's corpse. Barbra, who emerges intermittently from her stupor to reinvoke Johnny, is eventually killed by him and his fellow zombies when they invade the farmhouse. The next morning, the sole survivor, Ben, mistaking the sound of a police siren for a sign of safety, emerges from the cellar only to be shot by one of the vigilantes combing the countryside with police and German shepherds on a militaristic "search-and-destroy operation against the ghouls." Ultimately, although institutional forces of law and order have seemingly regained control of the landscape, the restoration of their dominance constitutes equal murderousness, causing the demise of the Black hero, whose body is burned on a pyre of zombie corpses, indistinguishable to the police from the true monsters.

The distinctly American nature of the trauma is foregrounded not only by the iconography of the flag and references to Vietnam, but the western imagery overlaid on the political landscape as a genre of internecine warfare. *Night* centers on a group of besieged defending the rural homestead. In the film's conflated iconographies of conflict, the villainous threat to American society is mounted by the radioactivated, truly silent majority—emblematic of the conservative constituency Nixon would call upon the following year to support his "Vietnamization" policy. The lawless attackers bear the marks of establishment culture; the initial zombies are primarily middle-aged, suit-wearing males, a collective of classically referent automaton-like figures intent on cannibalizing the free-thinking living. Compounding the landscape's menace, part of *Night*'s horror is that what is defended in this "western" is already bereft. Lodged inside the homestead is another version of the living defunct, the equally frightening collective of the modern nuclear family constituting, as Wood notes, "the legacy of the past, of the patriarchal structuring of relationships, 'dead' yet automatically continuing" (Wood, *Hollywood* 116). Mirroring the silent majority outside is the loquacious figure of conservatism within, the horrifically small-minded Harry, patriarch of a fractious, dysfunctional family in rebellion against him.

Suit-wearing zombies constitute the vanguard of the silent majority attacking the American homestead in *Night of the Living Dead* (George Romero, Image Ten-Continental Films, Columbia). Personal collection of the author.

Grappling with this reactionary, the cross-section of American society that gathers in self-defense is troubled and problematized, a populace at odds with itself.

Night does, however, valorize certain figures. In a significant departure from classical convention, the status of hero is occupied by an African American. Immediately assuming leadership of the group, Ben is a figure not only of racial equality but of Black empowerment. Cultural beneficiary of the surging civil rights movement, the 1968 Civil Rights Act, and Sidney Poitier's portrayal of a detective-hero in the previous year's *In the Heat of the Night,* the assertive, outspoken Ben takes on uncontested authority (although Harry constantly disputes his strategy). In fact, Ben is a lone Black hero this year in which Hollywood understood itself to be searching for alternatives to Poitier (who starred in a romance, *For Love of Ivy*), yet was markedly bereft of releases featuring African Americans. However, although empowered, Ben defends mainstream culture. Reflecting the disturbing statistics that African Americans constituted a disproportionately high number of soldiers in Vietnam, he bears the burden of the group's security. Resonantly, for this he receives no recognition. Recalling the King assassination and the practices of police and vigilante brutality against civil rights activists, including the April slaying of Black Panther Bobby Hutton, the heroic Ben's misrecognition as a demon and his murder emblematize the disheartening inevitabilities of the civil rights movement. With similar cynicism, the film recuperates the image of youth culture: the teenage couple is depicted as figures of both mediation among the farmhouse group and bravery—in essence, rational activists—yet, in defiance of classical genre codes, matching the fate of the hero, the innocent young lovers do not survive either.

Whereas *Night* locates the horror of the historical moment in the politicized American landscape of the western, signaling a new aesthetic of visceral violence rooted in the stylistics of Vietnam War reportage, *Rosemary's Baby* investigates the urban horrific of contemporary domesticity, importing a European visual sensibility to the classicism of Hollywood convention and disclosing modern culture to be the site of gothic terror. Like *Night,* its economies of shock and disturbance transcended the movie theater: the film had magnetic audience appeal yet simultaneously attracted civic backlash, as the genre's normative embrace by a major studio and commodification to mainstream audiences became coupled with issues of heresy. In the wake of *Rosemary*'s release, the National Catholic Office for Motion Pictures (NCOMP) issued the film a C (condemned) rating; similarly, other domestic bastions of Catholicism excoriated the work as an assault on the church. Perceived as a critical test case of the public clout of institutions challenging the industry, the film proved the seventh highest grossing film of the year in the United States and Canada despite vigorous efforts at its circumscription.

Rosemary's Baby announces itself as a work of urban gothicism with an establishing shot that takes in a distinctly different American landscape than *Night*, panning the crowded Manhattan skyline before settling on a formidable Victorian apartment building. The young couple diminished by the immensity of this relic are prospective tenants Rosemary and Guy Woodhouse (Mia Farrow, John Cassavetes), who are shown a musty apartment full of dead, overgrown plants; heavy, outworn furniture; and enigmatic writing from its deceased previous occupant. The flat seems to Rosemary ideally suited for transformation into a domestic space, accommodating a future baby. Shortly thereafter, the mysteries begin to multiply when the Woodhouses' elderly friend Hutch (Maurice Evans) recounts the history of the building, revealing that the Bramford is a notorious site of witchcraft and perverse demises.

Rosemary redecorates the apartment while Guy, a struggling actor whose career is mired in television plays and commercials, auditions unsuccessfully. Guy's initial reluctance to dine with their eccentric elderly neighbors, Minnie and Roman Castevet (Ruth Gordon, Sidney Blackmer), alchemizes into a close association, and the couple begin to intrude upon the Woodhouses' affairs. Simultaneously, Guy's professional luck begins to change, and he suddenly becomes determined to have a child. On "baby night," Minnie interrupts to bring a strange-tasting chocolate mousse, which makes Rosemary dizzy. Rosemary falls asleep, haunted by a disturbing dream sequence in which she hovers between the surreal and the actual, announcing "This is no dream. This is really happening!" As the sequence climaxes, she envisions herself lying nude on a mattress surrounded by an unclothed coven of the Castevets and their elderly friends as symbols are painted on her body with blood, and Guy turns into a demonic beast, impregnating her. Rosemary subsequently becomes pregnant, upon which the overbearing, nosy Minnie prescribes as her obstetrician the venerated Dr. Sapirstein (Ralph Bellamy) and mixes Rosemary an odd daily drink. In a strange eschewal of modern practice, Sapirstein advises Rosemary to abstain from reading medical literature, ingesting vitamin pills, or conferring with friends. Almost immediately, Rosemary begins to suffer, alarming her friends, but not Guy, who insists that she not seek another doctor's advice. Hutch, who expresses his concern, suddenly dies, but he manages to bequeath Rosemary a book on witchcraft that confirms her suspicions by indicating that the Castevets practice sorcery. Rosemary suspects that the couple is part of a coven determined to make use of her baby for demonic purposes. In her final days of pregnancy, Rosemary fails at attempts to elude both Sapirstein and Guy, whom she has concluded is part of the plot, agreeing to exchange his first baby for professional success. She is forcibly sedated and, upon waking, informed that her child has died. Eventually, she surreptitiously enters the Castevets' apartment to find the coven convened with the infant in a cradle draped in black, whereupon it is revealed, much to Rosemary's shock, that she has given birth to the devil.

The numerous demons haunting Rosemary spring from the domain of domesticity. Viewed through the lens of what Lucy Fischer identifies as the "trauma" of pregnancy, the film constitutes an indictment of patriarchy's horrific institutionalization of the traditional spaces of the feminine. Rosemary experiences the condition of domesticity and parturiency as that of the female gothic, a state of captivity within the oppressive architectures of a castle-like manse and the dark structurations of patriarchy, contending with her enigmatic husband and the mysterious impenetrabilities of masculine culture, all of which constantly undermine her perceptions. While feminists were purportedly burning their bras in protest at the year's Miss America pageant (although none actually did so), Rosemary suffers increasing disempowerment and infantilization (e.g., she covertly eliminates her excremental mousse from the table by wrapping it in her diaper-like cloth napkin) by male culture, whose representatives conspire to prevent her from acquiring knowledge of her condition and its cultural context, forcibly imprisoning her in a coven of masculine anxiety. Concurrently, at the moment when establishment figures were locating the horrific in radical youth movements, Rosemary's malefic baby, like young Karen Cooper, who brutalizes her own parents in *Night of the Living Dead*, constitutes an image of juvenile diabolism haunting contemporary culture. Both films trace this fiendishness to inflictions by the older generation actively displacing its ills onto a child.

Yet simultaneously in this drama of multiple demons, the film identifies classical Hollywood cinema as an equally haunting specter of production. The source of the gothic threat is not solely patriarchal domestic culture but the studio system, whose habitués are equated with a coven. The Bramford is a cloying site of memory, containing antiquated classical genre plots and haunted by denizens of Hollywood's Golden Age. Among its inhabitants are well-known figures of 1930s and 1940s cinema: Elisha Cook Jr., Ruth Gordon, and Ralph Bellamy. A nostalgic site of the archaic studio system, the Bramford promises Hollywood success for the frustrated television actor,

but at the malevolent cost of indenturement. Guy's sacrifice of his repro-
ductivity carries additional resonance insofar as the actor playing the role,
John Cassavetes, was a noted New York director who eschewed Hollywood
to create such independent films as *Faces,* released that same year, but who
nonetheless acted in studio productions to finance his work. Mia Farrow,
who played Rosemary, also emblematized a certain dissociation from Hollywood. Farrow—who, during the film's production, was becoming dis-
engaged from Hollywood culture in a highly publicized divorce from Frank
Sinatra—represented a new type of female lead, whose nonclassical beauty
(by studio standards) resembled that of European art cinema actresses. This
European aesthetic extended to the stylistics of the film, which featured unconventional frame composition, a surreal nightmare scene, a stream-of-
consciousness sequence, and the unsettling use of sound, beginning with
the mournfully intoned lullaby accompanying the title sequence.

Counterbalancing genre films encoding the threat of the collective
within the conventions of horror were the year's multiple dramas depicting
the figure of the lone assassin. *The Boston Strangler* investigated the homi-
cidal individual as both psychological deviant and emblem of widespread
social pathology preoccupying contemporary discourse. Based on an actual
criminal case (as is *Targets*), the film foregrounds the horrific as an empirical condition of modern culture.

The Boston Strangler is a police procedural which, in the course of tracking down a single assassin, exposes the malady extant throughout patriarchy. Dramatizing the case of 1962–64 serial murderer Albert DeSalvo, the
film exhibits a populace committed to identifying the assassin as Other, yet
grimly forced to reperceive itself as the locus of widespread deviance and
terror. This condition is identified as symptomatic of the Vietnam era when
the chief investigator of the case remarks to a newscaster, "What more can
you expect from a society that itself spends 44 percent of its tax dollar on
killing?"

The film proceeds as a series of narrative and visual fragments; Boston
is the site of increasing panic as a murderer leaves a growing trail of single,
female victims who have succumbed to strangulation and deviant sexual
assault. Segments of the horrific crimes and the shocking discoveries of
dead bodies are intercut with sequences of the dogged yet inefficacious
efforts of the police to locate the perpetrator, images of zealous reporters
gathering at crime scenes, fragments of interviews and newscasts, and shots
of the isolated lives of local citizens. As the number of victims (whose apart-
ments the strangler enters in the guise of a repairman) and the level of
social anxiety mounts, so do the efforts of the police who, in their sweep of

possible suspects among sexual deviants, uncover the banality of perversion evident even in their own ranks, extending to the chief investigator, who commits police brutality and, finding himself unnaturally fascinated with the case, grapples with his own inner degeneracy. When the Strangler (Tony Curtis) mistakenly intrudes on a married couple, he is captured and imprisoned in a mental hospital, wherein psychiatrists determine that he is schizophrenic. In a series of interviews with the chief investigator, DeSalvo eventually begins to recognize his repressed identity as an assassin, leaving him in a permanent state of shock.

The Strangler is represented as a bearer of historical traumas and cultural ills. Evoking the image of a veteran in an olive drab jacket and pants as well as laced boots (DeSalvo in fact served in the army), he carries the burden of contemporary violence, its repression, and gender tensions through the streets of Boston.[1] His face is first disclosed as he watches a television newscast of President Kennedy's funeral, which constitutes one tripwire for his urge to violence. At the same time, as husband and father of a traditional nuclear family, the Strangler is a figure of conventional patriarchy, whose violent rage toward independent females is an index of male anxiety symptomatic of masculine backlash during this moment of emergent women's liberation activism, which itself reached pathological proportions in the near-fatal June shooting of Andy Warhol by one of his actresses, radical feminist Valerie Solanas. Concurrently, by graphically displaying and problematizing the female body as a site of desire and brutal suppression, *The Boston Strangler* resonates the year's many censorship battles. Foregrounding the schizoid nature of contemporary cultural attitudes, the film discloses the populace's prurient interest in, and the mass media's role as sensationalist purveyor of, explicit displays of violence and sexuality within the context of Boston's puritanical, hystericized desire for its circumscription.

As did multiple films of the year, *The Boston Strangler* merges realism with the illusory, representing empirical experience as a form of hallucination. Like the year's emblematic texts of new journalism, Norman Mailer's Pulitzer Prize–winning *Armies of the Night* and Tom Wolfe's *The Electric Kool-Aid Acid Test*, which employed methods of fiction to achieve reportorial accuracy, *The Boston Strangler* negotiates the slippage between the imaginary and the actual that seemed to define contemporary experience, representing "reality" as more phantasmagoric than fiction. (In fact, during the year Mailer experimented with the genre of the fiction film, producing, directing, and starring in *Beyond the Law* and *Wild 90*.) Influenced by Prague experimental theater, director Richard Fleischer pioneered a multipanel

One of the year's films depicting the killer as lone assassin, *The Boston Strangler* (Richard Fleischer, Twentieth Century Fox) evokes the image of the military veteran (Tony Curtis as Albert DeSalvo) carrying the burden of contemporary violence. Personal collection of the author.

matte technique that fractured the individual frame into multiple shots, a split-screen device that transmuted the single image into a montage. For example, as the Strangler embarks on a murder after witnessing the Kennedy funeral, an assemblage of three horizontal images in a single frame concurrently record the progress of his car as it cruises down the narrow streets of Boston, DeSalvo behind the steering wheel in medium close-up, and his glassy-eyed, literally disembodied stare exposed in an extreme close-up as he hones in on the apartment building that contains his quarry. This grouping is soon followed by another split-screen frame, cleft into vertical and horizontal images, the former tracking DeSalvo down a narrow, empty hallway in the building while the latter simultaneously envisages his victim behind one of the shut doors, a young blonde woman alone in her dingy apartment watching a portable television set perched on a skeletal stand. The plurality of simultaneous images not only constitutes the stylistic equivalent of the Strangler's schizophrenia, but also represents the fracture and fragmentation of modern life manifesting itself most pronouncedly in the condition of individual alienation.

Ultimately, the film identifies the malady haunting contemporary culture as that which originates in the problematic of memory. In order to function in his quotidian existence as family man and furnace repairman in Boston—in other words, to keep the home fires burning in the domestic cultural sites of both the patriarchal household and the American city—the Strangler must repress the recollection of his own monstrous deeds. Memory's imperative, emblematized by the visual references to John Kennedy's assassination and Vietnam veterans, and embodied by the chief investigator, who, in his many conversations with the Strangler, exhorts the suspect to remember, must necessarily be censored for the individual to survive. When DeSalvo begins to recall, what surfaces is his own submerged heinousness and he devolves into a state of catatonia, a prisoner of warring memory who will never be released.

Offensives

If for no other reason, this was a pivotal year for American cinema insofar as, at last catching up to the historical moment, Hollywood explicitly acknowledged the conflict that haunted so many films by releasing the decade's only feature on the Vietnam War. At the height of U.S. military involvement as well as casualties, the thick of antiwar protests, and the moment at which the ability of the United States to prevail was cast into public doubt by the Tet Offensive, John Wayne mobilized his iconic status to rescue right-wing ideology in *The Green Berets*. Deploying his emblematic screen image as a frontier and war hero, Wayne (who co-directed and starred in the film) rearticulated the conflict in nostalgic terms, staunchly defending U.S. military policy via the conventions of the World War II combat film and the western. Yet, in its status as rhetoric, commercial enterprise, and generic text, the film proved immensely problematic, a work whose flaws foreground fissures in both domestic prowar doctrine and, as *New York Times* critic Renata Adler recognized, the status of Hollywood's classical strategies of fantasization.[2]

The Green Berets wages two wars: one against the North Vietnamese and the other against American skepticism. Manifestly inserting itself into the tempestuous discursive battle over U.S. military involvement, the film chronicles the geographical and ideological journey of a reporter (David Janssen) who accompanies a Green Beret unit overseas to witness the conflict firsthand. During a year in which highly respected CBS news anchor Walter Cronkite declared in a network documentary after visiting Vietnam, "We have been too often disappointed by the optimism of the American leaders, both in Vietnam and Washington, to have faith any longer in the silver linings they find in the darkest clouds. . . . To say that we are mired in stalemate seems the only realistic, yet unsatisfactory conclusion," the *Berets'* journalist sees only the "good fight" being waged effectively against unmitigated Asian evil by brave and compassionate men of hawkish resolve. With Hollywood's archetypal patriot, Wayne (playing Colonel Kirby), as his guide, the initially dubious reporter is alchemized into an abettor of U.S. military efforts in Vietnam.

Referring nostalgically at the outset to the former president, *The Green Berets* begins with a shot of a banner demarcating the "United States Army John F. Kennedy Center for Special Warfare." Unlike other films that reference the assassination as a haunting trauma, *The Green Berets* appropriates the name in service of perpetuating violence, encoding the war as a Kennedy legacy. A dissolve reveals that the JFK Center, a stateside military base, houses soldiers whose initial onscreen marches are for purposes not of training but choreographing propagandistic images for the press. In the press conference that follows, lower-ranking officers—excised of political doubt and moral dilemma—display their talents at speaking German, left to defend U.S. foreign policy as a matter of Cold War anticommunist doctrine.

One of the journalists, Beckworth, follows Kirby and his detachment to a makeshift military camp in Vietnam, site of a bricolage of classical generic iconography referring to Wayne's screen history as a western and war movie hero. Resonantly dubbed "Dodge City" and featuring a watchtower reminiscent of cavalry outposts, the camp is populated by the conventional assortment of soldiers, a melting pot of personalities, albeit few races and ethnicities. This collective includes the uncontainable "flotsam" of American brutality, a Vietnamese orphan (Craig Jue) tellingly named Hamchunk, who adopts American soldier Peterson (Jim Hutton) as a father figure. The outpost is run by Captain Nim (George Takei), a dedicated South Viet-namese officer who proves his loyalty to the American cause not only via his hard-line anticommunist rhetoric, but through the activity of rooting out a Vietcong traitor, whose off-camera shooting is rationalized by Kirby with the discourse of frontier justice: "Out here, due process is a bullet."

Beckworth is drafted physically and ideologically as the outpost is raided by the Vietcong (whose tactics and savagery resemble that of the tra-ditional western's Native Americans) and the unit goes on a mission to evacuate a village in order to save its inhabitants, only to find them brutally massacred by the VC. Endorsing U.S. war efforts, Beckworth eventually both displaces culpability onto the press for its myopic liberalism and opts to reenlist for a tour of duty with another unit. The final mission, to cap-ture a North Vietnamese general, proves a success, although the cost in-cludes the shocking death of Peterson, who leaves Hamchunk an orphan again. As Kirby breaks the news, the boy asks, "What will happen to me now?" Foregrounding the establishment's failure to provide an answer, Kirby responds with paternalistic rhetoric, "You let me worry about that, Green Beret. You're what this is all about," and in a final classical image of closure, they stroll down a beach in the light of a red sunset.

This film, which from the outset announces its subject to be discourse, foregrounds and links the problematic status of both prowar doctrine and the codes of classical Hollywood cinema in the mediation of the Vietnam experience. In *The Green Berets'* mission to enunciate the conflict in con-ventional screen images of patriotism, neither the nostalgic terms of the western and combat genres nor Wayne's star image brings coherence, con-tainment, or closure to the Vietnam War. Instead, the film is marked by discord among the urge to "correct" antiwar discourse, classical genre en-codement, and what Rick Berg points out as its "insist[ence] upon the pri-macy of sight and the authority of experience" (Berg 54). In the course of the film, Kirby comments to Beckworth, "It's pretty hard to talk to anyone about this country until they've come over and seen it." Such rhetoric, intended to foreclose the protests of stateside dissenters, instead emphasizes the film's status as a fictionalized depiction of the war—one, in fact, shot entirely in the United States. As Colonel Kirby and Hamchunk walk down a California beach representing Vietnam—a site where dusk is marked by the light sinking in the east of the artificial South China Sea, rather than the empirically correct west—the film concludes in Wayne's Hollywood, another land of the setting sun.

As a broadside in defense of U.S. policy that pointedly inserted itself in the public debate about the war, *The Green Berets* became the target of widespread critical and public excoriation. This Hollywood film, whose production was assisted by the Pentagon, became emblematic of the worst of the establishment's illusory prowar rhetoric. Upon its release, antiwar activists demonstrated at theaters in New York and Germany. In fact, in the wake of the war, dissent, and social violence, the institution of cinema itself was under assault from left-wing forces. Overseas, the Cannes Film Festival was shut down by filmmakers acting in solidarity with political protestors in France. Following King's assassination, the Oscar ceremonies were delayed and race riots resulted in the temporary closure of movie theaters. *Variety* estimated that civic protest and violence accounted for $100 million in property loss for movie theaters in the course of the year (Green, "Show Biz" 56).

The divisiveness of political sentiment about the war that fractured the social and political landscape was replicated in the thematic and formal conflict between studio and independent releases. Although the U.S. military produced a handful of prowar releases, Wayne's *The Green Berets* were vigorously challenged by peaking quantities of independent antiwar films. Employing oppositional forms of documentary, screened at film festivals, benefits, small art houses, and occasionally on television rather than major exhibition circuits, these films constituted their own guerrilla efforts (signaled by the newly established leftist documentary production and distribution company, Guerrilla Newsreel) against U.S. involvement in Vietnam.

Constituting what director Emile de Antonio described as a "film weapon," the antiwar documentary *In the Year of the Pig* waged battle against American military policy by attacking the administration's chauvinistic production of authenticity and memory. The film reconstructs Vietnam's past and the U.S. government's representation of its involvement by assembling often oppositional segments of political rhetoric, documentary witness, and historical and cultural analysis in order to expose the fallacies of America's involvement in Indochina. Formally adopting the stylistics of conflict in a dialectical counterposition of discourses, images, and sounds, *In the Year of the Pig* not only foregrounds the war as a rhetorical struggle but interjects itself into the sphere of mass cultural signification as a radical departure from the unity of classical cinema and establishment ideology.

The film takes the radical form of collage, pitting myriad discursive and graphic representations against each other to formulate a textual reflection of Vietnam as a site of competing discourses and the contested authorship of memory. Composing Vietnam's violent past from archival footage, television newscasts, Eastern European documentaries, presidential speeches, press conferences, and interviews with both U.S. and foreign scholars, politicians, journalists, soldiers (including one who deserted the Green Berets), and veterans, the film reconstitutes the country's turbulent history and exposes American political pronouncements as an aggregate of dissemblances. De Antonio's Vietnam is geographically and discursively a space of endless lexical and militaristic invasion, contestation, and, ultimately, appropriation. Juxtaposing American political and military claims against images of combat atrocities and Asian domestic misery, the film implicates the American government in the increasingly destructive and fictionalized defense of U.S. intervention.

Vietnam is represented as the site of not only a military but a media offensive: footage of a Buddhist monk burning to death in antiwar protest is accompanied by a former State Department official commenting, "It was so dramatic. It hit the headlines all over the world." Video images depict the staging and stagecraft of a procession of South Vietnamese puppet governments; public statements of military success and the provocation of armed offensives by President Johnson, Secretary of Defense Robert McNamara, and others are undercut by newsreel footage and the eyewitness accounts of the Gulf of Tonkin incident and other events, underscoring the illusory nature of political discourse. Ultimately, the film constitutes a metatext about history as a struggle of the imagination. Amidst this fractious conflict, one of the conjunctive urges of the film is the longing for nostalgia, a vacuum that the director fills with the romanticized figure of nationalism, Ho Chi Minh. De Antonio's Ho represents a yearning for a historical condition of unification never experienced, not Vietnam's true interventionist past but, as a Marxist, a figure of foreign ideological colonialization.

Although an independent production, de Antonio's film was also indicative of Hollywood's new, post-HUAC era liberal activism. It was financed in part by actors Robert Ryan and Paul Newman, one of several stars who campaigned for presidential candidate Eugene McCarthy (others stumped for Kennedy), and television performer Steve Allen. As a distinctly political text, like *The Green Berets*, the film also became a site of social conflict as theaters screening the film became targets of protest.

Beyond the Vietnam War film, the tension between liberal explicitness and agents of conservatism centered most dramatically on issues of censorship. Graphically erotic and anti-establishment domestic and imported releases were targets of intense civic and legal efforts at restriction as exhibition challenges reached the Supreme Court from Dallas and Chicago, and lower courts ruled on cases in Indiana, Maryland, and Miami. As the emblems of a newly sexually liberated culture mounted, NCOMP issued more "condemned" ratings during this year than any previous one. U.S.

customs seized such erotic foreign films as the 1967 Swedish work *I Am Curious (Yellow)*, and the exhibition of Frederick Wiseman's 1967 documentary about negligent and abusive practices in a Massachusetts mental institution, *Titicut Follies*, was banned by the state's supreme judicial court.

Emerging en force from the sexual revolution, Robert Aldrich's X-rated *The Killing of Sister George* was among a surging number of both studio and independent releases that depicted lesbianism, homosexuality, and bisexuality, including *The Detective, The Queen, The Lion in Winter, Flesh, The Legend of Lylah Clare, P.J., Vixen!, Rachel, Rachel*, and *The Sergeant. The Odd Couple*, a mainstream feature that broached the issue of queer domesticity comedically by pairing two heterosexual males as roommates, was the year's fifth highest grossing film in the United States and Canada. Among the multiplicity of films displaying graphic nudity and employing explicit language in what had become common enunciative codes for adult features, these works exhibited sexuality with a new, albeit not wholly nonjudgmental candor. *Sister George* discloses lesbianism with an openness previously unexhibited in a studio film, uncloseting the private lives of gay women as well as the integration between lesbian culture and the mainstream community; nonetheless, the film depicts queer sexuality as a pathology and source of almost unmitigated discontent. Concurrently, the film addressed issues of censorship that would embroil its own release.

The Killing of Sister George charts the incipient and eventual termination of a middle-aged British lesbian actress (Beryl Reid) from the BBC soap opera in which she plays a starring role as a nun. The linkage between character and actress constituted by their corollary eschewal of heterosexuality is fractured by queerness of disposition; Sister George's warm and ever-cheery onscreen persona is a complete departure from the performer's brash temperament. Off camera, George is a domineering, foul-mouthed alcoholic who exercises sadistic control over her live-in girlfriend, the much younger "Childie" (Susannah York), whose infantilization is explicitly denoted by her baby doll nightwear and her attachment to dolls. After George displays increasingly vulgar and uncontainable behavior on and off the set, including the sexual assault of nuns in the back of a taxi and belligerence toward the cast, crew, studio executives, and her young lover—all symptomatic of her anxiety at the prospect of losing professional and domestic attachments—the progressively troubled BBC kills off her character. But George does not leave quietly; at a studio going-away party, she verbally assails BBC executives, including one who offers her as a sop the role of the voice of Clarabell the Cow in a children's series. In the ironic unhappy ending, graphic sexuality is both appropriated and subsumed by the BBC, as a female television executive (Coral Browne) engages in explicit sex with Childie in George's flat and takes the younger woman away to her own apartment, an assuredly more discreet location for lesbian eroticism. George eventually accepts a more closeted fate as well, as the mass-distributed caricaturized female bovine voice. Revisiting the soap opera's empty set, in a final rampage George topples the props that once sustained her presence and now demarcate her extermination from mainstream culture, demolishing her character's coffin. At last she settles down to articulate her pain in a series of final, plaintive "Moo's."

Albeit banking on the appeal of graphic lesbian sexuality, *Sister George* reconstitutes the painful struggle between display and repression by uncloseting the main character's rage against her marginalization in mainstream culture and domestic life. While exhibiting the variegated nature of lesbianism—the domesticity of the couple, the social atmospherics of the lesbian bar (the film is Hollywood's first production not only to include a lesbian bar scene but to shoot one on location), and her working life in heterosexual culture—*Sister George*, like the year's other films depicting homosexuality, represents queerness as both torturing and tortured state. Defiantly insuppressible in her appetites and attitudes, George's conventional penchants for acceptance and affection—revealed only occasionally in the film—are disguised by uncouth humor, dykish bullying, and abusive eroticism (for example, she commands Childie to eat the butt of her cigar as an act of penitence). At the same time, George's eventual containment is naturalized by means of its alliance with imperatives of contemporaneity both in the spheres of mass entertainment and domesticity. As an older performer, George must face her pending obsolescence within the BBC, which, according to the director, is searching for "youth . . . new blood"; as an older lover, George's jealous rages belie a fear of replacement by younger sexual partners.

Sister George's diegetic struggles mirror those the film faced in the sphere of exhibition and distribution. Released approximately one month after the instatement of the ratings system, the film was the sixth to receive an X rating from the MPAA, and its advertisements were widely censored. Although Aldrich initially challenged the rating in court, he eventually accepted this method of commodification, agreeing to "self-apply" the classification.

Nostalgia Revisited

Retreating to former strategies of economic revival and themes of nostalgia, the major studios returned to the classical musical, releasing big-budget productions set in the past. Columbia, Warner Bros.,

Twentieth Century Fox, Universal, and United Artists each produced musicals in the decade's final, collective vestige of the blockbuster strategy. Nowhere was the tension between contemporaneity and nostalgia as pronounced as in this genre. The backstage musicals *Funny Girl* and *Star!*—biopics of Ziegfield Follies comedienne Fanny Brice and British music hall performer Gertrude Lawrence—featured female stars Barbra Streisand and Julie Andrews in reflexive leading roles as strong, talented, independent women, contextualizing issues of feminism—specifically, ambivalence about the women's liberation movement—in historicized narratives. At the same time, the backstage musical *The Night They Raided Minsky's* returned to the 1920s vaudeville stage to address contemporary issues of censorship in a plot about the invention, and attempted suppression, of the striptease.

Concurrently, the musical's efforts to appeal to youth culture was undergoing a significant change. While Elvis Presley's film career was stalled in what had become his own exhausted subgenre of rock 'n' roll musicals (*Speedway* and *Stay Away, Joe*) that continued to sanitize his image, the genre underwent an aesthetic renaissance with the emergence of the rockumentary. Chronicling the decade's then-largest group concert, the 1967 Monterey International Pop Festival, independent filmmaker D. A. Pennebaker produced the first rock festival documentary, *Monterey Pop*. The innocently hedonistic groups of young beachgoers, racetrack fans, and school dance crowds of the musical teenpic become, in this rockumentary, an ethnography of the counterculture. Studying the concertgoers' colorful codes of dress, blissful countenances, and the various orders of communality and communal living, the film presents an idealistic image of youth culture as its own peace movement (as does the countercultural musical, *You Are What You Eat*), emblematizing anti-establishment rebellion, political protest (manifest in a shot of antiwar posters), liberated sexuality, and drug use. Counterbalancing the highly contextualized, classically contained performances of Hollywood stars Streisand, Andrews, and the clearly antiquated Fred Astaire, who starred in *Finian's Rainbow*, rock performers like Janis Joplin and Jimi Hendrix proved to be unrestrained figures of contemporary visceral immediacy: the former, as James Monaco notes, an emblem of female empowerment, and the latter, an icon of Black power, whose uninhibited sexuality and anti-establishment rage are graphically evident in his erotic guitar playing, which climaxes in the burning and smashing of his instrument during the performance of "Wild Thing" (Monaco 266). Not only does *Monterey Pop* exhibit the sphere of rock music and its audience as anti-establishment forces, but, as direct cinema, it constitutes a form of stylistic counterculture as well. Eschewing formal conventions of the classical musical and the traditional documentary, as does de Antonio, the actively searching yet unobtrusive spontaneous cinematography, characterized by the mobile framing of portable shoulder-mounted cameras, quick pans, and frequent zooms, combined with rhythmic editing and elliptical cuts to convey the event's ambience in lyrical syncopation. The alternative stylistics of direct cinema's heightened realism were also practiced by Frederick Wiseman, whose *High School* disclosed the institution as one of almost militaristic authoritarianism.

In the course of the year, the ultimate escape fantasy was activated by NASA, which launched three spacecrafts, culminating in December's Apollo 8 mission, the first human orbit of the moon. In itself a nostalgic enterprise, dedicated to fulfilling President Kennedy's 1961 vision of a moon landing by the end of the decade, the Apollo missions fired the cinematic imagination. Negotiating the limits of envisionment, the space travel subgenre displaced contemporary struggles onto the spheres of memory and futurism, reconstituted as sites of harsh cultural critique. *Planet of the Apes,* the highest grossing science fiction film of 1968, centers on a cynical, time-traveling astronaut and his crew who land in a culture more primitive than the one they left twenty centuries earlier, becoming prisoners of a society run by primates. Darkly satirizing American political and social systems, the culture has institutionalized racism, class separation, and intolerance, violently silencing dissenters. The eventual discovery that this is the planet Earth dramatizes the failure of nostalgia thematically underlying many of the year's films.

The most visionary film to emerge from this traumatic year was Stanley Kubrick's *2001: A Space Odyssey,* a visually poetic work that exceeds the boundaries of both memory and contemporaneity, encompassing civilization from prehistory to the future. Informed by themes, motifs, and anxieties of the day, and articulated in pioneering aesthetics, the film coalesces the scientific, political, sociological, and spiritual. Kubrick combines the awe of outer space and modern technology with the search for universal connectednesss and peace, escapist fantasies envisioned in the stylistics of hallucinogenic liberation inspired by the drug culture with the tensions of the Cold War, and the anxieties of the burgeoning computer age.[3]

The film's initial Dawn of Man sequence locates the beginnings of humankind in the culture of the apes that, with the discovery of tools, shapes civilization into something both creative and destructive: the first ape to employ an implement—a bone—uses it as a murder weapon. The discovery of tools is prompted by the appearance of a vertically placed rectangular black monolith, a figure of magnetic appeal and inspiration (and, as Gerald Mast points out, the first of numerous screen-like shapes

2001: A Space Odyssey (Stanley Kubrick, MGM) evokes the image of the movie screen in the form of a rectangular monolith that links human history and civilization together through space and time. Personal collection of the author.

throughout the film) that prompts an exploratory mission to Jupiter. In an elegant elliptical cut, a shot of the ape's bone, thrown triumphantly into the air, metamorphoses into a future spacecraft carrying a NASA scientist (William Sylvester) to an international space station. The scientist is on his way to the site of a monolith equally enigmatic and captivating, the subject of a cover-up on the part of the American military-government complex, which the Soviets attempt to penetrate. The final movements of the film detail a space flight on which two astronauts, Frank (Gary Lockwood) and Dave (Keir Dullea), contend with a humanized computer, HAL, which is responsible for sustaining all the flight's operations. HAL misdiagnoses a unit failure and then, in retribution for Frank's suggestion to Dave that a disconnection may be in order, causes the astronaut's death. Dave eventually unplugs HAL and flies through a hallucinogenic seam in time and space, the stargate corridor, at the end of which he ages in an elliptical time sequence and is then reborn in the form of a star child hovering in outer space, poised to renew humankind.

Kubrick juxtaposes the breathtaking physical beauty of the universe and spatial poetry of shapes in outer space with successive glimpses of history as that of hostility and contention. The film recounts the advent and evolution of civilization as a record of violence, divisiveness, and desensitization, reaching its apotheosis in HAL, the emotional scion of the tool-bearing apes, who becomes murderously intoxicated by his own power. Ironically, in a world in which astronauts are wholly depersonalized, the most mortal figure left is HAL, who embodies the anxiety not only of the domination of technology but of the computer glitch. In this futuristic world, to err is to be human, which is unacceptable for a computer; thus HAL must be euthanized when he blunders.

Conversely, *2001* celebrates the apparatus of cinema. The film is a technologically pioneering work that introduced to the mainstream special effects processes of large-format front projection and "Slit-Scan" imaging. The former entailed projecting outdoor scenes of Africa onto the screen behind the performers from the front of the set, rather than the rear, in order to create a more lifelike illusion of prehistory within the confines of a studio. The latter technique was used to create the Stargate corridor sequence, in which Dave hurtles through a seam in time and space, flooded by streams of colored lights. Through such visual poetics and hallucinatory special effects (the film was advertised as "the ultimate trip"), Kubrick recuperates cinema itself, foregrounding the medium's ability to captivate audiences by spectacle.

Ultimately, the film is about cinema's universal power. Foregrounding its ability to manipulate time and space through elliptical cuts, and positing as the most powerful member of the cast a lens—HAL, a figure of the director, stripped down to an eye and central nervous system—*2001* locates the force of unification in cinema itself. In a culturally traumatic and fractious year, when nostalgia provided no succor, the source of unification and inspiration became the monolith, a figure of a movie screen, through which intelligent life communicates through time and space, inspiring progress, and binding the universe together.

NOTES

1. Although the iconography of DeSalvo's wardrobe marks him as a veteran, he did not serve in Vietnam but principally in Germany from the late 1940s to the early 1950s. He left the army in 1956.

2. Adler was disheartened by what *The Green Berets* indicated about the conditions of "the fantasy-making apparatus in the country."

3. I am indebted here to the late Gerald Mast, whose analysis of *2001* has influenced much of my interpretation.

1969

Movies and the Counterculture

CHRISTIE MILLIKEN

On 20 July, Neil Armstrong was the first man to step onto the Moon's surface, an event captured live on television and broadcast to a worldwide audience. It represented both a high point for American technological innovation and a victory over the Soviets in the space race. Despite this achievement, the year was marked by continuing social and political unrest that had characterized much of the preceding decade. The counterculture, best symbolized by protests against the Vietnam War, was in full gear, and a mood of cynicism following several political assassinations filtered into many aspects of American life. Emerging from the disintegration of the Students for a Democratic Society, the Weathermen organized as a militant group to foment violent revolution, staging "Days of Rage" in Chicago in early October and then violently disrupting the national moratorium in Washington, D.C., in November when some 250,000 nonviolent antiwar protesters marched against the Vietnam War. The National Guard was brought in to control protesters (including the Weathermen) at the trial of the Chicago 7, who were indicted on charges of conspiracy to incite the infamous riots at the 1968 Democratic National Convention in that city. Fallout from the assassinations of Martin Luther King Jr. and Robert Kennedy in the previous year continued when James Earl Ray and Sirhan Sirhan, their respective murderers, had their days in court. Kennedy's brother, Ted, a young senator from Massachusetts, became embroiled in a murky legal case in which he was the driver in a car accident that killed his passenger, Mary Jo Kopechne (a campaign aide to his brother), near Chappaquiddick Island, Massachusetts, an unresolved event that forever cast a pall over his career. Conspiracy theories and profound pessimism ran amok.

Richard Nixon entered the first year of his presidency, succeeding the embattled Lyndon Johnson. Hoping to avoid his predecessor's turmoil via a policy of "Vietnamization," Nixon began to implement a plan to gradually remove American troops from combat and turn the burden of war over to the South Vietnamese army. Some 65,000 American soldiers were brought home during Nixon's first year in office at the same time that he began a vigorous bombing campaign of Vietnamese communist strongholds in Cambodia, a tactic initially kept secret from the American public but which was designed to impress Hanoi with the possibility that the new president would stop at nothing to win the war. In this year alone, some 10,000 Americans were killed in Vietnam. As well, the My Lai massacre, which took place in March 1968 under the leadership of Lt. William Calley, was finally revealed to the American public twenty months later by freelance journalist Seymour Hersh, though Calley and other soldiers had already been formally charged with various counts of premeditated murder. Graphic images documenting atrocities from My Lai were shown in *Life* magazine and elsewhere, and details of reported torture, rape, and a series of subsequent cover-ups filled the media with incontrovertible evidence of heinous American war crimes and the compromised ethics of those assigned to investigate them. As more and more Americans began to pay closer attention to events taking place overseas, antiwar sentiment and a broader cynicism about American foreign policy and deception continued to rise. The violence of the images from Vietnam shown on the nightly news was certainly regarded as one cause of the increasing violence depicted on motion picture screens at this time. Another was the media coverage of Charles Manson and his "family" of apocalyptic followers (branded as hippies of a sort) who brutally murdered director Roman Polanski's wife, actress Sharon Tate, their unborn child, and four others in Los Angeles in August.

Culturally, this was also a year of hugely influential and symbolic music events. The Beatles gave their last public performance in January on the rooftop of Apple Records in London. Later in the year, John Lennon and Yoko Ono conducted their famous "Bed-In" at the Queen Elizabeth Hotel in Montreal and recorded their antiwar anthem, "Give Peace a Chance." In August, the Woodstock Festival treated a gathering of between 300,000 and 500,000 music fans to many of the biggest names in sixties rock music, including Jefferson Airplane, Janis Joplin, Jimi Hendrix, the Grateful Dead, and the Who, while the Rolling Stones' tour of the United States culminated in their infamous Altamont concert in December. These two events have taken on mythic status as iconographic of the apex and demise of the counterculture, respectively, and both were captured on film and released as important documentaries the following year.

The politicized struggle of the women's movement continued, with sizable protests staged at San Francisco's Bridal Fair (decrying the five-billion-dollar–a-year industry), outside New York's Marriage License Bureau (with leaflets telling women the "real terms" of the contract they are entering into), and at various Playboy clubs, as well as marches demanding the repeal of abortion laws. It was the Stonewall Riots in June in New York City, however, that marked the most significant sex/gender-issue protest of the year. Indeed, Stonewall is commonly seen as inaugurating the modern gay liberation movement, with a vociferous and public outcry against systemic homophobia. One Hollywood film that addressed the period's ethos of sexual liberation, though from a pointedly heterosexist perspective, was *Bob & Carol & Ted & Alice*. Tackling the trend toward swinging lifestyles, the film begins as a dramatic comedy/social satire about the efforts of a young couple to challenge their bourgeois, upper-middle-class, monogamous values through self-actualization therapy and sexual experimentation outside of their marriage, but it ends in their realization of the pain and complication that their swinging lifestyle has cost them.

The year is pivotal in the history of the American film industry, most notably because it immediately followed the imposition of the new age-based ratings system that took effect in November 1968 following the scrapping of the Production Code. The new system provided excellent public relations for the movie industry, was widely accepted by audiences, and enabled more diverse representations to emerge, particularly with respect to violence and sexuality. For many viewers this meant that Hollywood cinema could finally deal more directly with mature themes that reflected and responded to contemporary social, political, and cultural realities. In this vein, the theme of cynicism, even despair, is characteristic of the apocalyptic tone of many of the year's films. *The Rain People*, Francis Ford Coppola's foray into the woman's film genre, is about a pregnant woman, Natalie (Shirley Knight), who runs away from her empty life of domestic servitude to try to figure out what to do about her pregnancy and her marriage. Through guilt and compassion, Natalie reluctantly takes on a mothering role to Jimmy (James Caan), a brain-injured hitchhiker who ends up dying accidentally at the hands of a young girl in the film's final moments. Set in Depression-era America, *They Shoot Horses, Don't They?* chronicles the painful spectacle of an unending dance competition among a cluster of impoverished and desperate partners who focus their energy on the pursuit of the cash prize dangling before them. When one of the competitors, played by Jane Fonda, comes to understand the full extent of the organizers' corruption (interpretable as a fairly direct comment on the corruption of the establishment), she quits the competition and asks her dance partner to shoot her in the head. He obliges and is arrested. Like *Easy Rider, The Rain People, The Wild Bunch, The Lost Man, Medium Cool,* and *Butch Cassidy and the*

Sundance Kid, the film ends with the violent death of its protagonists. Even the year's James Bond installment, *On Her Majesty's Secret Service,* has the notoriously promiscuous Bond (played one time only here by George Lazenby) uncharacteristically fall in love and get married, only to have his wife shot dead beside him in his car as they depart for their honeymoon. *Salesman,* Albert and Davis Maysles's cinéma vérité documentary, chronicles the spiritual death of its four protagonists, lonely and desperate Bible salesmen who tour the South ruthlessly trying to sell overpriced copies of that book to very poor believers.

The influence of documentary shows up in Woody Allen's directorial debut, *Take The Money and Run,* set up as a mock documentary/biopic of the life of a hapless would-be thief, Virgil Starkweather (Allen), spanning from childhood to incarceration for bank robbery. The plot is ultimately set up around a series of gags and sketches with various characters, including Virgil's parents, parole officer, and relatives, giving talking-head accounts of his life. As with many of Allen's films, Jewish ethnicity plays an important backdrop for much of the humor. Another film to deploy this tactic is the bittersweet romantic comedy *Goodbye, Columbus,* based on a Philip Roth novella that chronicles a summer romance between a poor Brooklyn librarian (Richard Benjamin) and his wealthy Jewish princess girlfriend (Ali McGraw) with disapproving parents. An unlikely studio biopic of the year, *Che!* also utilizes interview-style talking heads, though for unintended comic effect. With Omar Sharif in the title role and Jack Palance playing Fidel Castro, this fabulously awful film shows little interest in the Argentinian revolutionary's life, an accurate portrait of Castro, or the Cuban Revolution that Che helped to orchestrate. Other, intended light fare, such as the western musical comedy *Paint Your Wagon,* with Lee Marvin, Clint Eastwood, and Jean Seberg, and *Sweet Charity,* a musical staring Shirley MacLaine and inspired by Fellini's *Nights of Cabiria* (1957), bombed at the box office. *Topaz,* an Alfred Hitchcock thriller based on a Leon Uris novel, used the backdrop of the Cuban missile crisis for an ultimately flat and sprawling film. Both John Huston's *A Walk with Love and Death* and Jerry Lewis's *Hook, Line and Sinker* also reflect the lesser work of two differentially talented men with long-established Hollywood careers, while the campiness of the special effects in *Marooned,* starring Gregory Peck, did little to advance the technological ability of Hollywood to imagine the future.

While direct reference to Vietnam was virtually absent from Hollywood feature films during the sixties, tangential and metaphorical references to the war and to growing cynicism about political deception more broadly are revealed in a number of the year's films. Of the many westerns released, including *True Grit, The Undefeated* (both starring John Wayne), *Young Billy Young, MacKenna's Gold,* and *Tell Them Willie Boy Is Here,* at least two, *The Wild Bunch* and *Butch Cassidy and the Sundance Kid,* may be read as metaphors for America's misguided imperialist and deceptive participation in the war. Arthur Penn's curious portrayal of the countercultural left, *Alice's Restaurant,* stages Arlo Guthrie's attendance at a draft board to humorous effect, incorporating lyrics from his famous song of the same name into the narrative. The film references the war without naming it when Arlo meets up with an old friend (a former G.I.) at a hippie commune and inquires about his hook hand. In *Medium Cool,* protagonist/cameraman John Cassellis, who grows to realize his complicity in the media/military complex he imagines himself to stand apart from, has on the wall of his apartment the famous image of a Saigon police chief shooting a suspected Vietcong member in the head at point-blank range.

In a more humorous but certainly no less cynical vein, the independent film *Putney Swope* depicts the corporate rise of a token African American executive at an all-white Madison Avenue advertising agency who, through a fluke in the chain of command, becomes the new head of the firm when the old chairman drops dead in a board meeting. Swope decides to revolutionize the agency, firing all the staff (save one token white employee), renaming it Truth and Soul, Inc., and terminating all accounts with tobacco, alcohol, and munitions manufacturers. The ads that he and his new staff of Black "radicals" produce for such products as cereal and acne remedies are so hugely successful that the new firm becomes a target of government operatives as a threat to national security.

Poised on the cusp of the blaxploitation era, this was an interesting year for a number of lesser known films about race. *The Learning Tree,* directed by Gordon Parks Sr., is a coming-of-age story infused with both nostalgia and pessimism based on his 1963 autobiography about life in a small Kansas town during the 1920s. Billed as the first Hollywood studio production (Warner Bros.–Seven Arts) directed by an African American, *The Learning Tree* dramatizes the life of fifteen-year-old Newt (Kye Johnson), a sensitive young boy who must learn to cope with sexual awakening, poverty, loss, and racial injustice. Ed Guerrero describes the importance of the film both for expanding the possibilities of Black filmmaking by challenging the limitations of Hollywood genre classification and for employing a Black crew at all levels of production (Guerrero 81). *The Lost Man* has Sidney Poitier countering his "ebony saint" persona with the portrayal of a Black militant who organizes an armed payroll robbery to acquire money for an unnamed group. The job goes awry when he accidentally kills a police officer and is forced to go into hiding. His attempt to leave Philadelphia is facilitated by an upper-middle-class white social worker who also briefly becomes his lover, though both are ultimately doomed. Dismissed by some critics as an inferior remake of Carol Reed's *Odd Man Out* (1947), *The Lost Man* nevertheless shows Black militants and civil rights demonstrators from a sympathetic perspective.

From a position of economic crisis earlier in the decade when the number of features produced by Hollywood hit an all-time low, the year showed significant recovery with the production of 230 features (Monaco 39). In many ways, the corporate conglomerates that gradually acquired the old studios from the middle of the decade onward ultimately saved Hollywood by the late 1960s. At the same time, however, the takeover of MGM by Las Vegas financier Kirk Kerkorian, the sole example of a buyout of one of Hollywood's "majors" during the 1960s that actually hurt the studio, resulted in a deemphasis of film production in favor of other leisure-related investments (Monaco 38). Alongside the cancellation of many feature productions in that year, a callous reminder of the end of Hollywood's Golden Age was marked by Kerkorian's ruthless sale of the motion picture branches of MGM, as well as the back lot, props, and music library. Certainly the unevenness of the studio product this year is a reflection of this changing economic structure of the studios as well as a response to the opportunities afforded by the new rating system, especially the ability to target films more directly and precisely to age-based demographics.

Documenting the Counterculture: Sex, Drugs, and the Rocky Road

The latter half of the decade was characterized by Hollywood's attempt to capture the youth market and to exploit the newly restructured industrial practices. After the colossal box office failures of several lavish studio productions earlier in the decade, the financing and distribution of cheaper features appealing to specific demographics became the preferred model for business. Placing greater emphasis on financing and distribution of motion pictures and less on production led to an increased market for acquiring and financing smaller budget, independent features that the studios hoped might turn a huge profit. Influenced by companies such as American International Pictures, which specialized in cheaply made films explicitly for the youth market, many films reflected the counterculture and Hollywood's brief flirtation with overt left-leaning subject matter.

Two films that epitomized this ethos are *Medium Cool*, directed by cinematographer Haskell Wexler, and *Easy Rider*, the directorial debut of actor

Dennis Hopper. Produced by Paramount, *Medium Cool* was a significant critical success, possibly the most influential American movie of the late 1960s (Arthur 45). *Easy Rider* was a quasi-independent feature with a sparse budget provided by Columbia Pictures that allowed the crew virtual freedom during production. The deal included Columbia's rights to distribute the film, which became one of the most commercially successful films of the decade. *Medium Cool,* the lesser known of the two films, is a fascinating document of its time. Shot in and around Chicago in the spring and summer of 1968, the film captures a range of hugely symbolic historical events, including footage of the Democratic National Convention that year and the antiwar protests there which erupted into violence. The film weaves these and other events into a fictional story about a cameraman, John Cassellis (Robert Forster), who learns a great deal about the ethics of his work and his life as he watches (and films) events unfolding before him. For Ethan Mordden, *Medium Cool* "isn't just a movie; it's a weapon. The whole thing is about the shooting of cameras and the shooting of guns, and about the feelings of those shot and those shooting" (Mordden 238). As a fiction-documentary hybrid inflected with European modernism, most pointedly Jean-Luc Godard's *Weekend* (1967), *Medium Cool* is significant not only for the degree to which it captures and chronicles events at a pivotal historical moment, but for its provocative, didactic interrogation of this moment's complex politics as well as the politics of filmmaking and film viewing. It also, briefly, became a *cause célèbre* due to its initial X rating, levied not for sexual content but for inflammatory crowd noise such as "Fuck the pigs!" "Pigs are whores!" and "Pigs eat shit!" As Wexler says on the DVD audio commentary, the rating was a "Political X." That the tone of the film is ultimately infused with pessimism and despair is certainly reflective of the mood at the end of the decade, especially among those who, like the director, had strong affiliations with the New Left.

The film begins as Cassellis and his soundman/buddy, Gus (Peter Bonerz), approach the scene of a car accident along a freeway and immediately start to record it, even as we hear faint murmurs from one of the victims. Not until they go back to their car do they radio in for an ambulance. The car from which they send a message for help reveals that the duo is employed by a local television station. They then nonchalantly get into the car and drive away from the bloody scene as the credits roll. This immediately sets up a series of questions around the politics of documenting, a debate that is staged literally in a scene soon to follow where various media people talk about their work during a cocktail party. One journalist talks to a cluster of people about the political and commercial problems of contemporary cinema: "I've

Cassellis (Robert Forster) and his soundman Gus (Peter Bonerz), a television news crew, film a freeway car accident before calling for an ambulance in *Medium Cool* (Haskell Wexler, Paramount). Digital frame enlargement.

made films on all kinds of social problems and the big bombs were the ones where we went into detail and showed why something happened. Nobody wants to take the time. They'd rather see thirty seconds of someone getting his skull cracked, turn off the televisions set, and say, 'Boy, wasn't that bad' and 'Get me another beer.'" Cassellis is shown talking about how nobody wants to see someone sitting "doing nothing," justifying his attention to the "drama" and "violence" in the world around him. The scene plays as a fascinating snapshot of various arguments and justifications for newsworthy reportage, with myriad questions posed about ethical choices.

The episodic structure of *Medium Cool* captures a fascinating array of images. One sequence, for example, documents a series of training exercises of the Illinois Army National Guard as it stages mock civil disturbances. Some recruits don hippie wigs and disingenuously chant "Make love not war" while their colleagues perform crowd control. Here and elsewhere in the film talking-head interviews invoke documentary techniques, though which interviews are staged remains uncertain. An officer for the National Guard tells us that the exercises we witness are part of the work of "Emergency Operation Headquarters" set up the previous winter specifically to deal with "planning and controlling operations in the event of civil disturbances"—a direct reaction to the violent civil rights riots that had recently rocked Chicago. Elsewhere, a group of young students are interviewed about the political work they are doing for Senator Robert Kennedy, whose image is plastered on the windows of a building behind them. Both Kennedy and Martin Luther King Jr. were assassinated during the course of the shoot, and footage referring to these events is carefully woven into the film. For example, a famous RFK speech is broadcast to racially and ethnically mixed low-wage workers performing their various duties in a restaurant kitchen. The scene ends abruptly as several men in suits (political aides?) rush into the kitchen, which may signal that the footage is being filmed simultaneously with the speech (as part of the California primary, after which Kennedy was assassinated). These workers represent a demographic that Kennedy's politics and policies had promised to help, making the scene immediately following—John and Gus in Washington filming the funeral—all the more poignant. Later in the film, Martin Luther King's famous "Promised Land" speech is broadcast on television as part of a network special commemorating the lives of JFK, RFK, and King, which is depicted as preempting "The Beverly Hillbillies" for the night. As Cassellis and his new girlfriend, the Appalachian war widow Eileen (Verna Bloom), watch the broadcast, King's speech inspires Eileen to reflect upon her religious reawakening (shown in flashbacks), while John's reaction is dramatically (and ironically) different: "Jesus, I love to shoot film."

Cassellis's education continues in the scene where he goes to the apartment of a Black cab driver, Frank (Sid McCoy), who was harassed by city cops for turning in an envelope containing $10,000 in cash left in his taxi. Suspicious of such honesty, particularly in a poor Black man, the white cops are shown ruthlessly interrogating him. Against the will of his boss at the TV station, Cassellis decides to do a follow-up story about Frank and comes across far more than he bargained for. Before he arrives at the apartment, Frank is shown hosting an informal meeting of a group of Black militants who question the wisdom of his returning the money in the first place, pointing out how much ammunition it could have purchased. He is accused by one of his friends/colleagues of "acting as a negro" rather than "as a Black man" by returning it. This distinction underscores the much more militant brand of racial politics characteristic of civil rights activism in the late 1960s, especially in a city marked by racial tension and rioting throughout the period. Again, the film moves into a talking head sequence as various militants are shown in direct address confronting Cassellis (and, by implication, us) about the motives for his visit to their neighborhood. The scene ends as another man talks about the potential virtue of violence in making the "invisible" poor Black man famous ("You make him an Emmy; the TV star of the hour") with the final threat that "somebody is gonna get killed," and is juxtaposed with an interview conducted at a shooting range filled only with white people. The owner of the club (Peter Boyle) talks to Cassellis about the increased interest in handgun ownership during recent years as a white middle-class woman awkwardly (and dangerously) wielding a gun comes up to ask for his assistance with the weapon.

The contrasting images of the Democratic convention (as staged circus) and the protests outside it that erupt into violent chaos as the National Guard and local police aggressively bear down on the protesters, bystanders, and journalists play in the background as Eileen looks for her son Harold, who failed to return home the night before. In a bright yellow dress, she stands out against the crowd of protesters and riot police. Various protesters yell, "The whole world is watching!" as others chant "Stay with us, NBC!" to the news cameras passing before them. A curious incident in which tear gas is dispensed into the crowd portrays an added layering of documentary "realism" when an offscreen voice warns the director/cameraman: "Look out, Haskell, it's real!"[1] When Eileen finally tracks Cassellis down, the two set out by car in their search. The final minutes of the film foretell their destiny aurally as a radio broadcast announces that they are in a tragic car accident in which she is killed and he is badly wounded. After this, we witness the accident, portrayed in a chilling series of rapid cuts followed by a black screen for several protracted seconds. In the next scene, a car passes by and stops just long enough for a young boy in the back seat to take a snapshot of the burning wreckage, a curious bookend to the film's opening sequence. The film ends with a tracking shot that pulls back from this wreckage along the road, eventually panning laterally to capture Wexler himself, a man with a movie camera. Shown atop a scaffold, Wexler pans his camera from what perspectively would be the accident onto the camera shooting him (and us as viewers). The final image moves our camera eye into his viewfinder, followed by blackness again, as "The whole world is watching" continues to be chanted.

Like *Medium Cool, Easy Rider* represents one of the most socially significant attempts at capturing the rebelliousness and countercultural lifestyle of the 1960s. Initially conceived by Peter Fonda while on the road promoting *The Trip* (1967), in which he co-starred with Dennis Hopper, *Easy Rider* was developed in the spirit of Roger Corman's American International Pictures exploitation quickies about rebellious bikers such as *The Wild Angels* (1966), in which Fonda had also starred. Indeed, Corman nurtured the careers of Hopper, Fonda, and Jack Nicholson throughout the 1960s during a period when they were having difficulty finding work in mainstream Hollywood productions.[2] Fonda reportedly imagined *Easy Rider* as a modern western, substituting John Wayne or Gary Cooper on horses with two hip guys traveling across America on bikes. Instead of being motivated by a quest to reinstate justice or exact revenge, as is typical of the western, Captain America/Wyatt (Fonda) and Billy (Hopper) seem set primarily on experiencing the freedom of the road.

With production costs just under $375,000, *Easy Rider* became a runaway hit, earning over $19 million and making it the fourth highest grossing film of the year (Hill 30). Eventually it became a global symbol of the "New American Cinema," characterized as challenging the traditional Hollywood model and emphasizing the creative vision of the director/auteur with low-budget productions featuring small casts and targeted at the late adolescent and college-age audience (Monaco 188). The film is also credited with being the first hit feature to truly integrate rock music into its entire story line, thereby merging the "enormous transformation of American music during the 1960s with the motion-picture industry's sudden discovery of the more youthful audience for theatrical motion pictures" (Monaco 188). The music in *Easy Rider* is nondiegetic but is clearly meant to be heard, less as commentary on the narrative than to "foster generational solidarity" (Shumway 38). With songs from Steppenwolf, Jimi Hendrix, The Byrds, and the Holy Modal Rounders, among others, the sound track album was the first multi-artist record of its kind to become a significant sales success (Shumway 38).

Easy Rider begins in Mexico, where Wyatt and Billy, whose names echo western legends Wyatt Earp and Billy the Kid, acquire a large quantity of cocaine that they in turn sell to a dealer/middleman (played by music industry producer Phil Spector) upon their arrival in Los Angeles. Interestingly, the transaction takes place at the end of a runway along L.A.'s International Airport and with no expository dialogue against the overbearing roar of jet engines. From here, the two men carefully pack their earnings into a tube inserted into Wyatt's gas tank and hit the road. At the edge of a desert landscape, Wyatt and Billy contemplate the vista; Wyatt looks at his watch, removes it, and tosses it away in a series of quick zooms and jump cuts followed by the swell of Steppenwolf's "Born to be Wild" as the titles begin. *Easy Rider* vacillates between a romanticization of their journey, emphasized by many sequences that highlight the beauty of the southwestern terrain, and the foreboding demythologization of their quest telegraphed via increasingly tainted/industrialized landscapes and the many bigots they encounter as they head farther east. Early in their journey, for example, they venture through the red rocks of Arizona. With the Band's "The Weight" as an aural backdrop, a montage sequence covers the span of bright daylight and expansive blue sky to dusk amidst the sumptuous, majestic beauty of Monument Valley, gorgeously shot by cinematographer László Kovács. Later in their travels, with George Hanson (Jack Nicholson) in tow, they travel through several quaint southern towns, passing endless cemeteries and stately mansions, then on to more impoverished rural areas where most of the inhabitants are Black. A form of bigotry certainly applies to Wyatt and Billy as well: early in their road trip they are refused a bed at a motel, presumably because of their hippie appearance and their bikes, a motif repeated throughout the film.

The dystopic vision of America that the film ultimately portrays is telegraphed early on by the west-to-east trajectory of their journey, one that reverses the conventions of the frontier ethos and implies its ultimate closure. This directional reversal—seen in many revisionist westerns of the era—signals the end of the frontier and the hopes it held for individual freedom and national progress. Wyatt and Billy never reach their destination, though they do encounter several curiosities on their journey: sharing a meal with an old white farmer living a traditional life off the land with his Mexican wife and children; taking a hitchhiker to a hippie commune where they briefly stay; and meeting up with George Hanson after being jailed for "illegally" joining a small-town parade on their motorbikes. The commune is particularly interesting for the way in which it depicts its members as urban dropouts living one particular brand of 1960s utopian idealism but who clearly have little hope of success, despite Wyatt's inexplicable observation that "they're gonna make it."

Hanson is a kind of moral compass in the film. An alcoholic black-sheep lawyer in his small town, his preference for defending ACLU cases places him outside the values of the parochial, racist community in which he lives; at the same time, he is clearly not a hippie like Billy and Wyatt. In opposition to their sparse and often stilted dialogue, the garrulous Hanson offers a poignant meditation on freedom and the current state of America. "They're gonna talk to you, and talk to you, and talk to you about individual freedom," he says. "But they see a free individual, it's gonna scare 'em. . . . It makes 'em dangerous." The accuracy of his perception is quickly confirmed soon after the three men fall asleep when they are assaulted by several rednecks from the town out of which they have just been driven and Hanson is beaten to death.

Later, Wyatt and Billy visit a famous brothel in New Orleans, yet their experience here and elsewhere in the city against the backdrop of Mardi Gras highlights urban decay and the depravity of capitalist America. With two prostitutes, they share the LSD given to them by the hitchhiker from the commune, but the experience proves to be anything but peaceful and enlightening hedonism. Instead of exuberant revelry, the drug seems to induce in all four characters painful memories of failure, loss, and loneliness as they roam aimlessly around an old cemetery. After George's death, several flashforwards begin to prepare us for the violent end that the duo will meet. During the film's final campfire scene after they have left New Orleans, Wyatt remarks to Billy, "We blew it." Like so much of what he says, his meaning is cryptic: is he referring to their misguided quest or does he mean America blew it? Or both? In any case, it seems that the violent death of Hanson, the experience of the not-so-open road, and the dissatisfying bacchanal of Mardi Gras have taken their toll on him.

As they head toward Florida from New Orleans the next day, both are suddenly and shockingly gunned down by a pair of rednecks. The final image of the film is an aerial shot that pulls away from the burst of flames engulfing Wyatt and his bike alongside the country road. This aerial perspective, which contrasts smoky fire against the verdant landscape, is evocative of so many contemporary images of American planes carpet bombing in Vietnam that appeared regularly on television news programs and documentaries (Hill 51). The pastoral green of the landscape gradually overwhelms the flames as the shot moves away from this shocking site of violence. As the shot pulls back far enough to incorporate a river, it has the paradoxical effect of making this sudden and catastrophic event also somewhat banal, dwarfed in the expanse of landscape that fills the screen as Roger McGuinn's "The Ballad of Easy Rider" plays over the film's final credits. Although the song speaks of freedom and the grandeur of the American landscape, the film as a whole suggests something else entirely, that "heading out on the highway," as Steppenwolf sings, is a foredoomed adventure in the politically charged climate of the time.

▪ Dead Myths and Frontiers of Doom

While *Easy Rider* certainly alludes to many elements of the western, it is clearly a hybrid of youth pic and biker film, road movie and buddy formula. In fact, the popularity of (male) buddy films in the late 1960s prompted many critics to read them as an appropriation of the woman's film. Molly Haskell reads these buddy films as indicative of the marginalized role of women during the period, in part as a response to anxieties provoked by second wave feminism (Haskell 187–88). *Butch Cassidy,* with its rapport between Paul Newman and Robert Redford, was the most commercially successful movie of the 1960s. Stylistically, the film reflected the tendency to manipulate formal screen elements characteristic of the period, alternating between the use of black-and-white and color cinematography, freeze frames, sepia-tinted imagery, and quick zoom shots; narratively, the film simultaneously deployed conventions of the classic western and satirized them in a lighthearted way.

Like *True Grit*, *Butch Cassidy* sets out to debunk certain aspects of the western only to reaffirm them. Butch (Newman) and Sundance (Redford) enjoy the constant playful bickering long associated with heterosexual couples in romantic comedies. For example, when faced with the prospect of gunning down a group of Bolivian bandits who clearly outnumber them, Butch (legendary outlaw that he is) reveals that he has never actually shot anyone before, and they humorously spat in the midst of danger. Of course, this debunks Butch's image somewhat as a macho western hero, but only briefly, since the two ultimately unite and kill the bandits. Like the final freeze frame that ends *True Grit*, symbolizing both Wayne's character's resilience and the actor's iconic status, *Butch Cassidy* ends with a violent shootout, freezing on the two heroes in the moment before their death. The sound track (if not the image) assures us that they will be killed: they are absurdly outnumbered by the Bolivian cavalry who have come in to kill the *"bandidos yanquis,"* as several rounds of fire are heard over their gun-wielding image. The freeze frame gradually pulls out into an extreme long shot and turns to a sepia tone, reinstating their mythic status already implied by the film's opening sequence, which plays a silent film version of their exploits as "The Hole in the Wall Gang."

Richard Slotkin positions *Butch Cassidy*, *The Wild Bunch*, and *The Undefeated* in the tradition of what he calls "Mexico Westerns." Their difference from earlier versions of the subgenre is the degree to which they "mythographically" express what he calls the "cognitive dissonance" that characterized America's response to Vietnam in the wake of the Tet Offensive and the My Lai revelations (Slotkin 591). These films depict the adventure of American gunfighters in Mexico (Bolivia in the case of *Butch Cassidy*), only here the negative aspects of the adventure are more explicit. While *Butch Cassidy*'s comic tone marks its difference from the others, it also utilizes the "last of the outlaws" theme and explicitly shows that the American frontier has become closed to the protagonists. Even the once-friendly sheriff to whom they turn for help warns them: "You're gonna die bloody. . . . All you can do is choose where." In Bolivia, Butch and Sundance never consider playing a counterinsurgency role (as the Wild Bunch do); they are strictly professional robbers, out for their own pleasure and profit. Despite its playful tone, Slotkin reads the film's reversal to a tragic ending for Butch and Sundance as a parable for U.S. involvement in Vietnam: "their success as despoilers of the natives isolates them among a frightened and hostile population. In the end they will be destroyed by a whole regiment of regular Bolivian cavalry. . . . The number of latinos required to kill them testifies to their superiority as Anglo warriors; yet in the end it is the numbers and solidarity of the natives that destroy them" (Slotkin 592).

More explicitly than *Butch Cassidy and the Sundance Kid, The Wild Bunch* is a film firmly situated in the "apocalyptic phase" of American cinema so characteristic of the end of the decade (Wood, *Hollywood* 28). Its unprecedented display of graphic violence most consistently dominated early discussions of *The Wild Bunch,* with critics arguing either that it was a landmark work offering a scathing indictment of America, or that the film's excessive violence was merely gratuitous exploitation bordering on the obscene and immoral (see Prince "Aesthetic"). The two extended battles that open and close *The Wild Bunch* mark a decisive shift in American cinema toward the aestheticization of "ultraviolence."

The appeal of powerful visuals and accelerated editing that came to dominate American cinema in the late 1960s has been interpreted as having particular resonance with much of the new, younger audience whose impact on the box office became increasingly significant (Monaco 196). The transition to accelerated editing techniques is empirically supported by Barry Salt's historical analysis of average shot length (ASL), which demonstrates that from 1958 to 1969, ASL decreased from 11 to 7.7 seconds—barely two-thirds of what it had been just a decade before, reaching the shortest ASL in film history since the silent period of the 1920s. As movies became faster paced and more graphic, there was a paradigm shift in American motion pictures from an "aesthetic of sentiment" to a "cinema of sensation" (Monaco 2). *The Wild Bunch* is certainly illustrative of this faster-paced aesthetic. Sam Peckinpah shot his battle sequences with multiple cameras running film at normal and differential rates of slow motion. Along with a multitude of rapid-fire cuts from extreme close-ups of faces and eyes to long shots to subjective shot-reverse shots, and the use of parallel editing and eye-line matches, editor Thomas Lombardo created a montage effect unlike anything seen before in American cinema.[3] A collision of shot speeds, angles, and camera distances combined with Peckinpah's innovative use of squib technology to simulate exploding bullets as they hit the body enabled a highly stylized, kinetic rendition of violence. For example, minutes into the heist that begins the film, the botched robbery erupts into a town massacre—hardly the conventional western shoot-out. Comprising literally hundreds of shots, one small section of the massacre shows a young blond boy and girl embracing each other in the middle of the massacre. They are first shown at a distance with pillars on either side of them, literally imprisoning them in the violent mayhem. There are cuts to a range of images (thirty shots in thirty-four seconds): Thornton aims; Pike's horse is shot; it rears, presented also as a subjective point-of-view of Pike atop the animal; a brief series of slow motion long and medium shots depict a man shot (with copious blood) and dragged by his horse; and so on. The series of killings is intercut with seven images of the children watching the events around them with strikingly complex and ambiguous expressions of intrigue, fear, and excitement. Many critics have claimed that Peckinpah brought a more "realistic" depiction of violence to American cinema, but Stephen Prince argues that this misses the director's point, that such stylization is not merely a highly formalized aesthetic but is political in its intent. Because of the constant exposure to the violent television imagery of the Vietnam War, viewers, in Peckinpah's view, had become desensitized to violence more generally. By heightening violent imagery through stylization, he hoped to generate more conscious awareness of it (Prince, "Aesthetic" 176).

Beginning with a gesture toward the classical western, the film shows Pike (William Holden) and his gang enter into the town of Starbuck, Texas, dressed as cavalry and thus, possibly, representatives of the law. But by the time the gang enters into the crowded railway office they plan to rob, their outlaw status and ruthlessness become apparent. The robbery goes awry and the bloody battle that ensues dramatically undermines classic plotting, since neither the Bunch nor the bounty hunters waiting to ambush them have any regard for the innocent townsfolk who get caught in the violent crossfire. This makes audience identification with characters and their moral integrity problematic from the very beginning of the story. Whereas classical westerns often delineate heroism on the basis of crucial differences between warring, violent men, even the Bunch (who typically might otherwise signify heroism) are shown using women as shields to protect them from gunfire. Harrigan (Albert Dekker), the capitalist railway boss who hires the bounty hunters, ostensibly operates on the side of the law, but his methods are ethically and morally bankrupt since he fails to warn the townsfolk of the ambush. The bounty hunters he has hired are mere vultures, scavenging the dead bodies after the shootout for boots, gold teeth, money, guns—anything of value. The one man of honor among them is possibly Deke Thornton (Robert Ryan), Pike's oldest friend and former member of the Bunch, now being blackmailed by Harrigan to hunt them down in exchange for his release from prison. When the five surviving members of the Bunch reach their rendezvous point after the heist, they

The Wild Bunch walk toward their final ultraviolent confrontation with Mapache in *The Wild Bunch* (Sam Peckinpah, Warner Bros./Seven Arts). Left to right: Tector Gorch (Ben Johnson), Lyle Gorch (Warren Oates), Pike Bishop (William Holden), Dutch Engstrom (Ernest Borgnine). Digital frame enlargement.

realize they have been duped: the sacks of coins they have stolen are in fact only worthless metal washers. With the failure of this "one last big heist" and the frontier closing in on them, they retreat to Mexico.

In Aqua Verde, they strike a deal with a corrupt Mexican general, Mapache (Emilio Fernandez), to rob a U.S. Army supply train and sell him the rifles in exchange for gold. Mapache has ravaged the hometown of Angel, the sole Latino of the Bunch, and the woman he loves has become one of the general's prostitutes. After seeing her, Angel shoots her in a jealous rage, which complicates but does not terminate the negotiations. The robbery is a success, but Mapache learns of the gift of some of the munitions to Angel's revolutionary comrades, and upon delivery of the guns takes Angel hostage and viciously tortures him by dragging him behind a car. The spectacle of Angel's violent torture prompts Pike to make one last claim to honor: the gang returns to Aqua Verde to rescue him, thereby instigating the final bloodbath.

Pike shoots Mapache, then his German consort, to the shock and silence of the townspeople and the army surrounding him. Mayhem ensues, with this final battle scene, like the first in the film, deploying a range of filmic techniques. During the fight, the only name that Pike calls to any of the numerous people who try to kill him is "Bitch!" to a prostitute (the only female)—a moment that stands out in a film that marginalizes women so completely and focuses on the group culture of men. Further, Pike is ultimately killed by a young boy (loyal to Mapache) who shoots him in the back. The capacity of children to commit violence runs through Peckinpah's work and is telegraphed early in the film as the Bunch ride into Starbuck, passing a group of children who torture two scorpions with a colony of ants. As the Bunch leaves town after the bloodbath, the sequence ends with the kids burning the maimed scorpions with burning hay, an image with apocalyptic overtones. During the two battle sequences, children bear witness, some registering shock and dismay, others mimicking the gunplay they see, illustrating the film's depiction of a world in which corruption is so widespread that even children are not immune. Indeed, unlike classical westerns, no tension exists between wilderness and civilization in *The Wild Bunch*, for the savagery typically associated with the wilderness has so completely penetrated "civilization" as to make the two indistinguishable.

Slotkin reads in these bloodbaths a metaphor for the brutal slaughter of Vietnamese civilians at the hands of equally (if differentially) culpable foes, seeing *The Wild Bunch* in terms of capitalism's destruction of the society it ostensibly sustains and making it the perfect evocation of Vietnam-era "destroy-the-village-in-order-to-save-it" ideology (Slotkin 612). Does Pike fail to realize or does he care that killing Mapache for a personal vendetta will only unleash a series of retaliatory attacks by both the army and the townspeople who may (or may not) have found him to be a tyrannical despot, but who certainly have no loyalty (or trust) for "bandidos yanquis"? As in *Butch Cassidy*, it is the number and solidarity of the natives that destroy the Bunch. The final images of the film show survivors of the massacre leaving Aqua Verde as vultures—both avian and human, since the bounty hunters have arrived—descend upon the town. The one item Thornton is determined to retrieve is Pike's gun, a gesture that powerfully suggests the homosocial tension between the two estranged men.

It is possible to interpret *The Wild Bunch* as first demythologizing and then remythologizing the western insofar as Pike makes one last noble gesture to save Angel, and Thornton subsequently rides off into the sunset with a band determined to fight the revolution (Cawelti 5). But this reading necessarily makes light of Pike's myriad ethical breaches as well as his shortsightedness. In the case of Thornton, the ethical compromises that have brought him to Aqua Verde in the first place complicate his potential heroism. While the complexity of the film continues to invite numerous possible interpretations, what is clear is that it held up a dark mirror to the more troubling aspects of the West, posing deeply disturbing questions about its myths. As Christopher Sharrett states: "*The Wild Bunch* is involved in more than homage for a dead past; it is a recognition of how that past was probably always a deceit" (104).

■■■■■■■■ **Broken Dreams, Shattered Myths**

Released just a month before the Stonewall Riots, *Midnight Cowboy* became the first and only film designated with an X rating (for sexual content) to win an Academy Award for Best Picture.[4] As the title suggests, the film engages several themes of the western, framing Joe Buck (Jon Voight) as a cowboy-hustler on a journey directed eastward, out of the frontier (rural Texas) and into the urban metropolis (New York City). Again, this west-east trajectory is suggestive of the film's demythologization of the American western and the buddy film, particularly their valorization of American male sexuality. In his quest to conquer a new frontier, Joe faces not a land of open possibility but an already exploited center of global capitalism, a landscape tainted with abundant riches and misery alike.

Midnight Cowboy begins with a close-up of a large blank white screen, which is gradually revealed to be the screen of an old, dilapidated drive-in movie theater. This shot is accompanied on the sound track by stock cinematic sounds of cowboys and Indians on galloping horses. The flashback structure of the film reveals that this site is a crucial one in Joe's past. Indeed, he has internalized so completely a vision of American masculinity from the movies (especially the western) that he is completely out of step with the world around him. As he dons his new cowboy gear and heads to the diner where he is a dishwasher to retrieve his final paycheck and say his goodbyes, Joe is presented as an anachronism even to the townsfolk

Joe Buck (Jon Voight) shows compassion by taking the dying Ratso Rizzo (Dustin Hoffman) to Florida in *Midnight Cowboy* (John Schlesinger, United Artists). Digital frame enlargement.

here in the west, several of whom remark on his cowboy outfit. In fact, the only people we see wearing cowboy hats are several old men who, tellingly, sit inside an abandoned movie theater—now a used furniture store—which has the remnants of a film no longer playing on its marquee: J HN AYNE THE A AMO, a curious signposting of Wayne's anachronistic jingoism (Floyd 109). As his bus nears New York, Joe listens attentively to a radio talk show discussing women's views of the ideal man, as one caller confesses: "My ideal of a man is Gary Cooper, but he's dead." Joe's delighted/excited re-action demonstrates his failure to comprehend the implications of this statement: he interprets the woman's lament as an invitation to the mascu-line posture he hopes to offer older women in the city. The Gary Cooper of such classical Hollywood westerns as *The Virginian* (1929), *The Westerner* (1940), and *High Noon* (1952) is gone; Joe nevertheless offers himself up as a self-commodified emulation of John Wayne, a poster of whom he hangs on his hotel room wall. At first he believes this cowboy-hustler persona will earn him a fortune; instead it leads only to poverty and despair.

Although he appears to arrive in New York fresh-faced, naive, and opti-mistic about his prospects, various flashbacks that run though the film reveal Joe to be much more complex and troubled. Abandoned by his mother and raised by his grandmother, several flashbacks show a young Joe repeatedly left alone to eat TV dinners or, alternatively, in bed with his grandma as one of her many paramours dresses beside them. The inappro-priateness of their relationship is suggested even before he leaves Texas as he gazes into the abandoned beauty parlor she once owned. Here, we flash back to a prepubescent Joe massaging his grandma's neck to her highly eroticized pleasure. Over the course of the film, various flashbacks are intermittently woven together to suggest that both Joe and his former high school girlfriend, Crazy Sue, were viciously gang-raped by a group of town toughs. While Crazy Sue's assault is more explicitly conveyed, the fact that Joe's flashbacks recur during his homosexual encounters reveals his deeply troubled relationship to the version of aggressive masculinity by which he has been victimized himself.

Joe's sensitivity and deference—especially to women—completely contradicts the mythic image of the cowboy he wants to project. Joe has little success with the jaded women of New York. His first trick outsmarts him into loaning her money for cab fare after she pretends to be offended by his request for pay. He comforts her with compliments and gives her money instead. With his second pickup, whom he meets at an Andy Warhol Factory–inspired party, he is at first impotent, finally able to perform when she taunts him with the prospect of his being gay (she has witnessed his protective behavior and the closeness of his relationship with Ratso Rizzo [Dustin Hoffman]). The party is a curious glimpse of a subcultural world Joe is simultaneously intrigued by and an outsider to. Interestingly, he is invited to attend by one of Warhol's stable of Superstars, Viva, who makes a brief appearance in the film, and Warhol released his own underground film exploiting the cowboy image, *Lonesome Cowboys,* just a few months before *Midnight Cowboy* was released. In it, Warhol introduced Joe Dallesandro, former *Physique Pictorial* pin-up, to a covert subculture of gay men. Whereas *Lonesome Cowboys* makes explicit use of the cowboy image as gay icon, John Schlesinger's film is much more ambivalent in its portrayal of homosexuality. Reading *Midnight Cowboy* in the broader context of the increasingly radicalized and more visible urban gay male culture of the late 1960s, Kevin Floyd sees the films as appropriating the traditionally heterosexual image of the cowboy to offer what he calls a "deterritorialization" and subsequent "homosexualization" of the cowboy figure as part of its deconstruction of the western myth (Floyd 102). Far from the exuberant celebration of gay subculture in the Warhol film, however, Joe is dismayed to discover that it is primarily gay men who are drawn to his cowboy image and who solicit his attentions in *Midnight Cowboy*.

Insofar as the film conforms with many aspects of the male buddy film so popular at this time, it borrows yet another characteristic of the mainstream western only to push it into uncharted territory. Joe's relationship to Ratso Rizzo becomes the most significant relationship in his desperate world. Rizzo is a consummate low-life, a small-time scam artist, who is also strikingly vulnerable with his crooked limp, permanent cough, unkempt appearance, and general ill health. He first scams Joe, then invites his easy victim to live with him in an abandoned apartment building in which he is squatting, an offer Joe accepts after he runs out of money and is shut out of his hotel. Gradually, a reversal in the dynamic between them takes place as Joe starts to take care of the sickly Rizzo, who in turn begins to feel affection for Joe and whose declining health motivates his desire to move to sunny Florida. To secure money for their journey, Joe picks up an older man whom he viciously beats. The excessiveness of this scene—since he is clearly able to take the money and run from this rather passive trick—is interpretable in a variety of ways: as intense homophobia, as violently repressed self-loathing homosexuality, as a vicious reaction to the violence that was previously wrought upon him by sexually aggressive men. Though the scene is likely to compromise the viewer's sympathetic identification with Joe, his compassionate nurturing of Rizzo as they take the bus to Florida redeems him somewhat. At this point, Joe takes on a mothering role as he cradles, feeds, and changes the soiled clothes of the dying man. Joe himself changes clothes as well, throwing away the cowboy outfit he has worn until then. Like Wyatt and Billy in *Easy Rider*, Rizzo never reaches his destination (at least, alive), and Buck's gloomy, lost, and lonely arrival in the Sunshine State firmly situates the film within the pessimistic tone of so many films of the year.

NOTES

1. Audio commentary by Wexler on the DVD release of the film reveals that this piece of dialogue was actually added later, as the film was edited. Wexler claims that he remembers thinking it himself, and so had the line dubbed into the footage, another curious example of the film's blend of fiction and nonfiction modes.

2. Lee Hill argues that although Hopper and Fonda had been raised within Hollywood's studio system, they also shared the myriad interests and concerns of the 1960s counterculture to a degree that was stifling their careers, particularly given the expectations the studios still had of young actors with Middle American good looks: "It sounds like a joke now, but by simply growing their hair long, they had seriously impaired their careers in the eyes of studio casting agents and producers. Their choices were narrowing to exploitation pictures or supporting roles as misfits and villains" (Hill 11).

3. While Peckinpah claims not to have seen *Bonnie and Clyde* until after he completed *The Wild Bunch*, a number of historians suggest that this may not be true. He did, however, continually cite Akira Kurosawa (especially *Seven Samurai* [1954]) as a crucial influence. See Prince, "Aesthetic."

4. Tino Balio points out that although the film was released with an X, this was not the rating given by the MPAA but was self-imposed by United Artists, the film's producers. In part, it seems that the X rating was a way to safeguard against the film's treatment of homosexuality, although it also appears to have been used for marketing purposes, since UA eventually adopted the following line as a lead to its trade ads and news releases: "Whatever You Hear About *Midnight Cowboy* Is True" (Balio 291–92). *Midnight Cowboy* is an excellent example of how the transition to the new ratings system was a highly experimental period in Hollywood filmmaking as new limits to both violence and sexual representation were tested and set. Note also that *Bob & Carol & Ted & Alice* was edited in several places before its commercial release to avoid an X rating (Balio 292). I would like to thank Tom Kemper for drawing this to my attention.

1960 – 1969

Select Academy Awards

1960

Best Picture: *The Apartment*, The Mirisch Company, United Artists

Best Actor: Burt Lancaster in *Elmer Gantry*, United Artists

Best Actress: Elizabeth Taylor in *Butterfield 8*, MGM

Best Supporting Actor: Peter Ustinov in *Spartacus*, Universal-International

Best Supporting Actress: Shirley Jones in *Elmer Gantry*, United Artists

Best Director: Billy Wilder, *The Apartment*, The Mirisch Company, United Artists

Writing (motion picture story): Billy Wilder, I.A.L. Diamond, *The Apartment*, The Mirisch Company, United Artists

Writing (best-written screenplay): Richard Brooks, *Elmer Gantry*, United Artists

Cinematography (black-and-white): Freddie Francis, *Sons and Lovers*, Twentieth Century Fox

Cinematography (color): Russell Metty, *Spartacus*, Universal-International

Film Editing: Daniel Mandell, *The Apartment*, The Mirisch Company, United Artists

Music (song): "Never on Sunday," music and lyrics by Manos Hadjidakis, *Never on Sunday*, Melinafilm Production, Lopert Pictures

Music (scoring dramatic or comedy picture): Ernest Gold, *Exodus*, United Artists

Music (scoring musical picture): Morris Stoloff, Harry Sukman, *Song without End, The Story of Franz Liszt*, Columbia

1961

Best Picture: *West Side Story*, Mirisch Pictures, United Artists

Best Actor: Maximilian Schell in *Judgment at Nuremberg*, Stanley Kramer Productions, United Artists

Best Actress: Sophia Loren in *Two Women*, Embassy Pictures Corporation

Best Supporting Actor: George Chakiris in *West Side Story*, Mirisch Pictures, United Artists

Best Supporting Actress: Rita Moreno in *West Side Story*, Mirisch Pictures, United Artists

Best Director: Robert Wise, Jerome Robbins, *West Side Story*, Mirisch Pictures, United Artists

Writing (motion picture story): William Inge, *Splendor in the Grass*, NBI Production, Warner Bros.

Writing (best-written screenplay): Abby Mann, *Judgment at Nuremberg*, Stanley Kramer Productions, United Artists

Cinematography (black-and-white): Eugen Shuftan, *The Hustler*, Robert Rossen Productions, Twentieth Century Fox

Cinematography (color): Daniel L. Fapp, *West Side Story*, Mirisch Pictures, United Artists

Film Editing: Thomas Stanford, *West Side Story*, Mirisch Pictures, United Artists

Music (song): "Moon River," music by Henry Mancini, lyrics by Johnny Mercer, *Breakfast at Tiffany's*, Paramount

Music (scoring dramatic or comedy picture): Henry Mancini, *Breakfast at Tiffany's*, Paramount

Music (scoring musical picture): Saul Chaplin, Johnny Green, Sid Ramin, Irwin Kostal, *West Side Story*, Mirisch Pictures, United Artists

■ 1962

Best Picture: *Lawrence of Arabia*, Columbia

Best Actor: Gregory Peck in *To Kill a Mockingbird*, Universal-International

Best Actress: Anne Bancroft in *The Miracle Worker*, United Artists

Best Supporting Actor: Ed Begley in *Sweet Bird of Youth*, MGM

Best Supporting Actress: Patty Duke in *The Miracle Worker*, United Artists

Best Director: David Lean, *Lawrence of Arabia*, Columbia

Writing (motion picture story): Ennio de Concini, Alfredo Giannetti, Pietro Germi, *Divorce—Italian Style*, Embassy Pictures Corporation

Writing (best-written screenplay): Horton Foote, *To Kill a Mockingbird*, Universal-International

Cinematography (black-and-white): Jean Bourgoin, Walter Wottitz, *The Longest Day*, Darryl F. Zanuck Productions, Twentieth Century Fox

Cinematography (color): Fred A. Young, *Lawrence of Arabia*, Columbia

Film Editing: Anne Coates, *Lawrence of Arabia*, Columbia

Music (song): "Days of Wine and Roses," music by Henry Mancini, lyrics by Johnny Mercer, *Days of Wine and Roses*, Warner Bros.

Music (music score—substantially original): Maurice Jarre, *Lawrence of Arabia*, Columbia

Music (scoring of music—adaptation or treatment): Ray Heindorf, *Meredith Willson's The Music Man*, Warner Bros.

1963

Best Picture: *Tom Jones,* United Artists–Lopert Pictures

Best Actor: Sidney Poitier in *Lilies of the Field,* United Artists

Best Actress: Patricia Neal in *Hud,* Paramount

Best Supporting Actor: Melvyn Douglas in *Hud,* Paramount

Best Supporting Actress: Margaret Rutherford in *The V.I.P.s,* MGM

Best Director: Tony Richardson, *Tom Jones,* United Artists–Lopert Pictures

Writing (motion picture story): James R. Webb, *How the West Was Won,* MGM

Writing (best-written screenplay): John Osborne, *Tom Jones,* United Artists–Lopert Pictures

Cinematography (black-and-white): James Wong Howe, *Hud,* Paramount

Cinematography (color): Leon Shamroy, *Cleopatra,* Twentieth Century Fox

Film Editing: Harold F. Kress, *How the West Was Won,* MGM

Music (song): "Call Me Irresponsible," music by James Van Heusen, lyrics by Sammy Cahn, *Papa's Delicate Condition,* Paramount

Music (scoring of music—adaptation or treatment): André Previn, *Irma La Douce,* Mirisch-Phalanx, United Artists

Music (music score—substantially original): John Addison, *Tom Jones,* United Artists–Lopert Pictures

1964

Best Picture: *My Fair Lady,* Warner Bros.

Best Actor: Rex Harrison in *My Fair Lady,* Warner Bros.

Best Actress: Julie Andrews in *Mary Poppins,* Walt Disney Productions, Buena Vista

Best Supporting Actor: Peter Ustinov in *Topkapi,* Filmways Production, United Artists

Best Supporting Actress: Lila Kedrova in *Zorba the Greek,* International Classics

Best Director: George Cukor, *My Fair Lady,* Warner Bros.

Writing (motion picture story): *Father Goose,* story by S. H. Barnett, screenplay by Peter Stone, Frank Tarloff, Universal

Writing (best-written screenplay): Edward Anhalt, *Becket,* Hal Wallis Productions, Paramount

Cinematography (black-and-white): Walter Lassally, *Zorba the Greek,* International Classics

Cinematography (color): Henry Stradling, *My Fair Lady,* Warner Bros.

Film Editing: Cotton Warburton, *Mary Poppins*, Walt Disney Productions, Buena Vista

Music (song): "Chim Chim Cher-ee," music and lyrics by Richard M. Sherman and Robert B. Sherman, *Mary Poppins*, Walt Disney Productions, Buena Vista

Music (scoring dramatic or comedy picture): André Previn, *My Fair Lady*, Warner Bros.

Music (music score—substantially original): Richard M. Sherman, Robert B. Sherman, *Mary Poppins*, Warner Bros.

▬▬▬▬▬▬ 1965

Best Picture: *The Sound of Music*, Argyle Enterprises, Twentieth Century Fox

Best Actor: Lee Marvin in *Cat Ballou*, Columbia

Best Actress: Julie Christie in *Darling*, Embassy Pictures Corporation

Best Supporting Actor: Martin Balsam in *A Thousand Clowns*, United Artists

Best Supporting Actress: Shelley Winters in *A Patch of Blue*, MGM

Best Director: Robert Wise, *The Sound of Music*, Argyle Enterprises, Twentieth Century Fox

Writing (motion picture story): Frederic Raphael, *Darling*, Embassy Pictures Corporation

Writing (best-written screenplay): Robert Bolt, *Doctor Zhivago*, MGM British Studios

Cinematography (black-and-white): Ernest Laszlo, *Ship of Fools*, Columbia

Cinematography (color): Freddie Young, *Doctor Zhivago*, MGM British Studios

Film Editing: William Reynolds, *The Sound of Music*, Argyle Enterprises, Twentieth Century Fox

Music (song): "The Shadow of Your Smile," music by Johnny Mandel, lyrics by Paul Francis Webster, *The Sandpiper*, Filmways-Venice, MGM

Music (scoring of music—adaptation or treatment): Irwin Kostal, *The Sound of Music*, Argyle Productions, Twentieth Century Fox

Music (music score—substantially original): Maurice Jarre, *Doctor Zhivago*, MGM British Studios

▬▬▬▬▬▬ 1966

Best Picture: *A Man for All Seasons*, Columbia

Best Actor: Paul Scofield in *A Man for All Seasons*, Columbia

Best Actress: Elizabeth Taylor in *Who's Afraid of Virginia Woolf?* Warner Bros.

Best Supporting Actor: Walter Matthau in *The Fortune Cookie*, Mirisch Corporation, United Artists

Best Supporting Actress: Sandy Dennis in *Who's Afraid of Virginia Woolf?* Warner Bros.

Best Director: Fred Zinnemann, *A Man for All Seasons,* Columbia

Writing (motion picture story): *A Man and a Woman,* story by Claude Lelouch, screenplay by Claude Lelouch and Pierre Uytterhoeven, Les Films 13, Allied Artists

Writing (best-written screenplay): Robert Bolt, *A Man for All Seasons,* Columbia

Cinematography (black-and-white): Haskell Wexler, *Who's Afraid of Virginia Woolf?* Warner Bros.

Cinematography (color): Ted Moore, *A Man for All Seasons,* Columbia

Film Editing: Fredric Steinkamp, Henry Berman, Stewart Linder, Frank Santillo, *Grand Prix,* MGM

Music (song): "Born Free," music by John Barry, lyrics by Don Black, *Born Free,* Columbia

Music (scoring of music—adaptation or treatment): Ken Thorne, *A Funny Thing Happened on the Way to the Forum,* United Artists

Music (original music score): John Barry, *Born Free,* Columbia

 **1967**

Best Picture: *In the Heat of the Night,* Mirisch Corporation, United Artists

Best Actor: Rod Steiger in *In the Heat of the Night,* Mirisch Corporation, United Artists

Best Actress: Katharine Hepburn in *Guess Who's Coming to Dinner,* Columbia

Best Supporting Actor: George Kennedy in *Cool Hand Luke,* Warner Bros.– Seven Arts

Best Supporting Actress: Estelle Parsons in *Bonnie and Clyde,* Warner Bros.– Seven Arts

Best Director: Mike Nichols, *The Graduate,* Embassy Pictures Corporation

Writing (motion picture story): William Rose, *Guess Who's Coming to Dinner,* Columbia

Writing (best-written screenplay): Stirling Silliphant, *In the Heat of the Night,* Mirisch Corporation, United Artists

Cinematography: Burnett Guffey, *Bonnie and Clyde,* Warner Bros.–Seven Arts

Film Editing: Hal Ashby, *In the Heat of the Night,* Mirisch Corporation, United Artists

Music (song): "Talk to the Animals," music and lyrics by Leslie Bricusse, *Doctor Doolittle,* Twentieth Century Fox

Music (scoring of music—adaptation or treatment): Alfred Newman, Ken Darby, *Camelot*, Warner Bros.–Seven Arts

Music (original music score): Elmer Bernstein, *Thoroughly Modern Millie*, Ross Hunter, Universal

■ 1968

Best Picture: *Oliver!* Columbia

Best Actor: Cliff Robertson in *Charly*, American Broadcasting Companies–Selmur Pictures Production, Cinerama

Best Actress: [tie] Katharine Hepburn in *The Lion in Winter*, Avco Embassy, and Barbra Streisand in *Funny Girl*, Columbia

Best Supporting Actor: Jack Albertson in *The Subject Was Roses*, MGM

Best Supporting Actress: Ruth Gordon in *Rosemary's Baby*, William Castle Enterprises Production, Paramount

Best Director: Carol Reed, *Oliver!* Columbia

Writing (motion picture story): Mel Brooks, *The Producers*, Avco Embassy

Writing (best-written screenplay): James Goldman, *The Lion in Winter*, Avco Embassy

Cinematography: Pasqualino De Santis, *Romeo and Juliet*, Dino De Laurentiis, Paramount

Film Editing: Frank P. Keller, *Bullitt*, Warner Bros.-Seven Arts

Music (song): "The Windmills of Your Mind," music by Michel Legrand, lyrics by Alan Bergman and Marilyn Bergman, *The Thomas Crown Affair*, Mirisch-Simkoe-Solar, United Artists

Music (score of a musical picture—original or adaptation): John Green, adaptation score, *Oliver!* Romulus Films, Columbia

Music (original score): John Barry, *The Lion in Winter*, Avco Embassy

■ 1969

Best Picture: *Midnight Cowboy*, United Artists

Best Actor: John Wayne in *True Grit*, Hal Wallis Productions, Paramount

Best Actress: Maggie Smith in *The Prime of Miss Jean Brodie*, Twentieth Century Fox

Best Supporting Actor: Gig Young in *They Shoot Horses, Don't They?* Chartoff-Winkler-Pollack, Cinerama

Best Supporting Actress: Goldie Hawn in *Cactus Flower*, Columbia

Best Director: John Schlesinger, *Midnight Cowboy*, United Artists

Writing (motion picture story): William Goldman, *Butch Cassidy and the Sundance Kid*, Twentieth Century Fox

Writing (best-written screenplay): Waldo Salt, *Midnight Cowboy*, United Artists

Cinematography: Conrad Hall, *Butch Cassidy and the Sundance Kid*, Twentieth Century Fox

Film Editing: Françoise Bonnot, *Z*, Reggane Films–O.N.C.I.C. Production, Cinema V Distributing

Music (song): "Raindrops Keep Fallin' on My Head," music by Burt Bacharach, lyrics by Hal David, *Butch Cassidy and the Sundance Kid*, Twentieth Century Fox

Music (score of a musical picture—original or adaptation): *Hello, Dolly!* adaptation score by Lennie Hayton and Lionel Newman, Twentieth Century Fox

Music (original score): Burt Bacharach, *Butch Cassidy and the Sundance Kid*, Twentieth Century Fox

WORKS CITED

AND CONSULTED

Adler, Renata. "'Green Berets' as Viewed by John Wayne." *New York Times* 20 June 1968: 49.

"AIP 'Angels,' Like Monkees, to Exploit, Follow-Up Films." *Variety* 2 Aug. 1967.

Alloway, Lawrence. *Violent America: The Movies, 1946–1964*. New York: Museum of Modern Art, 1971.

Alpert, Hollis. "Anglicized Waltz." *Saturday Review* 28 July 1962: 31.

———. "SR Goes to the Movies." *Saturday Review* 27 Aug. 1966: 40.

Archerd, Army. "Just for Variety." *Variety* 7 Sept. 1965.

———. "Just for Variety." *Variety* 2 May 1966.

Ariès, Philippe. *Centuries of Childhood: A Social History of Family Life*, trans. Robert Baldick. New York: Alfred A. Knopf, 1962. Originally published as *L'Enfant et la vie familiale sous l'ancien régime*. Paris: Librarie Plon, 1960.

Arthur, Paul. "Jargons of Authencity." *Theorizing Documentary*. Ed. Michael Renov. New York: Routledge, 1993. 108–34.

———. "*Medium Cool*." *Cineaste* 27.3 (June 2002): 45–46.

Balio, Tino. *United Artists: The Company That Changed the Film Industry*. Madison: U of Wisconsin P, 1987.

Bart, Peter. "Hollywood Scholars: College Groups Try for Improvement in Screen Teaching Technique." *New York Times* 24 Aug. 1964: 2:7.

"Bat Man: Sunset at High Campabello." *Carryon Crier* 28 Jan. 1966.

Baxter, John. *Hollywood in the Sixties*. New York: A. S. Barnes; London: Tantivy, 1972.

Benshoff, Harry M. "Gay, Lesbian, and Queer Cinema." *Schirmer Encyclopedia of Film*, vol. 2. Ed. Barry Keith Grant. Detroit: Thomson Gale, 2006. 277–86.

Benshoff, Harry M., and Sean Griffin. *America on Film: Representing Race, Class, Gender, and Sexuality at the Movies*. Malden, Mass.: Blackwell, 2004.

Benton, Robert, and David Newman. "The New Sentimentality." *Esquire* 61 (July 1964): 25–31.

Berg, Charles Ramirez. "*Bordertown*, the Assimilation Narrative, and the Chicano Social Problem Film." *Chicanos and Film: Representation and Resistance*. Ed. Chon Noriega. Minneapolis: U of Minnesota P, 1992.

Berg, Rick. "Losing Vietnam: Covering the War in an Age of Technology." *From Hanoi to Hollywood*. Ed. Linda Dittmar and Gene Michaud. New Brunswick: Rutgers UP, 1990. 41–68.

"Big Rental Films of 1968." *Variety* 8 June 1969: 15.

Bogdanovich, Peter. "The Autumn of John Ford." *Esquire* 61 (April 1964): 102–07, 144–45.

Branch, Taylor. *At Canaan's Edge: America in the King Years, 1965–1968*. New York: Simon & Schuster, 2006.

Brown, Helen Gurley. *Sex and the Single Girl*. New York: Bernard Geis Associates, 1962.

Bruccoli, Matthew, and Dmitri Nabokov, eds. *Vladimir Nabokov: Selected Letters*. San Diego: Harcourt Brace Jovanovich, 1989.

Buford, Kate. *Burt Lancaster: An American Life*. New York: Knopf, 2000.

Bunzel, Peter. "Shocking Candor on the Screen, a Dilemma for the Family." *Life* 23 Feb. 1962: 88–101.

Butler, Judith. *Gender Trouble: Feminism and the Subversion of Identity*. New York: Routledge, 1990, 1999.

"Camelot (disambiguated)." *Wikipedia*. *en.wikipedia.org*/wiki/Camelot_%28disambiguation%29.

Carson, Rachel. *Silent Spring*. Boston: Houghton Mifflin, 1962.

Cawelti, John. "Chinatown and Generic Transformation in Recent American Films." *Film Genre Reader III*. Ed. Barry Keith Grant. Austin: U of Texas P, 2003. 243–61.

"Chicago Cops Confiscate *Chelsea Girls*; Theatre Manager Arrested 13th Time." *Variety* 16 Aug. 1967: 24.

Cleto, Fabio. *Camp: Queer Aesthetics and the Performing Subject: A Reader*. Ann Arbor: U of Michigan P, 1999.

Corliss, Richard. *Lolita*. London: BFI Publishing, 1994.

Corman, Roger, with Jim Jerome. *How I Made a Hundred Movies in Hollywood and Never Lost a Dime*. New York: Random House, 1990.

Crosby, John. "Movies Are Too Dirty." *Saturday Evening Post* 10 Nov. 1962: 8–10.

Crowther, Bosley. "*Flower Drum Song*." *New York Times* 10 Nov. 1961: 40:1.

———. "Forceful Portrait of a Man Born to Lose: Paul Newman Superb as 'Cool Hand Luke.'" *New York Times* 2 Nov. 1967.

———. "*Guess Who's Coming to Dinner* Arrives." *New York Times* 12 Dec. 1967.

———. "*Judgment at Nuremberg*." *New York Times* 20 Dec. 1961: 36:1.

———. "*One, Two, Three*." *New York Times* 22 Dec. 1961: 17:1.

———. "*A Raisin in the Sun*." *New York Times* 30 May 1961.

———. "The Screen: New *Children's Hour*." *New York Times* 15 March 1962.

———. "*Splendor in the Grass*." *New York Times* 11 Oct. 1961: 53:1.

———. "Theirs and Ours: Foreign Films Forging Ahead of American." *New York Times* 9 Dec. 1962: X5.

———. "*West Side Story*." *New York Times* 26 Oct. 1961: 39:3.

Dickstein, Morris. *Gates of Eden: American Culture in the Sixties*. New York: Basic Books, 1977.

Dittmar, Linda, and Gene Michaud, eds. *From Hanoi to Hollywood: The Vietnam War in American Film*. New Brunswick: Rutgers UP, 1990.

"Dubuque County Atty. Refuses to Cry 'Woolf' vs. Local Distributor." *Variety* 7 Sept. 1966: 5.

Durgnat, Raymond. "*Batman*." *Films and Filming* 12.7 (April 1966): 8.

Ebert, Roger. "*Bonnie and Clyde*." *Chicago Sun-Times* 25 Sept. 1967.

"The Edge of Violence." *Time* 5 Oct. 1962: 15–17.

Everett, Anna. "The Civil Rights Movement and Television." *Encyclopedia of Television*, 2nd ed. Vol. 1. Ed. Horace Newcomb. New York: Fitzroy Dearborn, 2004. 520–24.

Farber, Manny. *Negative Space*. New York: Praeger, 1971.

Feng, Peter. "Being Chinese American, Becoming Asian American: *Chan Is Missing*." *Cinema Journal* 35.4 (Summer 1996): 88–118.

———. "Recuperating Suzie Wong: A Fan's Nancy Kwan-dary." *Countervisions: Asian American Film Criticism*. Ed. Darrell Y. Hamamoto and Sandra Liu. Philadelphia: Temple UP, 2002. 40–56.

Fiedler, Leslie. *No! In Thunder*. New York: Stein and Day, 1960.

Finler, Joel W. *The Hollywood Story*. New York: Crown Publishers, 1988.

Fischer, Lucy. "Birth Traumas: Parturition and Horror in *Rosemary's Baby*." *Cinema Journal* 31.3 (Spring 1992): 3–18. Reprinted in *The Dread of Difference: Gender and the Horror Film.* Ed. Barry Keith Grant. Austin: U of Texas P, 1996. 412–31.

Floyd, Kevin. "Closing the (Heterosexual) Frontier: Midnight Cowboy as National Allegory." *Science and Society* 65.1 (Spring 2001): 99–130.

Frank, Gerold. *Judy.* New York: Harper and Row, 1975.

Friedan, Betty. *The Feminine Mystique.* New York: Norton, 1963.

Friedenberg, Edgar Z. "Calling Dr. Spock!" *New York Review of Books* 28 March 1968.

Friedman, Lester D., ed. *Arthur Penn's Bonnie and Clyde.* New York: Cambridge UP, 2000.

———. *Hollywood's Image of the Jew.* New York: Frederick Ungar, 1982.

Gitlin, Todd. *The Sixties: Years of Hope, Days of Rage.* New York: Bantam, 1987.

Goldstein, Richard. *The Poetry of Rock.* New York: Bantam, 1969.

Goudsouzian, Aram. *Sidney Poitier: Man, Actor, Icon.* Chapel Hill: U of North Carolina P, 2004.

Graham, Allison. *Framing the South: Hollywood, Television, and Race during the Civil Rights Struggle.* Baltimore: Johns Hopkins UP, 2001.

Green, Abel. "Guns-For-'Fun' and Tragedy." *Variety* 12 June 1968: 60.

———. "Show Biz Hurt by Violence." *Variety* 8 Jan. 1969: 1, 56, 58, 60.

Guerrero, Ed. *Framing Blackness: The African Image in Film.* Philadelphia: Temple UP, 1993.

Hamamoto, Darrell Y. *Monitored Peril: Asian Americans and the Politics of TV Representation.* Minneapolis: U of Minnesota P, 1994.

Harrington, Michael. *The Other America: Poverty in the United States.* 1962. Reprint, New York: Touchstone, 1977.

Haskell, Molly. *From Reverence to Rape: The Treatment of Women in the Movies.* 2nd ed. Chicago: U of Chicago P, 1987.

Hawkes, Terence. *Structuralism and Semiotics.* Berkeley: U of California P, 1977.

"He Flies Again: *Batman* New Camp Leader." *Los Angeles Times* ca. 1965.

Heffernan, Kevin. *Ghouls, Gimmick, and Gold.* Durham, N.C.: Duke UP, 2004.

Hersey, John. *The Algiers Motel Incident.* New York: Alfred A. Knopf, 1968.

Higashi, Sumiko. "*Night of the Living Dead*: A Horror Film about the Horrors of the Vietnam Era." *From Hanoi to Hollywood.* Ed. Linda Ditmar and Gene Michaud. New Brunswick: Rutgers UP, 1990. 175–88.

Hill, Lee. *Easy Rider.* London: BFI Publishing, 1996.

Hirsch. "*The Chelsea Girls*." *Variety Weekly* 18 Jan. 1967: 6.

Hoberman, J. *The Dream Life: Movies, Media, and the Mythology of the Sixties.* New York: Free Press, 2003.

Hopp, Glenn. *Billy Wilder: The Cinema of Wit, 1902–2002.* Los Angeles: Taschen, 2003.

"Hub's Judge Fines Exhib Who Shows 'Chelsea Girls.'" *Variety* 14 June 1967: 13.

Hunter, Allan. *Faye Dunaway.* London: W. H. Allen, 1986.

Hutchinson, Tom. *Rod Steiger: Memoirs of a Friendship.* London: Victor Gollancz, 1998.

James, David E. "Documenting the Vietnam War." *From Hanoi to Hollywood.* Ed. Linda Ditmar and Gene Michaud. New Brunswick: Rutgers UP, 1990. 239–54.

Jewison, Norman. *This Terrible Business Has Been Good to Me: An Autobiography.* Toronto: Key Porter, 2004.

Johnson, Lyndon Baines. "The Great Society." *http://www.tamu.edu/comm/pres/speeches/lbjgreat.html.* Accessed 18 Sept. 2005.

Kapsis, Robert. *Hitchcock: The Making of a Reputation.* Chicago: U of Chicago P, 1992.

Kauffmann, Stanley. "Stanley Kauffmann on Films: Booms and Busts." *New Republic* 8 June 1968: 26, 43.

King, Martin Luther Jr. *Why We Can't Wait.* New York: Penguin, 1964.

Kroll, Jack. "Movies: Underground in Hell." *Newsweek* 14 Nov. 1966: 109.

LaFeber, Walter. *America, Russia and the Cold War: 1945–1992.* 7th ed. New York: McGraw-Hill, 1993.

Lax, Eric. *Paul Newman: A Biography.* Atlanta: Turner Publishing, 1996.

Leff, Leonard J. "Hollywood and the Holocaust: Remembering *The Pawnbroker.*" *American Jewish History* 84.4 (1996): 353–76.

Leff, Leonard J., and Jerold K. Simmons. *The Dame in the Kimono: Hollywood, Censorship, and the Production Code from the 1920s to the 1960s.* New York: Grove Weidenfeld, 1990.

Lenburg, Jeff. *Dustin Hoffman: Hollywood's Anti-Hero.* New York: St. Martin's, 1983.

Lev, Peter. *American Film of the 70s: Conflicting Visions.* Austin: U of Texas P, 2000.

Lipsitz, George. *The Progressive Investment in Whiteness: How White People Profit from Identity Politics.* Philadelphia: Temple UP, 1998.

"*Lolita.*" *Films in Review* (Aug.-Sept. 1962): 426–27.

"*Lord Love a Duck.*" *Playboy* (April 1966).

MacAdams, Lewis. *Birth of the Cool: Beat, Bebop, and the American Avant-Garde.* New York: Free Press, 2001.

Macdonald, Dwight. *Dwight Macdonald on Movies.* Englewood Cliffs, N.J.: Prentice-Hall, 1969.

Magid, Marion. "Auteur! Auteur!" *Commentary* 37.3 (March 1964): 70–74.

Mahoney, John. "Andy Warhol's *Chelsea Girls*: Artistic, Non-Artistic, Lucid, Muddled, LONG!" *Hollywood Reporter* 30 March 1967.

Mamber, Steven. *Cinema Verite in America: Studies in Uncontrolled Cinema.* Cambridge, Mass.: MIT Press, 1974.

"Manhattan's Lower Depths." *Time* 27 July 1962: 69.

Marcus, Greil. *The Manchurian Candidate.* London: BFI Publishing, 2002.

Mast, Gerald. *A Short History of the Movies.* New York: Macmillan, 1986.

McBride, Joseph. *Searching for John Ford: A Life.* New York: St. Martin's, 2001.

Medina, Ann. "A Timeline of the Women's Liberation Movement." http://www.cwluherstory.com/CWLUAbout/timeline.html. 2000.

Mekas, Jonas. *Movie Journal: The Rise of a New American Cinema, 1956–1971.* New York: Collier Books, 1972.

Meyer, Moe, ed. *The Politics and Poetics of Camp.* London: Routledge, 1994.

Miller, Douglas T. *On Our Own: Americans in the Sixties.* Lexington, Mass.: D. C. Heath, 1996.

Monaco, Paul. *The Sixties: 1960–1969. History of the American Cinema, Vol. 8.* Berkeley: U of California P, 2001.

Mordden, Ethan. *Medium Cool: The Movies of the 1960s.* New York: Alfred A. Knopf, 1990.

Munshower, Suzanne. *Warren Beatty: His Life, His Loves, His Work.* New York: St. Martin's, 1983.

"The New Ocean." *Time* 2 March 1962: 11–16.

O'Brien, Geoffrey. *Dream Time: Chapters from the Sixties.* New York: Viking, 1988.

O'Steen, Sam, with Bobbie O'Steen. *Cut to the Chase: Forty-five Years of Editing America's Favorite Movies.* Studio City, Calif.: Michael Wiese Productions, 2001.

Pendergast, Tom, and Sara Pendergast, eds. *UXL American Decades: 1960–1969.* Farmington Hills, Mich.: Thomson Gale, 2003.

Petropoulos, Jonathan. *The Faustian Bargain: The Art World in Nazi Germany.* New York: Oxford UP, 2000.

"Pinkertons Enforce Juvenile Shutdown at 'Virg Woolf' Showings." *Variety* 28 June 1966: 7.

Prince, Stephen. "The Aesthetic of Slow-Motion Violence in the Films of Sam Peckinpah." *Screening Violence.* Ed. Stephen Prince. New Brunswick: Rutgers UP, 2000. 175–204.

———, ed. *Sam Peckinpah's The Wild Bunch.* Cambridge: Cambridge UP, 1999.

Quart, Leonard, and Albert Auster. *American Film and Society Since 1945.* 2nd ed. Westport, Conn.: Praeger, 1991.

Reid, Mark A. *Redefining Black Film.* Berkeley: U of California P, 1993.

Rogin, Michael. *Ronald Reagan, The Movie: and Other Episodes in Political Demonology.* Berkeley: U of California P, 1987.

Rosen, Marjorie. *Popcorn Venus: Women, Movies, and the American Dream.* New York: Coward, McCann, and Geoghegan, 1993.

Salt, Barry. *Film Style and Technology: History and Analysis.* 2nd ed. New York: Macmillan, 1992.

Sarris, Andrew. *The American Cinema: Directors and Directions, 1929–1968.* New York: Dutton, 1968.

———. "Notes on the Auteur Theory in 1962." *Film Culture* 27 (Winter 1962–63): 1–8.

Sayres, Sohnya, et al., eds. *The 60s Without Apology.* Minneapolis: U of Minnesota P, 1984.

Scheuer, Philip K. "Batman to Face 'Old Gang' in Film." *Los Angeles Times* 3 May 1966: 4:14.

Schlesinger, Arthur Jr. "America 1968: The Politics of Violence." *Harper's Magazine* (Aug. 1968): 19–24.

———. "The Crisis of American Masculinity." *Esquire* (Nov. 1958): 64–66.

———. *A Thousand Days: John F. Kennedy in the White House.* Boston: Houghton Mifflin; Cambridge: Riverside Press, 1965.

Schuster, Hal. *Batmania II.* Las Vegas: Pioneer Books, 1992.

Sharrett, Christopher. "Peckinpah the Radical: The Politics of *The Wild Bunch.*" *Sam Peckinpah's The Wild Bunch.* Ed. Stephen Prince. Cambridge: Cambridge UP, 1999. 79–104.

Shumway, David. "Rock 'n' Roll Sound Tracks and the Production of Nostalgia." *Cinema Journal* 38.2 (1999): 36–51.

Shurlock, Geoffrey. Memo dated 10 June 1965. MPPA files, Margaret Herrick Library, Los Angeles.

Simmons, Garner. *Peckinpah: A Portrait in Montage.* Austin: U of Texas P, 1982.

Slotkin, Richard. *Gunfighter Nation: The Myth of the Frontier in Twentieth-Century America.* New York: HarperCollins, 1993.

Smith, Jack. "The Perfect Filmic Appositeness of Maria Montez." *Film Culture* 27 (Fall-Winter 1962/63): 28–32.

Sontag, Susan. *Against Interpretation and Other Essays.* New York: Delta, 1966.

Spoto, Donald. *Stanley Kramer: Film Maker.* New York: G. P. Putnam's Sons, 1978.

Stearns, Peter N. *American Cool: Constructing a Twentieth Century Emotional Style.* New York: New York UP, 1994.

"Summer 'Camp' Note." *Los Angeles Herald-Examiner* 25 April 1966.

"This Righteous Cause: First Negro to Attempt to Register." *Time* 21 Sept. 1962: 23.

Thomas, Kevin. "Batman Marathon Too Much." *Los Angeles Times* 28 Jan. 1966: 4:8.

Tube. "*The Children's Hour.*" *Variety* 6 Dec. 1961.

———. "*Flower Drum Song.*" *Variety* 1 Nov. 1961.

———. "*Judgment at Nuremberg.*" *Variety* 11 Oct. 1961.

———. "*One, Two, Three.*" *Variety* 16 Nov. 1961.

———. "*A Raisin in the Sun.*" *Variety* 29 March 1961.

———. "*Splendor in the Grass.*" *Variety* 25 Aug. 1961.

"Understanding Violence." *Newsweek* 17 June 1968: 43–46.

Von Doviak, Scott. "The Bottom Shelf: Bad Trips." http://www.highhat.com/Nitrate/004/bottomshelf.html. Accessed 3 June 2007.

Walker, Martin. *The Cold War: A History*. New York: Henry Holt, 1995.

Walker, Michael. "*Home from the Hill.*" *Cineaction* 63 (2004): 22–35.

Wanat, Matt. "'Fall in Behind the Major': Cultural Border Crossings and Hero Building in *Major Dundee.*" *Sam Peckinpah's West: New Perspectives*. Ed. Leonard Engel. Salt Lake City: U of Utah P, 2003. 87–113.

Warhol, Andy (with Pat Hackett). *POPism: The Warhol '60s*. New York: Harper and Row, 1983.

Wasko, Janet. *Movies and Money: Financing the American Film Industry*. Norwood, N.J.: Ablex Publishing, 1982.

Weiler, A. H. "Education Notes." *New York Times* 6 Dec. 1964.

Wertham, Fredric. *Seduction of the Innocent*. New York: Rinehart, 1953.

West, Adam, with Jeff Rovin. *Back to the Batcave*. New York: Barkley Books, 1994.

Westbrook, Brett Elizabeth. "Second Chances: The Remake of Lillian Hellman's *The Children's Hour.*" *Bright Lights Film Journal*. http://www.brightlightsfilm.com/29/childrenshour1.html.

Wexler, Haskell. Audio commentary to *Medium Cool*. Paramount DVD 06907. 2001.

Wharton, Don. "How to Stop the Movies' Sickening Exploitation of Sex." *Reader's Digest* (March 1961): 37–40.

"What You Believe In." *Time* 8 June 1962: 25–26.

Whit. "*West Side Story.*" *Variety* 14 Sept. 1961 .

"Who? What? When? Where? Why? A Report from Vietnam by Walter Cronkite." CBS News Special. 27 Feb. 1968.

"Who's Afraid. . . ." *Newsweek* 4 July 1966: 84.

"*Wild Angels* Banned in Denmark." *Los Angeles Times* 3 Feb. 1967.

"Will There Be War? The Question the World Is Asking." *New York Times* 28 Oct. 1962: E3.

Wolf, William. "*The Chelsea Girls.*" *Cue* 17 Dec. 1966.

Wood, Robin. *Arthur Penn*. New York: Praeger, 1970.

———. *Hitchcock's Films*. New York: A. S. Barnes; London: Zwemmer, 1965.

———. *Hollywood from Vietnam to Reagan*. New York: Columbia UP, 1986.

———. "'Shall We Gather at the River?' The Late Films of John Ford." *John Ford Made Westerns*. Ed. Gaylyn Studlar and Matthew Bernstein. Bloomington: Indiana UP, 2001. 23–41.

"Woolf Too Hot For Nashville Cop; Grabs Reel." *Variety* 19 July 1966: 22.

Wylie, Philip. *Generation of Vipers*. New York: Holt, Rinehart and Winston, 1955.

Youngblood, Gene. "*Batman* in Campville." *Los Angeles Herald-Examiner* 6 Feb. 1966: 1, 8.

———. "Warhol and His Spitting Images." *Los Angeles Herald-Examiner* 26 March 1967: F4.

CONTRIBUTORS

LESLIE H. ABRAMSON teaches film studies at Lake Forest College. Her work has appeared in *Literature/Film Quarterly*, and her essay on Mia Farrow will appear in the forthcoming volume *Star Decades: The Sixties* (Rutgers University Press). She is currently at work on a book about the films of Alfred Hitchcock.

HARRY M. BENSHOFF is an associate professor of radio, television, and film at the University of North Texas. He has published essays on numerous topics, including "Dark Shadows" fan culture, blaxploitation horror films, Hollywood LSD films, the reception of *The Talented Mr. Ripley* (1999), and Homo-Military films of the 1960s. His books include *Monsters in the Closet: Homosexuality and the Horror Film* (1997), *America on Film: Representing Race, Class, Gender and Sexuality at the Movies* (2004), *Queer Cinema: The Film Reader* (2004), and *Queer Images: A History of Gay and Lesbian Film in America* (2006).

DAVID DESSER is a professor of cinema studies and comparative literature at the University of Illinois. He received his Ph.D. in cinema studies from the University of Southern California. He is the co-author of *American Jewish Filmmakers* (1993, rev. ed. 2004) and the author, editor, and co-editor of numerous books on Asian cinema. He provided the commentary on the Criterion Collection DVD of *Tokyo Story* and contributed to commentary for the special edition of *Seven Samurai*.

ANNA EVERETT is a professor of film, television, and new media studies and director of the Center for Black Studies at the University of California at Santa Barbara. Her books include *Returning the Gaze: A Genealogy of Black Film Criticism, 1909–1949* (2001), *New Media: Theories and Practices of Digitextuality* (with John T. Caldwell, 2003), and the forthcoming *Digital Diaspora: A Race for Cyberspace*. She founded the journal *Screening Noir: A Journal of Film, TV, and Digital Culture*.

BARRY KEITH GRANT is a professor of film studies and popular culture at Brock University, Ontario. He is the author, co-author, or editor of numerous publications, including *Voyages of Discovery: The Cinema of Frederick Wiseman* (1992), *The Dread of Difference: Gender and the Horror Film* (1996), *Film Genre: From Iconography to Ideology* (2007), and *Film Genre Reader* (1986, 1995, 2003). His work has appeared in numerous journals and anthologies, and he serves as editor of the Contemporary Film and Television series for Wayne

State University Press and the New Approaches to Film Genre series for Blackwell Publishing.

JOE McELHANEY is an assistant professor of film studies at Hunter College. He is the author of *The Death of Classical Cinema: Hitchcock, Lang, Minnelli, and the Decline of Classical Cinema* (2006) and *Albert Maysles* (forthcoming).

CHRISTIE MILLIKEN is an assistant professor in the Department of Communications, Popular Culture, and Film at Brock University, Ontario. She is the author of *Generation Sex: Reconfiguring Sexual Citizenship in Educational Film and Video* (forthcoming). Her published essays have been included in *Spectator, Velvet Light Trap*, and the *Journal of Lesbian Studies* as well as in several anthologies, including *Lesbian Sex Scandals; Sugar, Spice, and Everything Nice: Cinemas of Girlhood*; and *Cultural Sutures: Essays on Medicine and Media*.

JAMES MORRISON is the author of *Broken Fever*, a memoir, and *The Lost Girl*, a novel, as well as several books on film, including *Roman Polanski* (forthcoming). He is an associate professor of film and literature and chair of the Literature Department at Claremont McKenna College.

MURRAY POMERANCE is a professor in the Department of Sociology at Ryerson University and the author of *Magia d'Amore* (1999), *An Eye for Hitchcock* (2004), *Johnny Depp Starts Here* (2005), and *Savage Time* (2005). He is editor of numerous volumes, including *Enfant Terrible! Jerry Lewis in American Film* (2002), *American Cinema of the 1950s: Themes and Variations* (2005), *Cinema and Modernity* (2006), and *City That Never Sleeps: New York and the Filmic Imagination* (2007), and is co-editor of *From Hobbits to Hollywood: Essays on Peter Jackson's Lord of the Rings* (2006). He edits the Horizons of Cinema series at the State University of New York Press and, with Lester D. Friedman and Adrienne L. McLean, respectively, co-edits the Screen Decades and Star Decades series at Rutgers University Press.

ERIC SCHAEFER is an associate professor in the Department of Visual and Media Arts at Emerson College in Boston. His essays have appeared in *Cinema Journal, Film History, Film Quarterly, Journal of Film and Video*, and *The Velvet Light Trap* as well as several anthologies and encyclopedias. He is the author of *Bold! Daring! Shocking! True!: A History of Exploitation Films, 1919–1959* (1999) and is completing *Massacre of Pleasure: A History of the Sexploitation Film, 1960–1979*.

CHRISTOPHER SHARRETT is a professor of communication at Seton Hall University. He is the author of *The Rifleman* (2005) and editor of *Crisis Cinema: The Apocalyptic Idea in Postmodern Narrative Film* (1993), *Mythologies of Violence in Postmodern Media* (1999), and co-editor with Barry Keith Grant of *Planks of Reason: Essays on the Horror Film* (revised 2004). His work has appeared in *Film International, Cineaste, Cinema Journal, Film Quarterly, Journal of Popular Film and Television,* and numerous anthologies. He is currently working on a book on neoconservative Hollywood cinema.

INDEX

Page numbers in italics indicate illustrations.